Critical Mapping for Sustainable Food Design

This book introduces critical mapping as a problematizing, reflective approach for analyzing systemic societal problems like food, scoping out existing solutions, and finding opportunities for sustainable design intervention.

This book puts forth a framework entitled "wicked solutions" that can be applied to determine issues that designers should address to make real differences in the world and yield sustainable change. The book assesses the current role of design in attaining food security in a sustainable, equitable, and just manner. Accomplishing this goal is not simple; if it was, it would not be called a wicked problem. But this book shows how a particular repertoire of design tools can be deployed to find solutions and strategize the development of novel outcomes within a complex and interconnected terrain. To address the wicked problem of food insecurity, inequity, and injustice, this book highlights 73 peer-reviewed design outcomes that epitomize sustainable food design. This includes local and regional sustainable design outcomes funded or supported by public or private institutions and local and widespread design outcomes created by citizens. In doing so, this book sets the stage for an evidence-driven and evidence-informed design future that facilitates the designers' visualization of wicked solutions to complex social problems, such as food insecurity. Drawing on an array of case studies from across the world, from urban rooftop farms and community cookers to mobile apps and food design cards, this book provides vitally important information about existing sustainable food design outcomes in a way that is organized, accessible, and informative.

This book will be of great interest to academics and professionals working in the field of design and sustainable food systems. Students interested in learning about food and sustainability from across design studies, food studies, innovation and entrepreneurship, urban studies, and global development will also find this book of great use.

Audrey G. Bennett is the Director of the Design for Social Innovation and Sustainability (DESIS) Lab at Penny W. Stamps School of Art and Design and an inaugural University Diversity and Social Transformation Professor at the University of Michigan, Ann Arbor. She is also a former Andrew W. Mellon Distinguished Scholar of the University of Pretoria, South Africa. She studies the design of transformative images that, through interactive aesthetics, can permeate cultural boundaries and impact the way we think and behave towards good social change. She was awarded the 2022 AIGA Steve Heller Prize for Cultural Commentary.

Jennifer A. Vokoun is an Associate Professor of Graphic Design at Walsh University, Ohio, USA. She is the founder and Director of The Center for Sustainable Food Design, formerly the Food Design Institute, facilitating community engagement and leading participatory design research on food systems issues, and serves as a faculty leader for the university's Blouin Global Scholars, an interdisciplinary cohort focused on food, sustainability, and hunger in a local and global context. Her research focuses on design and social innovation applied to sustainable food systems and food insecurity issues.

Routledge Studies in Food, Society and the Environment

Critical Mapping for Sustainable Food Design
Food Security, Equity, and Justice

Audrey G. Bennett
Jennifer A. Vokoun

Routledge
Taylor & Francis Group
LONDON AND NEW YORK

earthscan
from Routledge

Designed cover image: © Getty images

First published 2023
by Routledge
4 Park Square, Milton Park, Abingdon, Oxon OX14 4RN

and by Routledge
605 Third Avenue, New York, NY 10158

Routledge is an imprint of the Taylor & Francis Group, an informa business

British Library Cataloguing-in-Publication Data
A catalogue record for this book is available from the British Library

Library of Congress Cataloging-in-Publication Data
Names: Bennett, Audrey, author. | Vokoun, Jennifer A., author.
Title: Critical mapping for sustainable food design: food security,
equity and justice/Audrey G. Bennett, Jennifer A. Vokoun.
Description: New York, NY : Routledge, 2023. | Includes bibliographical references and index. Identifiers: LCCN 2022052778 (print) | LCCN 2022052779 (ebook) | ISBN 9781032118895 (hardback) | ISBN 9781032118888 (paperback) | ISBN 9781003222026 (ebook) Subjects: LCSH: Food security. | Food supply.
Classification: LCC HD9000.5 .B4487 2023 (print) | LCC HD9000.5 (ebook) | DDC 338.1/9--dc23/eng/20230313
LC record available at https://lccn.loc.gov/2022052778
LC ebook record available at https://lccn.loc.gov/2022052779

ISBN: 978-1-032-11889-5 (hbk)
ISBN: 978-1-032-11888-8 (pbk)
ISBN: 978-1-003-22202-6 (ebk)

DOI: 10.4324/9781003222026

Typeset in Goudy
by Deanta Global Publishing Services, Chennai, India

Contents

Foreword
by Ron B. Eglash

When Professor Audrey Bennett first mentioned to me that she was using the phrase "wicked solution" I was intrigued. The term "wicked problems" was precisely defined as dilemmas characterized by the impossibility of having "a solution" as we typically think of it. For example, one of the first uses of the term was by Rittel and Webber (1973), who specified what constituted wicked problems in social policy. They offered the example of poverty:

> Consider, for example, what would be necessary in identifying the nature of the poverty problem. Does poverty mean low income? Yes, in part. But what are the determinants of low income? Is it a deficiency of the national and regional economies, or is it deficiencies of cognitive and occupational skills within the labor force? If the latter, the problem statement and the problem "solution" must encompass the educational processes. But, then, where within the educational system does the real problem lie? What then might it mean to "improve the educational system?" Or does the poverty problem reside in deficient physical and mental health? If so, we must add those etiologies to our information package, and search inside the health services for a plausible cause. Does it include cultural deprivation? Spatial dislocation? Problems of ego identity? Deficient political and social skills?—and so on.
>
> (161)

The above quote concerns only their definition of a wicked problem in terms of its first characteristic, which is "no definitive formulation"—there are ten characteristics in total, each building a portrait of the diffuse complexity that makes wicked problems intractable in every normal sense of what we mean by "solution."

But I soon found out that what Audrey had in mind by "wicked solution" was exactly that same sense of diffuse complexity; that is, the solution would have to be an emergent property of the system in which it is embedded. By emergent property I am referring to the results of self-organization in the context of complex adaptive systems. Nature has some of the best examples. For instance, how do you keep 300-foot-tall trees like Sitka spruce from toppling over? A human engineer creating similar artificial structures would attempt to impose order from above, blasting large boulders, moving tons of earth, and pouring truckloads of cement. But nature's solution is an emergent root structure that winds its way around boulders, strengthens the earth instead of flattening it, and whose complex woody fibers deliver water and nutrients as well as perform a structural miracle. Similar challenges in nature are met with the same emergent phenomena. No nutrient run-off from the land in tropical oceans? The solution was the emergence of coral reefs, made possible by the symbiotic relation of coral polyps and algae living inside them. This hyper-efficient mutualism recycles "waste" from plant to animal and animal to plant *inside the same organism*, and the resulting physical structures then enable them to bootstrap an entire ecosystem into existence. Even the process that allows you to read these words, the hyperconnected neural nets of the brain, operate in a bottom-up fashion. Indeed, our new obsession with AI that actually works (as opposed to several decades and billions in research on top-down AI that could not even beat humans at chess) is only possible because we copied an emergent approach. If switching to a bottom-up approach worked for machine learning, could we similarly apply a bottom-up approach to food justice, at least insofar as analyzing the enormous variety of current projects documented in the literature?

In the case of AI, bottom-up neural networks are often referred to as *robust algorithms*, meaning that they are remarkably adaptive to new patterns. Once you train a neural net to navigate its robot in thousands of different spatial situations, you can throw it into a building it has never seen and it will (if properly trained) adapt. The word "robust" comes from the classical Latin "rōbustus," meaning "made of oak." The tree that bends but does not break has strong roots, for all the reasons mentioned above. Whether we are talking about neural pathways self-organizing to adapt to the data set, or root pathways emergently adapting to rocks and soils, their strength in the face of challenges—robustness—is a direct consequence of their bottom-up configuration. Surely any analysis of the wicked problem of food insecurity will also need this kind of robust search through the possibilities, implementing as wide a scope as possible as the solutions (which themselves will include top-down as well as bottom-up, local as well as global) are buffeted by climate change, capitalism, state imperialism, and similar challenges.

But this emergent process of covering the solution space as broadly as possible is only one part of the wicked solution. The second part is analytic mapping. Suppose you did find that there are hundreds of small trial-and-error experiments taking place to address food issues such as inequity, inaccessibility, unsustainability, and injustice. How could you track which ones are working, develop collaborations to link them horizontally, disseminate best practices to share knowledge and techniques, and implement policy changes to deliver support in financial, legal, institutional, and other domains?

In the past, many pressing problems were more uniform in nature, and so the mapping of possible solutions could be carried out in a more uniform way. Polio, for example, crippled millions in childhood; when the polio vaccine was introduced it was hailed as the "silver bullet." COVID-19, by comparison, was a

Figure F.1 Root system as an emergent phenomenon. Image courtesy of Ron Eglash.

confusing mess. An "anti-vaxxer" movement opposed vaccinations, a rising alt-right political movement weaponized the refusal to wear masks, and so on. It was, in short, a wicked problem. The solution was equally complicated: competing methods ("whole virus" approaches, RNA, mRNA, non-replicating vectors, protein subunits, etc.), each with different implications for political, economic, and health dimensions. It was, in other words, a wicked solution. This book is about an even more complicated problem domain, that of food insecurity.

If we are to find its wicked solution, we too will need a mapping tool that can help us navigate a landscape of political, cultural, economic, and ecological attributes without reducing them in ways that other frameworks might. A purely Marxist framework, for example, would nicely point out the humanitarian and ecological crisis caused by putting profits before people but would have little to say about how to keep your business afloat. Conversely, business advice, even when social justice-oriented, can be limiting. When I attended one of the Lemelson Foundation's "triple bottom line" business-for-social-good workshops, the keynote speaker told the audience "don't treat your business any differently than any other," explaining that above all else we needed to make sure we had sufficient profits: but how is that any different from the old single bottom line?

Unlike nature, our food systems do not have ready-made information trackers like the genetic code that can be passed between generations, or a system like biological evolution that can create and filter mutations. We have to impose such structures artificially. Hence the second aspect of this book's wicked solution framework: a simple two-axis grid by which we can begin to map the fundamental dimensions of that multitude of real-world experiments.

The first of the two dimensions might be described as "follow the money." Some projects are sponsored by a government program, following from policy and implemented through funding, resources, advising, and other means. Others are corporation-sponsored, perhaps not as much policy-oriented as simply a matter of creating public good will, publicity, and so on. Both of those cases are characterized as top-down. And at the other end of this axis we find its complement, bottom-up, where projects enjoy the grassroots grounding of citizen and community-based efforts. That of course comes at a price: they are often more restricted by budget, expertise, or other factors, but, for many, that's a price worth paying for the authenticity and local control self-funding ensures.

The second dimension is especially appropriate for our historical moment when so many activities are web-based, and yet "localism" in the form of urban farms, farm-to-fork eating, and so on has received new attention. Bennett's term "memetic" for those established through geographically spread networks is not, of course, limited to the web—think of seed-saver networks that existed by postal service in the past—but it nicely responds to the phenomena of the digital era.

Why these two dimensions? I think there are two ways of answering that. As a descriptive analysis, it simply reflects the kind of diversity of approaches one sees in the world. The point of a wicked solutions framework was to capture the real-world complexity of possibility. But it is equally important, I think, to ask if this is also prescriptive. As an advocate for more radically democratic futures, I often stress the importance of radically democratic structuring, that is to say, both things that are localized and things that are bottom-up emergent. But even in purely natural systems, one sees an interesting tendency for certain kinds of scaling effects.

Take, for example, adaptation. Darwin described how a species adapts over millennia through genetic evolutions. But we now know that there are also epigenetic effects that can happen over a few generations. For example, in many organisms, a restriction in mothers' diets results in undersized babies. This effect (changing DNA methylation) allows adaptation to short-term ecological changes (a decade-long drought for example) before genetics (which takes many centuries) can etch these changes in stone. Over a single lifetime, we adapt as individuals by changing muscle mass, and over even shorter time spans we adapt with things like calluses (days), behaviors (minutes), and so on.

Politics in a sense plays a similar role in allowing adaption over many scales. Changing the Constitution is often the result of decades-long change, but federal law can happen more quickly. State laws, county laws, city laws—our house rules about chore distributions—all exist in a scaling array of adaptations and commitments. As in the biological case, the most profound changes need to be those that take the longest, that have the deepest commitment. If the body needs to abandon gills for lungs, or the nation needs to abandon slavery for abolition, that has to happen in ways that cannot be simply un-done on a whim.

For those reasons, I suspect that the two dimensions in this wicked solutions analysis are not merely descriptive. Society needs memory spans and commitment levels at many different scales, across both time and space. But obviously the devil is in the details. In the biological case, we know which aspects of the system need to be linked to long-term adaptations (e.g., DNA) and which short-term (e.g., calluses require corneodesmosin). When these are misaligned, disaster strikes: let DNA take on short-term changes and the results are cancer. Can we find aspects of the food system that are similarly at their best—more just, equitable, sustainable—at specific scales in time and space?

Of course asking this particular set of questions is merely one of a myriad of ways of utilizing the wicked solutions framework. Other approaches might be to look at transformations across quadrants—speculative or design fiction approaches that offer thought experiments with counterfactual reassignments ("what if localized urban farms were memetic?"), ideas about fluidity and circulation along dimensions, and so on. I hope the readers will enjoy this means of grasping wicked complexity without reduction, but in nonetheless graspable form, and find it as profoundly useful and "good to think with" as I did.

Preface

It is common, when discussing sustainable food design research, as design scholars and visual communication designers, for people to assume that food design is only about what they see on their plates. Some may even think that we work directly with food, in a kitchen, as part of our research (we do not). After all, entire media channels are dedicated to food, with cooking shows like *Chopped*, where food as a multisensory phenomenon becomes a mode of designing for entertainment. In these shows, the taste and texture of food are seriously considered, and so, too, are the plating and the visual presentation. For those who consider this spectacle to be food design, they are not wrong; in a literal sense it is food design. The plates, the utensils, and the cooking tools that clutter our kitchen drawers and counters, designed by industrial designers, product designers, and engineers, can all be considered a form of food design as well. So, too, are the signs, logos, cook-books, menus, and other materials related to food created by graphic designers and others considered food design. But in the past 20 years or so, design as a field and a process has expanded to be more intentionally applied to social systems and processes, resulting in an examination and expansion of what food design is, and what it could be. What has slowly emerged is the field of food design that is transdisciplinary and inclusive of a wide range of disciplines. It is into this space, as visual communication design scholars and environmental stewards, working in the United States, and focused on social justice and sustainability, we have entered to expand food design to sustainable food design, with a broad defini-tion of what constitutes sustainable and a charge to designers to embrace this emerging sub-discipline and the collaborative design research process required to conduct inquiries in this transdisciplinary and cross-cultural space.

The act of designing has evolved from a lone designer conceptually facing down challenges afforded by the blank canvas or the printed page to designers working collaboratively to address complex human challenges within built, natural, and socio-cultural environments. Within these new problem-solving spaces, one finds designers and other stakeholders grappling with confounding social issues like the inequities in economic and environmental sustenance, housing, food secu-rity, quality education, and healthcare experienced by many and exacerbated for those who are underserved. Today, design practitioners and researchers are being trained to apply their creativity, critical thinking, and applied technical skills and methods to problem-solve almost any societal challenge by coordinating with experts from other disciplines and the community as needed to develop viable solutions.

Within these collaborative spaces designers scope problems, take in information, see patterns, and synthesize solutions through creativity, community-engagement, reflection, and iteration. With these thinking, making, and social abilities we bring the understanding of how to both zoom in and zoom out of the context to focus on minute details and to see the whole, the gestalt, and make relationships between seemingly disparate concepts. If we focus too narrowly on a singular idea, we can miss opportunities to bridge gaps and see connections that can expand an idea and strengthen the design outcome. However, if we only look from an expansive perspective, the view can be too generalized and overwhelming to venture deeper.

Relatedly, the challenge with sustainable food design is that it can be difficult to fathom the vast scope of the converging fields of food, design, and sustainability. However, as the pandemic, social disruptions, political conflicts, and climate change continue to impact the world around us, it becomes clear that this wide scope cannot deter us. Design research for social innovation is needed now, maybe more than ever. So, where does a designer start? Answering this question is so daunting that it motivated the writing of this book.

The good news is that the canvas is not blank. Work has been done, and new work continues to be done in design to address wicked problems in society. However, due to the dysfunctional state of the system, when one begins the design research process, it is not always clear what has been done and what needs to be done. What is clear though is that we live in a hyper-connected world and while ever-increasing digital and technological innovations create novel ways for us to interact socially and professionally, they also create disconnects and discords between us. It's as if by having so many avenues of connection, we often fail to see what is right in front of or beside us. Critically mapping a wicked solution to food insecurity provides the tools to understand how to both zoom in and zoom out, to see the individual nodes (sustainable food design outcomes) in the food system, and how they connect and interact to form a more resilient, sustainable food system in the world that delivers food security in a just and equitable manner.

We want to emphasize that connection and interaction are key, in a sustainable community, in the food system, and in a collaboration. In September 2018, we both attended and separately presented on design research at AIGA's (the professional organization for design) Design Educators Community's conference, Decipher. Audrey Bennett presented "Defining and executing a graphic design research agenda (if only for the sake of justice)," and Jennifer Vokoun presented, along with Anne Berry, Penina Acayo Laker, and Sarah Rutherford, "We are not alone: Navigating design research and writing challenges with group support." It was at this conference, in the hallway of the Art and Architecture building of the Penny W. Stamps School of Art and Design at the University of Michigan, where we met for the first time and discovered a mutual interest in food security, design research and writing, social justice, and sustainability. Converging at the intersection of these mutual interests, our new design research collaboration was formed.

The initial fruits of our collaboration were presented just prior to the onset of the pandemic in the United States in February 2020 at the College Arts Association conference in Chicago. Together we presented a paper titled "Places to Intervene in the Global Food System: Defining Problems that Designers *Should* Address" on the Design Studies Forum panel titled "Diversifying Diversity: Addressing Marginalized Global Communities through Design." Soon after presenting, with the pandemic fully engulfing the world and anti-Black racism rearing its ugly head, again, we set about to expand our research jointly, recognizing the critical juncture and the ravaging impact of the worldwide pandemic on the food system. We worked remotely and met weekly via Zoom for at least 15 minutes but no more than an hour to discuss our progress by reading an extensive array of gray and scholarly literature on food, design, and sustainability. We grappled with how to interpret some of quantitatively dense food findings we encountered. We also vented with each other about the devastating impact of COVID on our professional and personal lives. We discussed alarming statistics and news regarding the state of food insecurity in our local communities and around the world. Then, we wrote and rewrote together using Google Docs. After one year, the result is this book.

We have worked diligently to curate a set of sustainable food design peer-reviewed design outcomes that make up the wicked solution to food insecurity. Like many design processes, it has been muddled at times. Emerging fields, like sustainable food design, often lack the defined edges that help to navigate uncharted spaces. As designers we are used to making sense of this type of ambiguity, and the hope is that this work provides a structure and framework to help other designers, broadly speaking, move forward to collaboratively design solutions that take a bigger bite out of a wicked problem like food insecurity.

Parts of this preface were adapted from Bennett, A. 2019. "Defining and Executing a Graphic Design Research Agenda (If Only for the Sake of Justice)." In *Dialogue: Proceedings of the AIGA Design Educators Community Conferences: Decipher, Volume 1*, edited by Kelly M. Murdoch-Kitt and Omar Sosa-Tzec, 372–387. Ann Arbor, MI: Michigan Publishing Service.

Acknowledgments

Thanks to our dear families for their understanding and emotional support through a demanding one-year research and writing process.

Thank you to those who awarded our book project resources to support its production, including the University of Michigan's Office of the Vice President of Research, the Penny W. Stamps School of Art and Design, and Walsh University. Thanks to Jimmy Brancho for his keen eye for detail while copyediting our book.

We thank everyone who permitted us to reprint their artwork, visuals, or text in our book. Thanks to the Creative Commons and Wikipedia Commons contributors who allow general reuse of their work with limited restrictions. Thank you also to Alberto Rigau and the AIGA Design Educators Community (DEC); Björn Steinar Blumenstein; David Allen Burns and Austin Young of Fallen Fruit; Carolien Niebling; Hillary Savage of Bread and Puppet; Johanna Seelemann; Koen Vanmechelen; M. Farley Nobre; Maia Neumann of Yumbox; Mumo Musuva; Rebecca Fowler of Humane Borders, Inc.; Poonam, and the Daily Dump Team; and the Food and Agriculture Organization. Their graciously allowing us to reprint their work does not mean that they endorse the book or its contents.

Writing a book together remotely during a pandemic had its many challenges. We are grateful to have learned that we think alike, which made the process much easier.

Acronyms and Abbreviations

AFM:	alternative food movement
AIN:	Aquaculture for Income and Nutrition
ANAPQUI:	Asociación Nacional de Productores de Quinua (The National Association of Quinoa Producers)
ARS:	Agricultural Research Service
BIP:	Business Innovation Platform
BIPOC:	Black, Indigenous, People of Color
Black Oaks:	Black Oaks Center for Sustainable Renewable Living
BMI:	body mass index
BMPs:	best management practices
BMS:	Brazilian Mandala System
BSAS:	The Brisbane Aboriginal Sovereign Embassy
CEASE	(Communities, Engagement, Actions, Shareability, Ecosystem) Design Thinking Tool
CERES:	Centre for Education and Research Environmental Strategies
CFN:	civic food network
CIRAPIP:	Center for Information, Research & Action for the Promotion of Farmers Initiatives
COCAMP:	Cooperativa dos Assentados da Reforma Agrária do Pontal (Agrarian Reform Settlers' Cooperative in the Pontal)
CSA:	Community Supported Agriculture
CSFSP:	Canada-Saskatchewan Farmer Stewardship Program
DO:	design outcome
DT:	design thinking
DSMG:	Duncan Street Miracle Garden
EC:	Egg of Columbus
ERS:	Economic Research Service
EU:	European Union
FAO:	Food and Agriculture Organization
FDA:	Food and Drug Administration
FF:	Fleet Farming
FFOC:	Free Food on Campus!
FIES:	Food Insecurity Experience Scale

FTA:	The Food Trade Apparatus
GFJI:	Growing Food Justice for All Initiative
GHG:	greenhouse gas
GPN:	generative production network
GUI:	Graphical User Interface
HHFKA:	Healthy Hunger-Free Kids Act of 2010
HQCP:	high-quality cassava peels
ICIPE:	International Center of Insect Physiology and Ecology
IHRG:	Indigenous Health Research Group
IITA:	International Institute of Tropical Agriculture
ILRI:	International Livestock Research Institute
IYA:	IITA Youth Agripreneurs
LMV:	La Mesa Verde
Meadow Well:	Meadow Well Food Hub
MST:	Movimento dos Trabalhadores Rurais Sem Terra (Rural Landless Workers' Movement)
NFW:	Northern Friesian Woodlands Association
NGO:	non-governmental organization
NJCHS:	New Jersey Child Health Study
OPT:	Obesity Prevention Tailored
PAR:	participatory action approach
PPB:	participatory plant breeding
PPD:	postharvest physiological deterioration
PPF:	Parks and People Foundation
REC:	Rural Enterprise Center
RPP:	researcher-practitioner partnership
RRVP:	Rock River Valley Pantry
SFI:	Slow Food International
SFUW:	Slow Food University of Wisconsin-Madison
SLU:	Swedish University of Agricultural Sciences
SPD:	speculative participatory design
SSCA:	Saskatchewan Soil Conservation Association
SUMI:	Software Usability Measurement Inventory
SWF:	Sweet Water Foundation
SWO:	Sweet Water Organics
UA:	urban aquaponics
UN:	United Nations
UNDESA:	United Nations Department of Economic and Social Affairs
URF:	urban rooftop farming
USAID:	United States Agency for International Development
USDA:	United States Department of Agriculture
WHO:	World Health Organization
ZFarming:	Zero-acreage farming

Introduction

Today, our worldwide struggles—against climate change, socio-economic and environmental disparities, political divisions, conflicts, trade struggles, and health issues—show the need for more sustainable design moving forward. Attaining sustainability requires transdisciplinary coordination and collaboration from all fields, and across a spectrum of design areas, including architecture; engineering; communication; marketing; visual arts; visual communication, information, and graphic design; product design; interaction design; experience design; and others.

In this book, we look specifically at sustainability in food security through the lenses of equity and justice. Grubinger et al. (2010, as cited in Chase and Grubinger 2014), define food as a system:

> an interconnected web of activities, resources, and people that extend across all domains involved in providing nourishment and sustaining good health, including production, processing, packaging, distribution, marketing, consumption, and disposal of food. The organization of food's system reflects and responds to social, cultural, political, economic, health, and environmental conditions and can be identified at global scales, from a household kitchen to a city, county, state, or nation.
>
> (6)

This view of food makes food insecurity the epitome of a "wicked problem" (Buchanan 1992; Rowe 1986; Rittel and Webber 1973; Churchman 1967). The term "wicked" refers to a daunting complexity, problems that take place within an evolving system of highly interlinked, deeply embedded, cross-cultural, and cross-disciplinary challenges. So, too, are the solutions within the wicked problem's system. Bennett (2012b) proposes that a wicked problem requires a wicked solution—an equally complex system of design outcomes (DOs) that address it. Figure I.1 illustrates a model of Bennett's wicked solution concept showing how social designers and innovators can contextualize existing DOs across a field of possibilities mapped by two sets of dimensions: top-down versus bottom-up and localized versus memetic.

Manzini (2014) introduces the top-down and bottom-up polarity[1] in design as where change starts; that is, it starts with those who are driving it (57).

DOI: 10.4324/9781003222026-1

Top-down interventions tend to come from private and public institutions. We receive some policies backed up by laws, and do our best to implement them or suffer the consequences. Or we receive some product that is too tempting not to use; the corporation gets compliance simply by making the alternative technologically unavailable to its users. Bottom-up interventions, in contrast, come from individuals, communities, networks of individuals, and so on. Whether that is a social movement that spreads across the nation, like Black Lives Matter, or just a neighborhood effort, like holding all the garage sales on the first Saturday of each month in a particular town, there is neither the force of state power nor the force of economic might behind it. Such people-powered phenomena feel different: more authentic perhaps, more voluntary, more like a "direct democracy" (Matsuska 2020) than representatives deciding for us, or marketing staff creatively scheming to create consumer loyalty and market exclusion (Bougette et al. 2019).

In addition to top-down vs. bottom-up, we can make a further distinction with the degree to which the solution is localized. In the case of Black Lives Matter, the movement began in an inherently decentralized, non-geographic fashion: across Twitter. Many movements and other phenomena today propagate in this meme-like spread, and for that reason, we will refer to it as *memetic*. At the opposite end of that spectrum, there are bottom-up phenomena that are highly localized and geographically specific: community events such as tailgate parties and sandlot baseball in the US (or pub night and a kick around in the UK), and so on. But it is indeed a spectrum, and we need to be able to consider all the forms that land somewhere in-between.

Thus, our map of wicked solutions has two dimensions. Along the vertical axis are DOs that emerge bottom-up by individuals and lay communities impacted by the wicked problem, or top-down from privately or publicly funded professionals. Along the horizontal axis lies DOs that range from decentralized memetic spreading to localized or those situated in a particular geographic context.

Why bother with this kind of mapping? Due to the complexity of both the problem and solution contexts, it is hard to see the system's state at any one moment. Critical mapping enables the visualization of the wicked solution in terms of its flow of control (top-down vs. bottom-up) and flow of communication (memetic vs. localized) without getting bogged down in the details before we are ready for them. Most importantly, it helps us to map changes over time. Moving from top right to left and down, DOs that populate quadrant A are top-down and localized, emerging from positions of economic power and may be implemented or regulated through large-scale commercial or cultural production that is limited to a geographic area (e.g., one nation or household). DOs that populate quadrant B are top-down and memetic and thus differ from quadrant A in that they may be implemented or regulated through large-scale commercial or cultural production that permeates global geographic boundaries (e.g., many countries or households). DOs that populate quadrant C are bottom-up and memetic and emerge from lay positions of power and authority (e.g., citizens) that may effectuate mass consumption through technological mediation and other forms of widespread

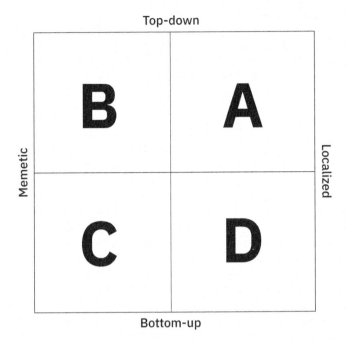

Figure 1.1 A wicked solution comprises an assemblage of existing DOs onto a grid of four quadrants, contextualized across two dimensions. Image courtesy of Audrey G. Bennett.

consumption or cultural production and appropriation. Finally, DOs that populate quadrant D are bottom-up and localized.

The wicked problem of food insecurity, inequity, and injustice can be described as a perennial state of pursuing but never attaining a sustainable balance where all of humanity gets sufficient healthy food within a productive environment. Instead, what prevails seemingly is the opposite: a lingering state of food insecurity amid environmental deterioration exacerbated within marginalized communities. Yet, as food insecurity continues to challenge the healthy sustenance of humanity, society has an evolving repertoire of existing, localized DOs scattered across the globe like disconnected nodes in a dysfunctional system. Lack of access to or knowledge about these existing food design assets—interventions, resources, and knowledge—perpetuates food insecurity, health problems, and environmental deterioration, particularly in underserved communities.

Food insecurity is one of many wicked problems in society that is garnering increasing attention within the design field. Flood and Sloan (2019)—at the "Food: Bigger Than the Plate" exhibit they curated at the Victoria and Albert Museum in Britain—note that design has been fundamental to food since industrialization, with design practitioners participating in every aspect of the commodification of food from its production to its consumption (13). Both Flood and

Sloan (2019) and Manzini (2014) provide ample examples of past and present, top-down and bottom-up designs addressing food worldwide. Designers who seek real-world problems affecting humanity and the environment may choose food insecurity as the problem to address based on perhaps a negative food-related experience they've had, other personal or professional interests unrelated to direct life experience, or even community needs identified through primary or secondary research.

Whatever their rationale for choosing food insecurity, designers[2] who pursue this wicked societal problem in their research undoubtedly will confront the question: where in the food system can design intervene to bring about more sustainable change? Answering this question effectively is a challenge as it requires knowledge of the current state of the food system in which DOs already exist that impact the food security problem but may not be accessible to a broad audience. Thus, the purpose of this book is to compile these DOs, organize them according to their relevance to a particular part of the food system, and by doing so, facilitate analysis and understanding that informs future sustainable food design development.

As critical thinkers and makers, designers are varied in their creative problem-solving approaches. Frequently, they may come to the design process with an outcome already formulated in their heads. Solution-focused design methods for addressing complex challenges like food and the outcomes they generate seem to dominate design processes; however, less time is given to the problem definition phase. How can one address a wicked problem like food insecurity if one cannot understand the problem or see the current state of the system? And even if an intervention is designed, how can one access the solution if its complexity rivals that of the wicked problem itself? Surely some means of mapping changes over time is required.

In solution-focused design methods for addressing complex challenges, conceptualizing and making the outcome arguably dominates most of the time in the design process, which limits time spent on problem definition. Critical mapping addresses this by letting us put problem definition, intervention design, and follow-up assessment on the same map. In doing so, we can resolve a tension that is built into the very notion of "design." On the one hand, if we cannot predict outcomes, why hire a design team? On the other hand, if we are not putting resources into tracking outcomes and making corrections, how can we call ourselves responsible professionals? Critical mapping is thus an organizational framework that assumes problem analysis, intervention creation and making, and outcome response need to be approached as an evolutionary process, allowing the design to be democratically modified and corrected by those most affected (Dorst 2019).

This book introduces a problematizing, reflective approach to the creative design inquiry process called critical mapping. Critical mapping entails compiling existing peer-reviewed DOs engaged in systemic interaction towards addressing a wicked problem, and organizing them visually and affinitively towards identifying places to intervene in the system to design a more sustainable future. In critical mapping, a wicked solution is visualized as a diagram onto which peer-reviewed DOs are charted for analysis. It is a problem-definition framework to critically analyze systemic societal problems like food insecurity and make evidence-based decisions towards a more sustainable future. In terms of food insecurity, critical mapping permits cognizance of the interaction and interdependence of effectuated and effective DOs in the food system towards identifying what environmental scientist Donella Meadows introduced as "leverage points … places within the system where a small shift in one thing can produce big changes in everything" (Meadows 1999).

Critical mapping begins with secondary research on the wicked problem and its current and evolving wicked solution. First, the wicked problem is named, operationalized verbally and visually with evidence, and grounded with statistical evidence. Then, the second step in critical mapping is to conduct a transdisciplinary and integrative literature review to identify and compile existing, peer-reviewed DOs that address the wicked problem. These DOs are then filtered to isolate those that are sustainable. The third step entails affinity diagramming— visually organizing and plotting the sustainable DOs onto a wicked solution grid visualized across a field of possibilities, towards identifying leverage points or gaps targetable by design innovation or appropriation. Along the vertical axis are DOs that emerge bottom-up from individuals and communities impacted by the wicked problem (e.g., artwork) or top-down from privately or publicly funded professionals (e.g., scholars). Along the horizontal axis lies DOs ranging from memetic (e.g., community gardens) to localized (e.g., sack gardens), that is, from widespread adoption to local use. In the next-to-final step of critical mapping, we analyze the wicked solution and identify the leverage points.

There is precedence for this kind of mapping framework in addressing wicked problems in a global society. For instance, in 2020, Johns Hopkins' Coronavirus Resource Center employed data visualization to show day-by-day infection and vaccination rates globally and hyper-locally (Dong et al. 2020). Health experts and laypeople could see where infection rates were spreading and at what rate. Relatedly, critically mapping existing sustainable DOs that address a wicked problem can enable designers to critically analyze the system to identify leverage points. From there, they can synthesize the impact of the existing solutions and see where lacunae exist to address human needs equitably and in a just manner; such solutions can potentially make a meaningful impact that propels society further towards sustainability and annihilating the wicked problem. Visualizing a wicked solution to food insecurity can arguably facilitate the identification of gaps in the complex food system that, when filled, can move us forward to creating a more sustainable future that is food secure, equitable, and just.

This book carries out the first four of the following five steps of critical mapping for food insecurity where we (1) name and operationalize the problem, (2) conduct a transdisciplinary and integrative literature review of peer-reviewed scholarship to identify and compile sustainable food DOs, (3) map DOs onto a wicked solution visualization, (4) analyze the wicked solution and identify gaps or leverage points for further innovation or appropriation, and (5) conduct primary research within communities grappling with the wicked problem to identify assets to include in the evolving wicked solution or adapt a sustainable food DO already included in the wicked solution to a new local context. Using food insecurity as the wicked problem, it compiles and maps existing sustainable food DOs from an integrative review of literature across disciplines and assesses the current state of the food system towards identifying leverage points or places where designers *should* intervene.

The first chapter, titled "Critically mapping a wicked solution to food insecurity," introduces, updates, and extends Grubinger et al.'s (2010) categories of the food system to include the additional categories of agriculture/aquaculture and access, with sustainability being integral to all of the categories. Thus, the proof-of-concept visualization of the wicked solution to food insecurity illustrated in Figure 1.10 includes eight food categories—agriculture/aquaculture, processing, production, distribution, communication (including recall, marketing, safety, and packaging), access, consumption, and waste. Each category comprises sustainable food DOs (listed and categorized in Appendix II) across two spectra—top-down (institutionally supported) to bottom-up (through citizen or community agency) and localized (affecting a limited amount of people) to memetic (widespread and affecting many)—that contribute to the wicked solution to the wicked problem of food insecurity. Chapter 1 discusses the following sustainability criteria for identifying existing sustainable DOs to populate each quadrant of the wicked solution to the food insecurity system: ethical, environmentally friendly, evidence-based, economical, ecological, effectuated, equitable and just, and enduring. Chapter 1's visualization of food insecurity's wicked solution provides the structure for the next four chapters of the book, where each corresponds to one of the four quadrants A, B, C, or D of the wicked solution. Chapters 2–5 discuss each of the four quadrants and the sustainable food DOs they hold. Each chapter represents one quadrant and includes descriptions of each sustainable food DO, identified from the transdisciplinary and integrative literature review of peer-review publications and our sustainability analysis. Each chapter concludes with an analysis of the quadrant to identify possible leverage points for future design innovation or appropriation.

In the second chapter titled "Quadrant A: Local, sustainable food design funded or supported by public or private institutions," we analyze the existing DOs of food insecurity's wicked solutions that are top-down and localized. Then, in the third chapter titled "Quadrant B: Widespread, sustainable food design funded or supported by public or private institutions," we describe and analyze existing DOs of food insecurity's wicked solution that are top-down and memetic. In Chapter 4, titled "Quadrant C: Widespread, sustainable food design created by citizens," we describe and analyze existing DOs that are bottom-up and memetic. Next, in Chapter 5, titled "Quadrant D: Local, sustainable food design created by citizens," we describe and analyze existing DOs that are bottom-up and localized. Chapters 2 through 5 each conclude with an analysis section titled "Places to intervene" that discusses the leverage points that emerged from the analysis of the existing DOs and the gaps between them to identify places within the food insecurity system that need intervention through design innovation or appropriation.

In the concluding chapter of the book, Chapter 6, we reflect on the analyses of the gaps in existing activities in the food system that may be inhibiting society's ability to yield a present reality of sustainable food. We discuss the limitations of our critical mapping process and propose how readers, through a research agenda, can engage with a variety of professional and community stakeholders to innovate or appropriate sustainable food DOs to address food insecurity. Then, we describe future work related to the fifth step of critical mapping, primary research with local communities on the further development of the wicked solution to food insecurity through multimodal communication of existing sustainable food DOs to communities who may lack the technological infrastructure to gain access to them.

Critical mapping, as a problematizing framework, has the potential to facilitate knowledge exchange around wicked problems (like food insecurity) and their existing wicked solutions (like sustainable food design) among professional design practitioners and researchers and other lay and professional stakeholders who may be situated remotely in different spaces, places, and times. This book, on a micro level, will be useful to anyone seeking insight into addressing the wicked problem of food insecurity in their private and public spheres of access, experience, power, and control. On a macro level, it sets the stage for a design future that facilitates the harvesting of wisdom from peer-reviewed scholarship towards social design, innovation, and appropriation that changes the world for the better by alleviating food insecurity in ways that are more equitable and just.

Notes

1 DESIS Network founder, Ezio Manzini, defines top-down stakeholders as experts, decision makers, or political activists, and bottom-up stakeholders as the people and communities directly involved in the social problem (57).
2 Manzini (2014; 2015), Benjamin (2019), and Costanza-Chock (2020) define the word "designer" broadly to include professionals with formal training in design as well as lay people doing design who do not have formal design training but fancy themselves as designers. We endorse their definitions in our own operationalization of "designer" to include laypeople and professionals (with or without formal design training) who may not self-identify as a designer but are producing, making, creating, and innovating technology and DOs. Thus, a designer is anyone who generates intangible and tangible outcomes through creative problem solving.

Bibliography

Benjamin, Ruha. 2019. *Race after Technology: Abolitionist Tools for the New Jim Code.* Medford, MA: Polity Press.
Bennett, Audrey G. 2012a. "Good Design is Good Social Change: Envisioning an Age of Accountability in Communication Design Education." *Visible Language* 46, no. 1/2: 66–79.

Bennett, Audrey G. 2012b. "Introduction: A Wicked Solution to the Global Food Problem." *Iridescent: Icograda Journal of Design* 2, no. 3: 2–10. https://www.tandfonline.com/doi/abs/10.1080/19235003.2012.11428510.

Bougette, Patrice, Oliver Budzinsky, and Frédéric Marty. 2019. "Exploitative Abuse and Abuse of Economic dependence: What Can We Learn from an Industrial Organization Approach?" *Revue d'economie politique* 129 no. 2: 261–286. https://doi.org/10.3917/redp.292.0261.

Buchanan, Richard. 1992. "Wicked Problems in Design Thinking." *Design Issues* 8, no. 2: 5–21. https://doi.org/10.2307/1511637.

Chase, Lisa, and Vern Grubinger. 2014. *Food, Farms, and Community: Exploring Food Systems.* Durham, NH: University of New Hampshire Press.

Churchman, C. West. 1967. "Guest Editorial: Wicked Problems." *Management Science* 14, no. 4: B141–B142. https://www.jstor.org/stable/2628678.

Costanza-Chock, Sasha. 2020. *Design Justice: Community-led Practices to Build the Worlds We Need.* Cambridge, MA: MIT Press.

Dong, Ensheng, Hongru Du, and Lauren Gardner. 2020. "An Interactive Web-based Dashboard to Track COVID-19 in Real-time." *The Lancet Infectious Diseases* 20, no. 5: 533–534. https://doi.org/10.1016/S1473-3099(20)30120-1.

Dorst, Kees. 2019. "Co-evolution and Emergence in Design." *Design Studies* 65: 60–77.

Flood, Catherine, and May Sloan, eds. 2019. *FOOD: Bigger than the Plate.* London: V&A.

Grubinger, Vern, Linda Berlin, Elizabeth Berman, Naomi Fukagawa, D. N. Kolodinsky, B. Parsons, A. Trubek, and K. Wallin. 2010. *University of Vermont Transdisciplinary Research Initiative Spire of Excellence Proposal: Food Systems.* Burlington, VT: University of Vermont.

Matsusaka, John G. 2020. *Let the People Rule.* Princeton, NJ: Princeton University Press.

Manzini, Ezio. 2014. "Making Things Happen: Social Innovation and Design." *Design Issues* 30, no. 1: 57–66.

Manzini, Ezio. 2015. *Design, When Everybody Designs: An Introduction to Design for Social Innovation.* Cambridge, MA: MIT Press.

Meadows, Donella H. 1999. *Leverage Points: Places to Intervene in a System.* Hartland, VT: The Sustainability Institute. https://donellameadows.org/wp-content/userfiles/Leverage_Points.pdf.

Rittel, Horst W. J., and Melvin M. Webber. 1973. "Dilemmas in a General Theory of Planning." *Policy Sciences* 4, no. 2: 155–169. https://www.jstor.org/stable/4531523.

Rowe, Peter G. 1986. *Design Thinking.* Cambridge, MA: MIT Press.

1 Critically mapping a wicked solution to food insecurity

Food sustains life, and without it, humanity would cease to exist. The Food and Agriculture Organization (FAO) of the United Nations (UN) at their 1996 World Food Summit in Italy defined food security as "a state where all people, at all times, have physical, social, and economic access to sufficient, safe, and nutritious food to meet their dietary needs and food preferences for an active and healthy life" (FAO 2008). Subsequently, in the report titled "An Introduction to the Basic Concepts of Food Security," the FAO introduces four dimensions of food security that operate simultaneously: availability, access, utilization, and stability. Availability refers to the physical supply of food daily through generative production, level of stock or inventory, and trade (1). Economic and environmental factors, like income and geographic location, respectively, determine household and individual access to the physical supply of food (1). Once an individual gains access to a food supply, how they utilize that food to retrieve the nutrients their body needs daily depends on their culturally based and cognitive "feeding practices, food preparation, diet, and intra-household" practices of distributing food along with their body's biological functionality and its ability to utilize the nutrients accordingly (1). To be food-secure requires balancing availability, access, and daily utilization to achieve the fourth dimension of food security, stability. A lack of equilibrium in the food system can bring about too little or too much food on an individual level; and both of these states can have negative health ramifications that, over time, can lead to preventable illnesses and mortality for human beings (1).

As food security is an overall life-or-death balancing act influenced by environmental, biological, political, economic, ethical, aesthetic, and socio-cultural factors, the FAO created a scale and household and individual survey instruments (see Appendix IV Food Insecurity Experience Scale Instruments) to assess the range of food security for households and individuals across the globe ("The State of Food Security and Nutrition in the World" 2018, 7). The FAO's measuring scale illustrated in Figure 1.1 strategically uses semiotic hues for danger and safety, ranging from green (food-secure) to green-yellow (mild food insecurity) to yellow-orange (moderate food insecurity) to orange-red (severe food insecurity).

Subsequently, in its 2021 update titled "The State of Food Security and Nutrition in the World: Transforming Food Systems for Food Security, Improved

DOI: 10.4324/9781003222026-2

Figure 1.1 FAO's food insecurity experience scale ranges from food secure to mildly food insecure to moderately food insecure to severely food insecure. It is used to measure the state of food security among people individually and in households across the globe. Image courtesy of FAO.

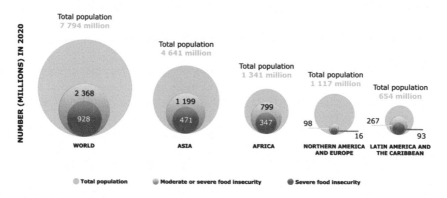

Figure 1.2 The concentration and distribution of food insecurity by severity differ significantly across the world's regions—Asia, Africa, Northern America and Europe, Latin America and the Caribbean—with food insecurity being most prevalent in Asia and Africa respectively. Image courtesy of FAO.

Nutrition and Affordable Healthy Diets for All," the FAO reports that "moderate or severe food insecurity has been climbing slowly since 2015 and, as of 2021, affects more than 30 percent of the world population" with over 900 million people experiencing severe food insecurity as shown in Figure 1.2 (19). As shown, "the concentration and distribution of food insecurity by severity differ greatly across the different regions of the world with food insecurity being more prevalent in Asia and Africa respectively" (20).

The United States Census Bureau estimates that of its approximate 300 million population (United States Census Bureau n.d.), 50% are female, and 31.9% are people of color experiencing high levels of food insecurity. According to the FAO (2021, 22), "globally and in every region, the prevalence of food insecurity is higher among women than men". In terms of race and ethnicity, the United States Department of Agriculture's (USDA) Economic Research Service (ERS) provides open access to its food security data online.[1] One chart titled "Trends in food insecurity by race and ethnicity, 2001–21" shows that Black (non-Hispanic) and Hispanic households have experienced substantially more food insecurity in the past decade than other racial and ethnic households. This reality grossly contradicts the aims of the FAO that, as noted previously, defines food security as "a state where *all* people, at *all* times, have...access to sufficient, safe and nutritious food to meet their dietary needs and food preferences for an active and healthy life" (2008, emphasis added). Penniman blames this disparity on age-old racism noting:

> Racism is built into the DNA of the US food system. Beginning with the genocidal land theft from Indigenous people, continuing with the kidnapping of our ancestors from the shores of West Africa for forced agricultural labor, morphing into convict leasing, expanding to the migrant guestworker program, and maturing into its current state where farm management is among the whitest professions, farm labor is predominantly Brown and exploited, and people of color disproportionately live in food apartheid neighborhoods and suffer from diet-related illness.
>
> (2018, 5)

In the edited book titled *Cultivating Food Justice: Race, Class, and Sustainability*, Alkon and Agyeman (2011) concur, discussing how "food is not only linked to ecological sustainability, community, and health but also racial, economic, and environmental justice" (15). Referencing Winne (2008), Alkon and Agyeman clarify that the injustice of food insecurity centers on access; communities of color tend to lack ease of access to healthy food due to geographic location and affordability—that is, healthy food that is available likely is too expensive and more costly than similar food in wealthier areas (Alkon and Agyeman 2011, 17). Undeniably, food insecurity is a pressing social justice issue in the present period of multiple social challenges, including climate change, COVID-19, war, and white supremacy. As good health depends mainly on food security for *all*, the next section discusses the negative ramifications of food insecurity on health.

Food insecurity and its dire health consequences

The World Health Organization (WHO) uses the term "malnutrition" to represent the negative impact of food insecurity on human health. WHO defines malnutrition (the "double burden of malnutrition") as:

> deficiencies, excesses, or imbalances in a person's intake of energy and nutrients. The term malnutrition addresses three broad groups of conditions: 1) undernutrition, which includes wasting (low weight-for-height), stunting (low height-for-age), and underweight (low weight-for-age); 2)

micronutrient-related malnutrition, which includes micronutrient deficiencies (a lack of important vitamins and minerals) or micronutrient excess; and 3) overweight, obesity, and diet-related non-communicable diseases (such as heart disease, stroke, diabetes, and some cancers).

(World Health Organization 2017)

Figure 1.3 illustrates how food insecurity can follow two distinct pathways to bring about malnutrition in individuals and households that can lead to mortality. The process of malnutrition begins with an individual's lack of or inconsistent access to food, whether by their agency or the impact of their household status. The consequences of this "uncertain food access" affect the quantity, quality, and continuity of their food consumption and even their mental health—the latter of which also negatively impacts the quantity, quality, and continuity of their food consumption (FAO 2018). On the one hand, if too few calories, proteins, vitamins, and minerals are consumed, malnutrition through undernutrition and micronutrient deficiencies ensues. On the other hand, if too many high calories and nutrient-poor foods are consumed, malnutrition through overweight, obesity, and diet-related non-communicable disease can occur.

As of June 9, 2021, WHO's webpage provides key facts on malnutrition estimates that 1.9 billion adults are overweight or obese, 462 million adults are underweight, 149 million children under five are stunted (too short for age), 45 million children are wasted (too thin for height), 38.9 million children are overweight or obese. In regard to race and ethnicity, as of 2020, 41.6% of Blacks, 38.8% of American Indian/Alaska Natives, 38.5% of Hawaiian/Pacific Islanders, 36.6% of Hispanics, 30.7% of Whites, and 11.8% of Asians in the United States were obese (United Health Foundation, n.d.). Foster (1992) and Leathers and Foster (2004) argue that malnutrition, specifically undernutrition, is a perennial challenge in developing nations. However, WHO's malnutrition webpage on malnutrition also notes that economically developed countries, too, are challenged by malnutrition through excess consumption that leads to obesity—the gateway physical state to life-threatening illnesses such as diabetes, cancer, and heart disease. This simultaneity of seemingly opposing health consequences (i.e., overweightness and undernutrition) at alarming rates caused by food insecurity contributes to it being a wicked problem, and the pervasiveness of food insecurity in communities of color makes it a critical social justice issue, further adding to the complexity of the problem.

While it is evident that malnutrition presents a significant and complex challenge in global society today, some argue that it will persist into the future. For instance, Nelson et al. (2018) predict that between now and 2050, when the world population grows to 10 billion, obesity and undernutrition will continue. That is in part because of "the 'nutrition transition' in many countries where, as incomes grow, diets shift away from traditional diets towards 'western' diets that are typically higher in saturated fat, sugar, and salt" (16). Thus the global food problem's focus will evolve to center more on micronutrient deficiencies exacerbated, in some regions, by climate change, increasing incomes,[2] and evolving diets. Their

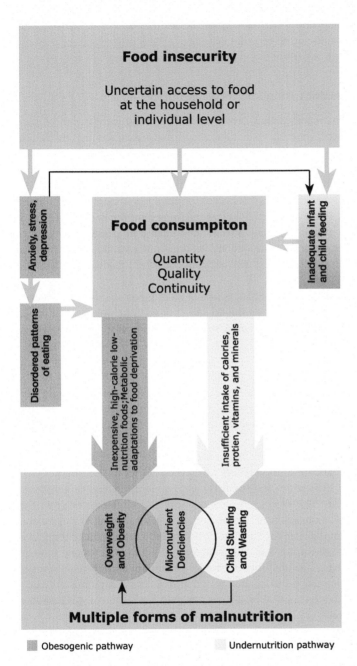

Figure 1.3 Pathways from food insecurity or inadequate food access to multiple forms of malnutrition. Image courtesy of FAO.

findings indicate that the global food problem in 2050 may be more about "providing nutritious diets rather than adequate calories" (Nelson et al. 2018). In the next section, we discuss the drivers that systemically undermine food security and malnutrition towards addressing food insecurity moving forward.

Factors driving malnutrition and food insecurity

In 2017, WHO also reported that there are socio-cultural, behavioral, biological, and environmental factors that influence an individual's nutrition (World Health Organization 2017, 4). Lifestyle habits and socio-economic status, food supply, portion sizes, and cost are some of the factors that constantly and simultaneously interact while influencing one's daily access to healthy food (5). While the drivers of the double burden of malnutrition might be thought of as a linear progression in time that cycles with no clear starting point, the reality of the situation with malnutrition is that it is arguably more the simultaneity of occurrence of these factors that influences one's nutrition. If malnutrition is an effect of food insecurity, then the factors driving malnutrition contribute to those driving food insecurity.

Recently, the USDA attempted to paint a broader picture of the food security system that includes the drivers mentioned earlier of malnutrition, and extended the repertoire to include climate change, political conflict, and even design (i.e., technology and innovation) (FAO 2021). As depicted in Figure 1.4, the FAO comprehensively illustrates food security as a system of activities composed of drivers affecting complex activities ranging from local to global, individual to institution. The complex activities occurring in the food system include subsystems of activities related to the production of food to its supply within environments where access to healthy food is influenced by numerous top-down and bottom-up drivers.

Attaining a state of food security means creating an equitable and just balance across the four dimensions of food security discussed earlier in this chapter (i.e., availability, access, utilization, and stability) and two more (agency and sustainability)[3] (FAO 2021, 53). Agency is "the capacity of individuals or groups to make their own decisions about what foods they eat; what foods they produce; how that food is produced, processed and distributed within food systems; and their ability to engage in processes that shape food system policies and governance" (190). Whereas, sustainability is "the long-term ability of food systems to provide food security and nutrition in a way that does not compromise the economic, social and environmental bases that generate food security and nutrition for future generations" (190).

The current state of the food system, however, is the opposite of the kind of food-secure balance that we seek. As the earlier statistics in this chapter reveal, populations worldwide are struggling to achieve food security due to major drivers, including political conflict, climate variability and extremes, economic slowdowns and downturns, unaffordability of healthy diets, and underlying poverty and inequality that emerge from top-down and bottom-up activities in the food

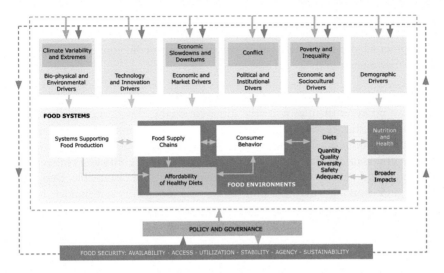

Figure 1.4 FAO's "food systems diagram…illustrates how the drivers behind recent food security and nutrition trends specifically create multiple impacts throughout food systems (food systems, including food environments), leading to impacts on the four [traditional] dimensions of food security (availability, access, utilization and stability), as well as the two additional dimensions of agency and sustainability. These drivers have impacts on attributes of diets (quantity, quality, diversity, safety and adequacy) and nutrition and health outcomes (nutrition and health)" (2021, 53). Image courtesy of FAO.

system. On the one hand, there are top-down institutional activities and natural factors (e.g., the environment and climate changes) that can cause poverty, economic recession, war and conflict, and varied and extreme climates that negatively impact the flow of the food system and create a state of food insecurity, inequity, and injustice for many communities, especially those of color. On the other hand, there are bottom-up demographic and environmental factors, including nutrition, health, income level, heritage, geographic location, and dieting habits that influence when, where, what, how, and how much an individual consumes, and thus can lead to prolonged experiences of food insecurity.

To mitigate the negative drivers on the food system towards food security for all, the FAO (2021, 88) outlines the following six possible pathways to intervene and transform the global food system towards food security:

1. Integrating humanitarian, development, and peacebuilding policies in conflict-affected areas.
2. Scaling up climate resilience across food systems.
3. Strengthening the resilience of the most vulnerable to economic adversity.
4. Intervening along the food supply chain to lower the cost of nutritional foods.

5. Tackling poverty and structural inequalities, ensuring interventions are pro-poor and inclusive.
6. Strengthening food environments and changing consumer behavior to promote dietary patterns that positively impact human health and the environment.

While the intent of providing these pathways may be for top-down intervention, we interpret them as potential interventional pathways for top-down *and* bottom-up activities within the realm of design for social innovation and appropriation. A secure food future depends on the continued development of innovative interventions that can disrupt drivers of food insecurity and redirect the system towards greater security that is equitable, just, and sustainable. Designers of all kinds working with other professional and community stakeholders in the food system, can play a vital role in creating such a future. In the next section, we discuss the need for three seemingly disparate fields—sustainability, food, and design—to come together to address food insecurity, inequity, and injustice through sustainable food design.

The convergence of sustainability, food, and design

With an increasing awareness of the environmental impact of development on the planet, sustainable development emerged as a mainstream concept with the publishing of *Our Common Future* in 1987 by the United Nations, often referred to as the Brundtland Report[4] (Du Pisani 2007). In the report sustainable development was defined as development that "seeks to meet the needs and aspirations of the present without compromising the ability to meet those of the future" (World Commission on Environment and Development 1987, 51). The report expressed concerns on future global equity and focused on the redistribution of resources to stimulate economic growth in poorer nations to ensure that basic needs were met for all humans. Sustainable development is based on the idea that social equity, economic growth, and environmental stewardship could be integrated in various areas including agriculture and food. The concept of the integrated sustainability lens of social, economic, and environmental would later be the basis for the concept of the triple bottom line (Du Pisani 2007). The triple bottom line is a sustainability construct, a framework that measures performance and organizational success in business based on three lines: economic, social, and environmental (Goel 2010). Elkington (2008) coined the concept and used the terms "profit," "people," and "planet" to reference the three pillars. The triple bottom line in sustainability is based on the integration of the social, environmental, and economic, and places an equality of emphasis on each of the lines (Alhaddi 2015).

Many sustainable development frameworks have been created and used in local, regional, and global contexts, based on the three components of the triple bottom line—social, economic, and environmental—and they vary widely in their scope and effectiveness (Orenstein and Shach-Pinsley 2017). The "three pillars" approach has been challenged due to the complexities within each system and the limits of compromise when trying to achieve balance among all three pillars (Miller 2014). Other sustainability paradigms have emerged, including the concepts of social sustainability (Eizenberg and Jabareen 2017; Vallance et al. 2011), "just sustainability" (Agyeman 2008; Agyeman et al. 2003; Sherriff 2009), and sustainable livelihoods (Chambers and Conway 1992; Knutsson 2006; Miller 2014). Social sustainability varies widely in its definition and scope in practice and theory. Eizenberg and Jabareen (2017) view the risks from climate change and its threat on social spheres as a key concept of sustainability and they offer that social sustainability seeks to address social issues while confronting these risks. Just sustainability considers social justice and environmental justice and recognizes the inextricable links between humans and the earth (Agyeman 2008; Alkon and Agyemen 2011; Sherriff 2009). Sustainable livelihoods include access to the tools and resources needed for living and being able to weather shocks and stressors, now and in the future (Chambers and Conway 1992).

As sustainable development concepts and applications emerged after the Brundtland Report, most focused on the environmental aspects, neglecting the components of poverty, equity, and health, even though these were addressed in the report (Eizenberg and Jabareen 2017). Design and sustainability were also initially focused on the environment with a particular emphasis in areas of product design and engineering (Bhamra and Hernandez 2021; Ceschin and Gaziulusoy 2016). Victor Papanek's book titled *Design for the Real World: Human Ecology and Social Change* introduced the impact of design on consumption and the environment and encouraged the design profession to transform (1985). As sustainable development frameworks and focus have expanded, sustainable design's emphasis evolved from a focus on the environment and the impact of a product to the emphasis on sustainability as a property of the system (Bhamra and Hernandez 2021; Ceschin and Gaziulusoy 2016). This shift in focus has expanded the role of the designer. Manzini (2015) writes about design and social change towards sustainability and the roles of both diffuse designers, non-experts using their natural abilities, and design experts, trained professionals. The designer's role in addressing complex social issues like food has expanded to social innovation and radical transformation. These everyday designers can make changes locally that can have a broader impact, or they may begin with a big vision and recognize the need to accomplish it by working locally (Manzini 2015). While this may happen as a matter of course, a vision and radical processes are necessary to achieve societal change (Reynolds 2017). The idea of radical innovation can lead to changing systems (Manzini 2015), which leads us back to food systems and design.

According to semiotician Roland Barthes (2018) in "Toward a Psychosociology of Contemporary Food Consumption," food is a system of communication composed of "signifying units" (24) that "imply a set of images, dreams, tastes, choices, and values" (23). As such, food falls within the intellectual scope of scholarly and creative production in design, even in its subdisciplines like graphic design, visual art, and visual communication and information design. However, in the College Art Association's panel presentation titled "Design History: The State of the Art" (2016), art historian Grace Lees-Maffei noted that even with the development of the International Food Design Society in 2009, nearly a decade later, food was still a "relatively unexplored area of design" (Lees-Maffei 2016). Yet, three years after Lees-Maffei's 2016 presentation, Flood and Sloan—in an edited collection that accompanies the 2019 food exhibit titled "Food: Bigger than the Plate" at the Victoria and Albert Museum in Britain—offer another perspective asserting that design has been fundamental to food since industrialization, with design practitioners participating in every aspect of the commodification of food, from its production to its consumption (2019, 13).

In fact, in the early twenty-first century, food design had been evolving steadily, with various definitions emerging to determine its scope. The use of the term "food design" was being used in academia in the early 2000s as intersections in design and food began to be explored.

For instance, the Association for the Study of Food and Society and the Agriculture, Food & Human Values Society (ASFS/AFHVS) have been holding professional conferences on food-related themes since 1987;[5] and their 2005 conference titled "Visualizing Food and Farm" was particularly groundbreaking in its focused exploration of the role of design through visualization in food knowledge production. The conference's program included the following scholarly talks:

- Lori S. Ball, Matthew Pottieger, and M. E. Deming presented "Revealing the Role of the Local Food System in the Formation of Landscape Patterns," making landscape patterns in the food system visible by collecting data through local farm visits, reviewing aerial photos and maps, then analyzing them to create new maps and compositions, creating a spatial phenomenon and revealing a narrative of the local food system.
- Also examining patterns, Daniel Block presented "Supermarkets, Ethnic Markets, and Corner Stores in Chicago: Geographic Patterns, Ties to Community, and Provision of Fresh Foods," an ongoing mapping project examining spatial patterns between types of markets and demographics in Chicago.
- Alison Grace Cliath presented on blue-green labeling and how it can help consumers make equitable, sustainable choices in "Seeing Shades: Ecologically and Socially Just Labeling." Utilizing visual sociology, Cliath explored blue-green labeling and the challenge created by some industries developing their own "greenwash" labels without actually being environmentally friendly or socially just.

Subsequently, Francesca Zampollo founded the International Food Design Society in 2009,[6] with the First International Symposium on Food Experience Design in 2010 in London.[7] Then, ASFS/AFHVS held another professional conference at Indiana University in 2010 that included separate food experience design lectures by Sonia Massari and Francesca Zampollo on the first food design panel in food system education (Massari 2017). Additional academic conferences on food and design propagated worldwide. For instance, the First International Conference on Designing Food and Designing for Food was held in London in 2012,[8] and the biennial conference titled "GLIDE'12: Global Interaction in Design Education" was organized by the first author in consultation with design consultants Michele Washington, Adream Blair, and Gloria Gomez. Hosted at Rensselaer Polytechnic Institute in Troy, New York, design scholars from around the world convened virtually, including Clinton Carlson, Whitney Peake, Sónia Matos, Karin Vaneker, Erwin Slaats, Sonia Massari, and others to contribute peer-reviewed, research findings on the use of visual communication design resources to address the global food problem. The conference culminated in the publication of a special issue titled "GLIDE'12: Consumed"[9] in *Iridescent*, the International Council of Design's journal on design research. In 2013 the Latin American Food Design Network[10] (red-LaFD) was established by Pedro Reissig and Daniel Bergara, with assistance from Francesca Zampollo. Additional relevant conferences then occurred including the First European Conference on Understanding Food Design in 2015, where the second author presented on "The Future of Food Design"[11] and also spoke at the preceding 2nd Food Design x Education (FDxE)[12] event, the Second International Conference on Food Design in New York City in 2015,[13] and the First International Food Design and Food Studies Conference in 2017 in Lisbon, Portugal.[14] Additional events and conferences on the topic have been held since then.

Interestingly, the International Food Design Society became inactive during this emergent period at which time its founder, Francesca Zampollo, shifted resources and efforts to the development of the *International Food Design Journal* in 2016. Today, the *International Journal of Food Design* continues and is dedicated to understanding food design. To wrestle with the broad definitions of food and design, Zampollo originally categorized food design into the subcategories of "design with food," "design for food," "food space design" (interior design for food), "food product design," "design about food," "eating design" (Zampollo 2013) and more recently "food design thinking" (Zampollo and Peacock 2016). Within each of these subcategories of food design research, food content knowledge experts interact with chefs, food scientists, architects, interior designers, product designers, and industrial designers. As more designers connect with food knowledge, the field of food design will continue to expand (Zampollo 2016). When the *International Food Design Journal* was first published in 2016, food design was still relatively new as an area of research; the journal has helped to expand the field and scholarship since then, though global research databases still reveal limited indexed publications specific to food design (Juri et al. 2022). The original guidelines for the journal stated that it is "open to any research and project that simply connects food and design" (8).

In the inaugural issue of the *International Food Design Journal* in 2016, editor Francesca Zampollo collected and presented definitions from professionals working in food and design, in addition to contributions from the editorial and advisory boards of the journal. The definitions range from reflecting a heavy focus on food as food design to wider, more systemic visions. Fabio Parasecoli, formerly Director of Food Studies Initiatives at The New School in New York City, and formerly the Director of the Food Studies PhD program at New York University, defined food design with a wider lens:

> Food design includes ideas, values, methods, processes, and activities aiming to modify, improve and optimize individual and communal interactions with and around food, including but not limited to edible materials, objects, experiences, natural and built environments, services, systems, and networks.
>
> (Zampollo 2016, 7)

Zampollo advocated against choosing one definition and instead embraced varied definitions for their complexity and intersections, a reflection of the field of food design (2016). Food design practitioner, social entrepreneur, and scholar Pedro Reissig (2017) invited the collective to shape the definition of food design, recognizing the oft-cited interpretation that food design solely means the aesthetic qualities of food; he proposed the following working definition:

> any "action" that can "improve" our "relationship" with food individually or collectively in diverse ways and instances, including the design of food products, materials, experiences, practices, technology, environments, and systems. By useful, I mean a definition that frames a way of thinking and acting, motivating open and critical thinking with a propositive attitude.
>
> (5)

Inherent in this definition of food design is the understanding that it is a platform that considers the complex; it requires an examination of relationships with foods from all aspects (Reissig 2017). However, as the food system comprises a complex system of activities that currently effects insecurity, inequity, injustice, and environmental damage, the scope of food design must expand to include impact through the inclusion of sustainability with social justice framing. In the proceedings of the 2nd International Food Design and Food Studies Conference, "Experiencing FOOD: Designing Sustainable and Social Practices," Pires acknowledged the growing need for design solutions that focus on sustainability and creativity in food systems, recognizing both the layered complexities in food systems and the need for inclusivity of diversity, culture, education, and history (Bonacho et al. 2021).

As Nicola Twilley notes, "food is an incredibly powerful tool for connecting seemingly disparate issues…If you design for food and food systems, you will inevitably address all considerations needed to create a sustainable, workable community" (*Urban Omnibus* 2010). Sustainability, food, and design are fields encompassing wide perspectives, methods, and contexts. Variations and cross-combinations of these subjects have been expanded upon in the literature in recent decades, including "sustainability transformation" (Abson et al. 2016; Artmann et al. 2020; Elmqvist et al. 2019; Dorninger et al. 2020), "sustainability transitions" (Köhler et al. 2019; Markard et al. 2012; Gaitán-Cremaschi et al. 2019; Gaziulusoy and Öztekin 2019), "food systems sustainability" (Béné et al. 2019; El Bilali and

Allahyari 2018; Haysom et al. 2019; Mourad 2016; Weber et al. 2020), "design of food systems" (Ballantyne-Brodie and Telalbasic 2017; Manzini 2015), "design for sustainability" (Bhamra and Hernandez 2021; Ceshin and Gaziulusoy 2016; Rocha et al. 2019; Spangenberg et al. 2010), "eating design" (Schouwenburg and Vogelzang 2011), "food experience design" (Massari 2012), and human food inter-action design (Choi and Blevis 2010; Comber et al. 2014; Dolejšová et al. 2020). Within this broad scholarly context, "food design" (Bordewijk and Schifferstein 2020; van Hinte 2016; Guixe et al. 2010; Juri et al. 2022; Massari 2017; Reissig 2017; Zampollo 2016) arguably solidified as a subset field of design. As the world-wide pandemic beginning in 2020 has significantly impacted all facets of the food system, positioning a more inclusive definition of sustainability within food design has gone from being a call to action to an imperative.

Underpinning this imperative, the 2015 United Nations 17 Sustainable Development Goals (SDGs) in its 2030 Agenda (United Nations, n.d.) announced the following 17 goals to design a sustainable world by 2030:

Goal 1. End poverty in all its forms everywhere.
Goal 2. End hunger, achieve food security and improved nutrition, and promote sustainable agriculture.
Goal 3. Ensure healthy lives and promote well-being for all at all ages.
Goal 4. Ensure inclusive and equitable quality education and promote lifelong learning opportunities for all.
Goal 5. Achieve gender equality and empower all women and girls.

Figure 1.5 Sustainable Development Goals.

Goal 6. Ensure availability and sustainable management of water and sanitation for all.

Goal 7. Ensure access to affordable, reliable, sustainable, and modern energy for all.

Goal 8. Promote sustained, inclusive, and sustainable economic growth, full and productive employment, and decent work for all.

Goal 9. Build resilient infrastructure, promote inclusive and sustainable industrialization, and foster innovation.

Goal 10. Reduce inequality within and among countries.

Goal 11. Make cities and human settlements inclusive, safe, resilient, and sustainable.

Goal 12. Ensure sustainable consumption and production patterns.

Goal 13. Take urgent action to combat climate change and its impacts.

Goal 14. Conserve and sustainably use the oceans, seas, and marine resources for sustainable development.

Goal 15. Protect, restore, and promote sustainable use of terrestrial ecosystems, sustainably manage forests, combat desertification, halt and reverse land degradation, and halt biodiversity loss.

Goal 16. Promote peaceful and inclusive societies for sustainable development, provide access to justice for all, and build effective, accountable, and inclusive institutions at all levels.

Goal 17. Strengthen the means of implementation and revitalize the Global Partnership for Sustainable Development.

It has been argued that all of the goals relate to food security (FAO 2018; Massari 2020) but SDG number 2 explicitly states the goal of ending hunger. Utilizing the wedding cake model theory of Rockström and Sukhdev (2016), Massari expands on how food design can have a positive impact on potentially all 17 SDGs by moving to a systemic or ecocentric approach from an anthropocentric approach for each of the three sustainability pillars, referred to in Rockström and Sukhdev's model as the biosphere, society, and economy (2020). In Rockström and Sukhdev's model, the biosphere is the base and supports the societal and economic layers. Adding sustainability to food design clarifies the broad definition of food design by embracing a clear intention of sustainability when designing with, for, or about any area of food (Massari 2020). Working from Parasecoli and Reissig's definitions, in this book we define sustainable food design as pursuing design outcomes (DOs) and processes for any area in a food system that seek to improve and optimize the environment, the economy, and society, both individually and collectively, through a systemic lens that centers equity and justice.

Looking forward to the professional playing field of sustainable food design, we propose that:

> the task and job of the food designer is not to grant the same vision for everybody, but to establish the conditions for different visions that can interact and lead to sustainable solutions. If in the last decade we've worked to

explain how to design the best food experiences and focused on the systemic approach in the food world, today more than ever we need to unify this knowledge into a common project: designing more sustainable food systems.

(Massari 2020, 31)

Our ever-changing food system, impacted by climate, socio-economic disparities, political divisions, trade, and health issues, highlights the need for sustainable, equitable, and just design solutions. To solidify this understanding of sustainable food design that considers the need to acknowledge the current state of insecurity, inequity, and injustice in the food system, we propose an extended definition of sustainability development beyond the three pillars. Other definitions of sustainability as a goal imply a destination, which is unrealistic with the global seismic shifts and inequities worldwide. The dynamic nature of society, the economy, and the environment require a lens that adjusts and adapts as necessary, moving towards greater food security that is equitable and just and facilitates balanced nutrition that leads to improved sustenance of all of humanity and the natural ecosystem. We therefore introduce the following eight dimensions of sustainability that we call the 8 Es of sustainability (8Es) and use as the criteria for assessing DOs, which include:

- Ethical: the DO does not harm humans or communities or the earth.
- Equitable and just: the DO facilitates greater inclusivity, that is, all people having access to resources and benefits in an equitable and just manner.
- Environmental: the DO improves the environment without harming it.
- Economical: the DO permits value to return to all actors in the system thereby yielding "generative justice" (Eglash 2016).
- Ecological: the DO contributes to the healthy balance of the social ecosystem.
- Enduring: the DO is durable and lasts a long time.
- Effectuated: the DO has been implemented within a public context.
- Effective: evidence shows that the DO works.

In the 8Es, all criteria interconnect, interrelate, and rely on integration and in terms of food security, consider food justice and food sovereignty as critical components of sustainable food design. Food justice is connected to food sovereignty with "food justice spurring short-term action and rights in domestic contexts, while food sovereignty movements support longer-term national, regional and international networks and political action" (Clendenning et al. 2016, 175).

Food justice focuses on examining and addressing inequalities within the food system that impacts race and class disproportionately (Gottlieb and Joshi 2010). Gottlieb and Joshi define food justice as "ensuring that the benefits and risks of where, what, and how food is grown and produced, transported, and distributed, and accessed and eaten are shared fairly" (2010, 6). While food justice can focus on many facets and issues of inequality within the food system, scholarship related to food justice is grounded in both ecological sustainability and social justice, or "just sustainability" (Agyeman 2008).

Food sovereignty is a related concept brought to the global stage by La Via Campesina,[15] an international peasant movement (Clendenning et al. 2016). In 2007 it was defined at the Nyéléni International Forum on Food Sovereignty:

> the right of peoples to healthy and culturally appropriate food through eco-logically sound and culturally appropriate methods, and their right to define their own food and agricultural systems. It puts the aspirations and needs of those who produce, distribute, and consume food at the heart of the food systems and policies rather than the demands of markets and corporations. It defends the interests and inclusion of the next generation.
>
> (Nyéléni 2007)

The social aspect of sustainability is expanded in the 8Es to include categories of ethics and inclusivity, which *feeds* into a more equitable and just society. That is, sustainability is not limited to the environment but also considers social, eco-logical, and ethical implications. Economic sustainability returns unalienated value equitably to all stakeholders within the system who contribute to creating it. Finally, to be sustainable, a DO ideally should be effective and endure, both actively and residually.

Meeting the 8Es criteria for sustainable food design is an incredible challenge for designers across disciplinary and cultural domains who are investigating food insecurity, as food insecurity is itself a wicked problem that is global in scope, multidimensional, multifaceted, and intercultural. The question then is: where *should* these designers intervene in the food system to create a more sustainable food future that is secure, equitable, and just? Addressing this question requires understanding what has been done in design across professional domains to address food insecurity to know what is needed moving forward. In the next sec-tion, we introduce a design method for seeing and analyzing the current state of the sustainable food design system to find leverage points or places to intervene to move the system towards greater security.

Critically mapping sustainable design: a design approach to addressing wicked problems

In the seminal 1982 text titled "Designerly Ways of Knowing," design scholar Nigel Cross grapples with the Royal College of Art's (RCA) assertion that gen-eral education lacks a "third area" (1982, 221). Reviewing opposing previous arguments that "design with a capital D" or "technology" should fill this lacuna in a future triad of general education, Cross posits that the missing area should be "designerly" ways of knowing that would contrast with the existing objective and subjective ways of knowing in the sciences and the humanities (including the arts), respectively (222). The inclusion of design in general education aimed to elevate design from the skills-based role it played in the middle to late twentieth century within technical or vocational training to a discipline that contributes to students' intellectual and character development.

In response to the RCA's report titled "Design in General Education" that states, "there are things to know, ways of knowing them, and ways of finding out about them that are specific to "design" (quoted in Cross 1982, 223), Cross posits that the designerly way of knowing entails using constructive thinking and codes in a solution-focused problem-solving process to tackle ill-defined problems (226). In differentiating the kind of problems that designers address from those that scientists and humanists/artists typically confront, Cross reveals a narrow view of design that summons the counter-argument this paper makes when he says:

> It is also now widely recognized that problems are ill-defined, ill-structured, or "wicked." They are not the same as the "puzzles" that scientists, mathematicians and other scholars set themselves. They are not problems for which all the necessary information is, or ever can be, available to the problem solver. They are therefore not susceptible to exhaustive analysis, and there can never be a guarantee that "correct" solutions can be found for them. In this context, a solution-focused strategy is preferable to a problem-focused one: it will always be possible to go on analyzing "the problem," but the designer's task is to produce "the solution".
>
> (224)

Cross's position that solution generation should dictate problem definition in designerly processes likely influenced the rise of "coevolution" (Maher et al. 1996), which contemporary designers generally define as "the re-interpreting of a design problem in the light of an exploration of possible solutions until a good 'fit' between problem and solution ('an idea') emerges" (Dorst 2019).

However, solution-focused designing has had a seemingly limited effect on wicked problems as nearly half a century later, society is still grappling with them and contemporary designers are still challenged by their complexity. One could argue that coevolution through solution-focused designerly inquiry has encouraged a contemporary mode of design that leads to superficial success. This success typically manifests as DOs that may reflect only incremental aesthetic changes supported by professional organizations and trade journals and imitated in design education but that ultimately lead to failure (Winkler 2009) or the perpetuation of societal problems.

Should we only be "celebrating failures"[16] (Poggenpohl and Winkler 2009) though, or also learning and adjusting from our successes by critically mapping them to identify lacunae, if any, surrounding them to determine which of the gaps we can—or rather should—fill through future design innovation or appropriation? Are coevolution, solution-focused design, and our relentless pursuit of novelty serving society well enough? One could argue that many contributions from solution-focused, designerly practices tend to enable, perpetuate, or contribute to food's systemic challenges with goals that are unsustainable. A quick visit to a local grocery store, for instance, can provide ample evidence affirming solution-based, designerly inquiry's questionable participation in food through food packaging design. One can readily observe a variety of brands of consumable goods with excess sugar, sodium, fat, etc., packaged with high aesthetics aimed at outselling the competition rather than honestly informing the consumer of the product's low nutritional value and the negative impact of consuming it. If a solution-based designerly inquiry is a way of knowing, then what's needed in design arguably is greater "accountability" (Bennett 2012) in the decision-making leading to an outcome and the impact of the DO on humanity and the environment.

Towards this end, it's been nearly half a century since the publication of Cross's text, and the discipline of design has matured in its cognizance of the societal impact of its outcomes. For instance, Berman (2008) shows that professional designers are taking responsibility for their creative actions. Even the design research community is now grappling with emerging principles of "design justice" (Costanza-Chock 2020) that include:

1. Using design to sustain, heal, and empower our communities, as well as to seek liberation from exploitative and oppressive systems.
2. Centering the voices of those directly impacted by the outcomes of the design process.
3. Prioritizing design's impact on the community over the designer's intentions.
4. Viewing change as emergent from an accountable, accessible, and collaborative process rather than as a point at the end of a process.
5. Seeing the role of the designer as a facilitator rather than an expert.
6. Believing that everyone is an expert based on their own lived experience and that we all have unique and brilliant contributions to bring to a design process.
7. Sharing design knowledge and tools with our communities.
8. Working towards sustainable, community-led and -controlled outcomes.
9. Working towards non-exploitative solutions that reconnect us to the earth and to each other.
10. Before seeking new design solutions, looking for what is already working at the community level. Honoring and uplifting traditional, indigenous, and local knowledge and practices.

Though the discipline of design is evolving to be more ethical and socially and environmentally conscious, society continues to battle lingering, ill-defined problems (e.g., poverty, food insecurity, sustainability, racism, climate change, etc.) along with emerging ones. For instance, our present-day battle with COVID-19 and the marriage of visualization to medical innovation reveals an interesting interdependency between problem-focused and solution-focused inquiries to save lives. At the outset of the pandemic, we relied heavily on visualizations to understand the spread of the virus and its symptoms as we worked expeditiously to design effective solutions through medical innovation—implementing strategies like social distancing, hand-washing and mask-wearing, medicinal appropriation, and finally, vaccination. This real-world reliance on visuals to navigate a societal problem may indicate a missed opportunity in the design discipline towards including rigorous problem-focused designerly thinking that centers around visual analysis to reveal design intervention opportunities or to "look for what is already working" (Costanza-Chock 2020, 7). We propose that such a pivot in designerly inquiry would enable designers to use their plenty and powerful visualization resources to identify more strategic places to intervene with designerly ways of knowing that yield substantive change in society's wicked problems. Indeed, the analysis of problems in design needs to become more salient as the discipline matures and hears the clarion call to use design's resources to identify and address societal problems (e.g., food insecurity), problems that are complex by nature—"ill-defined, ill-structured, 'wicked'" (Cross 1982, 224) and multidisciplinary and multicultural. We propose the design resource of mapping to serve this purpose.

Mapping in the fields of food and design

Mapping, in general, has been integral to research inquiries across disciplines, including food and design. In the field of food, it has been used in both educational and non-educational contexts as "an approach to understanding 'eco-agri-food systems'"(Zhang et al. 2018) and to define "food justice" (Loo 2014). Edwards and Mercer (2010, 156) bring to light the use of mapping pervasively in food to enable their students to see the urban agriculture system in Australia's local context. Additionally, they reviewed the use of food mapping across disciplines to "chart...food insecurity, food 'deserts' and poverty," show "the connections between food and transportation," and even "trace community commodity chains" locally to globally (156). In non-educational contexts, Edward and Mercer (2010) also disclose how New York City was the starting place for the participatory development of an ecological map by eco-designer Wendy Brawer. Known as the Green Map, Brawer's concept has been adopted by hundreds of other cities around the world (156).

Within the area of food, mapping has been used in a participatory manner to identify the causes of problems within food systems to determine how to effect change. For instance, Sedlacko (2014) discusses the participatory construction of "causal loop diagrams" for "knowledge brokerage" between research scientists and policymakers. In their system, they aim to link experts in different disciplines and professions.

Within the design disciplines, Zahedi and Heaton (2016) show how designers use mapping cognitively to understand their creative thinking and the interrelatedness of concepts. Whereas Jones and Bowes (2017) argue specifically for the use of "synthesis mapping" to address "socially complex problems," Sevaldson (2011) and Buchanan (2019) argue for the inclusion of systems thinking into design thinking processes that aim to address complex problems. Other studies (Frerichs et al. 2018; Kokotovich 2008; Eden 2004; Dorst 2019) argue for mapping specifically in the problem definition phase. For instance, Suoheimo et al. (2021) map different categories of problems—tame to complex to wicked—to the well-known Freudian iceberg model of the conscious and subconscious mind to enable deeper problem understanding in the design process.

Design historian Victor Margolin supports Flood and Sloan's perspectives on there being historical precedence for food design within the discipline of design, as he too implies an historical relationship between food studies and design studies (Margolin 2013). Indeed, within the design discipline's evolving oeuvre there exist countless food design assets, but sustainable food design at present is an emerging school of thought arguably due to the recent rise and impact of climate change, the COVID-19 pandemic, and other perennial social injustices that are compromising food security. Indeed, as food insecurity continues to ravage the health of communities locally and globally, society's evolving repertoire of existing food DOs is scattered across the globe like disconnected nodes in a dysfunctional system. Many of these DOs are not accessible or are known only among a local community with only a few of them attaining national or international prominence. We propose that compiling existing effectuated food DOs that address food insecurity, inequity, and injustice and visualizing them in an affinity diagram (a method first introduced by Japanese anthropologist Kawakita Jiro (Plain 2007)) can enable designers and other stakeholders to meaningfully stunt Nelson et al.'s (2018) dire predictions of society's food future. Such a visualization can enable designers to better determine places to intervene to tweak the system towards a more sustainable, secure, equitable, and just food future.

Overview of critical mapping

The *critical* mapping framework this book introduces facilitates knowledge exchange among transdisciplinary designers around societal problems involving cross-cultural and -disciplinary stakeholders about where to start a social innovation design process.

Compiling a wicked problem's existing sustainable DOs to create a wicked solution visualization—an approach we introduce as critical mapping—aids problem understanding and definition in the design process towards identifying opportunities for innovation of more sustainable designs. Critical mapping aims to visualize existing sustainable DOs as a system of interdependent nodes engaged in systemic interaction towards annihilating a wicked problem. The critical mapping approach compiles and organizes existing DOs that address the wicked problem sustainably. It is a problematizing, reflective approach to analyzing systemic societal problems like food insecurity to mediate more strategic innovation or appropriation within the system towards designing a more sustainable future.

Critical mapping begins with placing an intellectual boundary around the wicked problem, fencing it in, by naming and operationalizing it. This initial step of critical mapping includes compiling evidence (e.g., statistical information) that proves the societal problem is real and devastating to humanity, that it exists and is worthy of resources and time. For instance, part of step 1 of critically mapping a wicked solution to food insecurity has been done in the introduction to this chapter. In the second step, we conduct secondary research on the wicked problem to identify existing design solutions that are sustainable. To this end, an "integrative literature review" (Torraco 2005; Snyder 2019) is conducted to identify existing DOs that address the wicked problem and to assess their degree of sustainability. Sustainable DOs, in the third step, are then affinitively organized and plotted onto a wicked solution grid contextualized across a field of possibilities with two sets of dimensions: top-down or bottom-up and localized or memetic (i.e., widespread or passing from one to many). Along the vertical axis are sustainable DOs that emerge bottom-up by citizens and communities impacted by the wicked problem or top-down from a position of economic power (e.g., public or private institutions). Along the horizontal axis lie sustainable DOs that range from memetic to localized, that is, from being replicated globally to situated locally. In the fourth step of critical mapping, we analyze the data and look for gaps in need of design intervention through future innovation or appropriation. In the next section, we begin critical mapping by naming and operationalizing the wicked problem of food insecurity. In doing so, we take illustrative steps to depict the food system to see and analyze its actors and activities towards understanding the wicked problem of food insecurity.

Step 1: Naming and operationalizing the wicked problem of food insecurity

We cannot adequately address food insecurity until we understand it; and "to fully appreciate the magnitude of the challenges that we face and what will be needed to bring about a new food system in harmony with this human need *and* the environment, we need to understand and confront the social, economic, and political foundations that create—and maintain—the food system we seek to change" (Holt-Giménez 2015, 23–25). To understand the forces that influence the food system and perpetuate food insecurity, Jacobi et al. (2019) argue that knowledge of the "actors and activities" in the system is necessary. In their study of food systems in Kenya and Bolivia, they sought to make visible the actors that participated in four phases of food that they delineated as "agricultural inputs and production, processing and storage, distribution and trade, and consumption and recycling" (Jacobi et al. 2019, R4). Their stages of food supply—from creation to recycling—updates the linear process commonly thought of in global society's top-down, large-scale industrial system, that is creating food that travels long distances from a remote farm to the household plate and finally to the landfill. Instead, their stages of food imply a more circular process with a recycling process that redirects food waste to the generation of new food.

Deploying the design resource of visualization that includes the tool of mapping to understand the food system is a necessary next step because food is a complex system comprising what von Braun et al. (2021) call "interlinked systems" of global and local actors and activities (748). In other words, the food system includes "local food" (Granvik et al. 2017; Chase and Grubinger 2014) systems that are "interlinked" and interacting with the global food system to enable greater participation from local small-scale farms and even home gardens. Accordingly, Chase and Grubinger (2014) illustrate the food system with concentric circles to indicate interlaced and scaled levels of interdependent activities and actors that range from the individual (the inner circle) to the household, local, regional, national, and global spheres.

Grubinger et al. (2010) define a food system as:

> an interconnected web of activities, resources, and people that extend across domains involved in providing nutrition that sustains health, including production, processing, packaging, distribution, marketing, consumption, and disposal of food.
>
> (6)

Using both Jacobi et al. (2019) and Grubinger et al.'s (2010) definitions of the food system, we can operationalize the food system as a set of scaled and interdependent sustainable activities that occur across the following spectrum:

- Agri/aquaculture: planting and growing "raw food materials" and breeding and caring for animals that will be used for food. Other related activities include training and managing labor, land management, innovating or acquiring, maintaining and using farming technologies (Ericksen 2008, 238), and caring for "aquatic animals and plants" for food in "fresh, brackish and marine environments" (Pillay and Kutty 2005, 3). "A variety of factors determine these activities, from climate conditions to land tenure, input prices, agricultural technology and government subsidy provisions intended to protect or promote" (Ericksen 2008, 238).
- Production: harvesting crops and slaughtering animals (238).
- Processing: transforming raw food material (vegetable, fruit, animal) for trade by altering its appearance, storage life, nutritional make-up, and content (238).
- Distribution: moving processed food from one place to another, typically from place of origin to retail spaces for consumption. Activities in the distribution phase of the food system include various forms of shipping, governmental trade, and storage regulations (238).
- Communication: the visual and verbal communication technologies like symbols, apps, and educational training programs that contribute to the food system's functionality.
- Accessibility: one's ability to acquire enough healthy food to sustain life. The factors and activities that influence one's ability to acquire enough healthy food include:
  - Affordability: one's "purchasing power" that depends on "pricing policies and mechanisms, seasonal and geographical variations in price, local prices relative to external prices, the form in which households are paid, income, and wealth levels" (240).

   o   Allocation: governmental policies and social and political capital governing when, where, how, and how much food one can access at a given time in a given private or public space (240).

   o   Preference: social or cultural norms, heritage, and values (e.g., religion, season, advertising, preparation requirements, human capital, tastes, customs that influence consumer demand for certain types of food) (240).

• Consumption: choosing, purchasing, or otherwise acquiring, preparing, eating, and digesting food. Factors affecting these activities include price, income level, cultural traditions or preferences, social values, education, health, and household status among other things (238).

• Waste: composting, recycling, and disposal of expired and unconsumed but still-edible food and materials involved in its production and consumption.

While Grubinger's use of the term "production" may be inclusive of agriculture, we aim to bring clarity to the food system by separating early stages of food production into two phases: agriculture or aquaculture and production. We also added accessibility to include activities related to equity and justice and communication

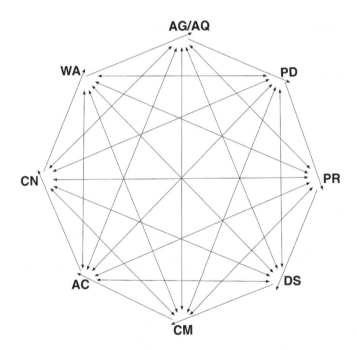

Figure 1.6 The interconnected food system comprising eight phases including agriculture/aquaculture (AG/AQ), production (PD), processing (PR), distribution (DS), communication (CM) (including recall, marketing, safety, packaging), accessibility (AC), consumption (CN), and waste (WA) where sustainability is integral to all eight categories. Image courtesy of Audrey G. Bennett.

and to further clarify the important role graphics, communication, and visual communication design plays or can play in the food system.

In our representation of the food system illustrated in Figure 1.6, there are eight phases of activities—agriculture/aquaculture (AG/AQ), production (PD), processing (PR), distribution (DS), communication (CM) (including recall, marketing, safety, and packaging), accessibility (AC), consumption (CN), and waste (WA). The activities of food systems reflect and respond to social, cultural, political, economic, health, and environmental conditions and can be identified at multiple scales, from an individual's plate to a household kitchen to a community restaurant to a regional foodbank to a nation (Grubinger 2010, 3).

In Figure 1.7 we show the flow of value that occurs between producers and consumers in large-scale, industrial food systems where a grand producer provides mostly processed food to a consumer at cost. The consumer has limited agency in the control of their food choices or what they eat, and that agency may be further compromised based on various factors (e.g., affordability and geographic location) affecting their access to healthier fresh and unprocessed options. Attaining food security depends on citizens becoming empowered to contribute to the production of the food they consume. In addition to large-scale, industrial, agricultural production, a food system thrives when there are also home gardens, community gardens, urban farms, and training. "Strip a system of redundancy, and you increase its efficiency; but you also reduce its adaptability and resilience" (Cockrall-King 2012, 59); a sustainable food system includes production actors inclusive of mainstream food businesses, small alternative food businesses, and citizen activists coordinated through strategic plans and policies.

A sustainable food system designed to address inequity and injustice engages consumers and producers (the actors) in all phases of the food system (as depicted in Figure 1.8).

Understanding these independent actors (i.e., producers, consumers, and consumer-producers) and the interdependency of their activities in the sustainable

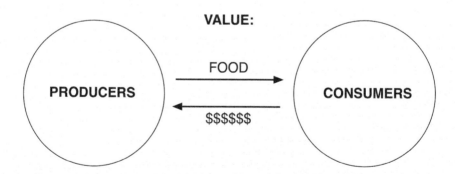

Figure 1.7 The food system visualized as producers providing food for consumers for profit which leads to a perennial wicked problem of food insecurity. Image courtesy of Audrey G. Bennett.

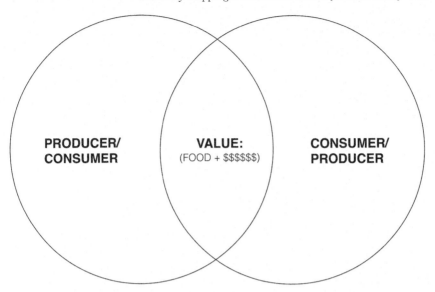

Figure 1.8 A sustainable food system where the producer and consumer engage in all phases of the food system leading to food security that is sustainable, equitable, and just. Image courtesy of Audrey G. Bennett.

food system is essential to mediating and supporting their interaction towards a more sustainable food-secure future. We argue that to attain this essential understanding and food-secure state where all people have access to healthy food daily should also entail compiling and analyzing the existing sustainable food DOs. Only then can one see the current state of the food system and where there may be gaps for design innovation or appropriation. In the next section we introduce the design method of critical mapping to assess the current state of the system of sustainable food design for food insecurity in order to find leverage points or places to intervene with design innovation or appropriation.

Step 2: Integrative literature review to identify sustainable food DOs

Which sustainable DOs currently comprise the wicked solution to food insecurity? Addressing this question entails conducting secondary research to glean existing sustainable food DOs that we then plot onto a wicked solution visualization modeled in Figure 1.9. In doing so, we aim to facilitate an analysis of the food system to identify what Meadows (1999) calls "leverage points…places within the system where a small shift in one thing can produce big changes in everything."

Our secondary research on the wicked solution to food insecurity entailed conducting an integrative literature review to find and compile a broad set of

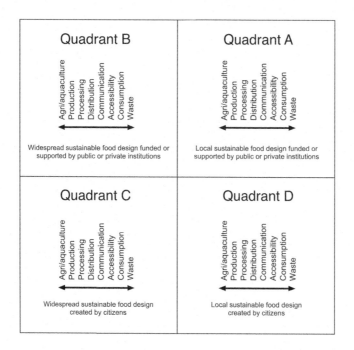

Figure 1.9 Bennett's wicked solution model applied to food insecurity. Image courtesy of Audrey G. Bennett.

peer-reviewed, sustainable food DOs that currently address food insecurity according to the 8Es of sustainability criteria. The integrative literature review was conducted using 123 databases available by way of ProQuest at the University of Michigan. We chose ProQuest instead of Web of Science as the former provides a multidisciplinary scope of scholarly articles inclusive of a broad array of humanities, arts, and design databases. The goal of using an integrative literature review instead of a systematic or semi-systematic one was to compile a multidisciplinary and inclusive set of scholarly articles focused on sustainable food design for security, equity, and justice.

To begin, we conducted a general ProQuest search of the individual terms "sustainable," "food," and "design" that yielded 790,974 results. Next, we modified the search to include full texts and only those that were peer-reviewed, and narrowed the results to 141,630 results. While ProQuest provides searches of newspaper and magazine articles, we limited our integrative literature review to peer-reviewed articles as we wanted the wicked solution proof of concept to consist of sustainable DOs that emerge from mostly peer-reviewed research and to make the literature review more manageable. In an effort to retrieve a more manageable set of peer-reviewed results within the scope of our research, we modified the search further to include only scholarly journals, and that change yielded almost the same quantity of results, 141,095.

The year 2009 was then used strategically as a start date to further narrow the results to correlate with the founding of the International Food Design Society in that same year. However, when we modified the search by adding the date range from 2009 to 2021, we still yielded a high 127,402 results. Thus, we modified the search for the exact phrase "sustainable food design," which yielded a singular result that, after a cursory review of the title, abstract, and subject keywords, we determined fit the scope of our research. However, with only one result, we reverted back to the most recent search terms and this time added the exact phrase "food security" and the previous 127,402 results dropped significantly to 22,881 results. Of those results, we selected those in English only, which narrowed our results down to 22,767 results. When we limited the search further to the location of the United States, the results dropped more significantly to 2,296 results.

With the goal to compile sustainable DOs generated from scholarly research, we specifically targeted peer-reviewed articles published in design and design research journals. A study conducted by Friedman et al. (2008) found the following five design and design research journals as the top venues for the dissemination of design research scholarship: *Design Studies, Design Issues, International Journal of Design, Design Journal,* and *Journal of Design History.* Subsequently, Mansfield (2016) conducted a similar study to identify the top design research journals based on the "highest ranked 'design' submissions" (904) and found the following journals to be the most popular "design-focused" journals: *The Design Journal, Applied Ergonomics, Ergonomics, Journal of Design Research,* and *Design Issues.* In an attempt to find results from the aforementioned design research journals on both Friedman et al.'s and Mansfield's lists, we broadened our search terms for design to include similar keywords in use in the discipline. Towards that end, we added the term "innovation" as a synonym for design to the search query of the 2,296 results previously found and consequently narrowed those results to a more manageable 886 results. Of these 886 results, after a cursory review of titles, abstracts, and subject keywords, we identified 25 articles that fit the scope of our research.

ProQuest conveniently allows the saving of searches, so we went back to the previous search that yielded 886 results with the added term "innovation" and replaced the term "food security" with "food equity," and yielded 22 results of which we identified one article that fit the scope of our research. Thus, again, we went back to the previous search that yielded 886 results and replaced the term "food security" with "food justice," and yielded 49 results of which we identified 22 articles that fit the scope of our research after a review of titles, abstracts, and subject keywords. Still, none of the journals from the ProQuest searches came from any of the flagship design journals. Thus, we returned to the previous search that yielded 2,296 results and replaced the term "innovation" with "appropriation" as another pseudo-synonym for design. Consequently, we yielded 88 results. Of those 88 results, we identified one relevant article after another cursory review of titles, abstracts, and subject keywords. Once again, we returned to the previous search that yielded 2,296 results and replaced the term "innovation" with "repair" as another pseudo-synonym for design. Consequently, we arrived at 131 results. Of those 131 results, we identified 6 relevant articles after a cursory review of titles, abstracts, and subject keywords that fit the scope of our inquiry.

Next, we conducted a new ProQuest search for design publications specifically: pub(design) AND ft(sustainable) AND ft(food) AND ti(design). This targeted search of design journals resulted in 76 articles of which 31 used the terms "sustainable," "food," and "design" in the text and were published in design journals. However, when we qualified the search further by adding the term "food security" the results narrowed to 14 including 6 articles that were also in the previous 31 results. After a cursory review of titles, subject keywords, and abstracts, we identified 5 articles as relating closely to the scope of our research inquiry. Then, when we modified the previous search that yielded 76 results further by replacing the term "food security" with "food justice," that resulted in 12 articles of which one fit the scope of our research. Again, we modified the previous search that yielded 76 results by replacing the term "food security" with "food equity," resulting in 8 articles of which only one fit the scope of our research and matched a previous article we had already found.

In our integrative literature review, we found a total of 62 peer-reviewed journal articles that fit the scope of our research after a cursory review of titles, abstracts, and subject keywords. To be more thorough and potentially garner a broader set of peer-reviewed publications from top-ranked, design research journals and publishers, we decided to conduct a second phase of the integrative literature review by conducting an exploratory search for articles and books using our university libraries' general search function and our own knowledge of publications within the disciplines of art and design. This second phase of our integrative literature review yielded additional journals and books helping us to meet our goal for a more thorough review. Texts in the second phase included an exhaustive review of the articles in all published issues of the *International Journal of Food Design*. After reading these articles and other publications in full to confirm fit with our research agenda we identified and extracted additional sustainable food DOs to further populate our wicked solution to food insecurity, providing the proof of concept illustrated in Figure 1.10. At times the found publication itself was the DO.

When reviewing all of the peer-reviewed articles in depth and evaluating the DOs they disclose for fit with sustainable food design we used categories from Figure 1.6. We used our sustainability criteria (i.e., the 8Es) to decide whether to include or not a DO in the wicked solution. The sustainable DOs in the wicked solution to food insecurity meet some but not necessarily all of the 8Es of sustainability criteria (see Appendix III). Our next step entailed categorizing each sustainable food DO according to its design form.

Heskett (2005) notes that "design should be the crucial anvil on which the human environment, in all its detail, is shaped and constructed for the betterment and delight of all" (1). Towards this end, Heskett categorizes design as:

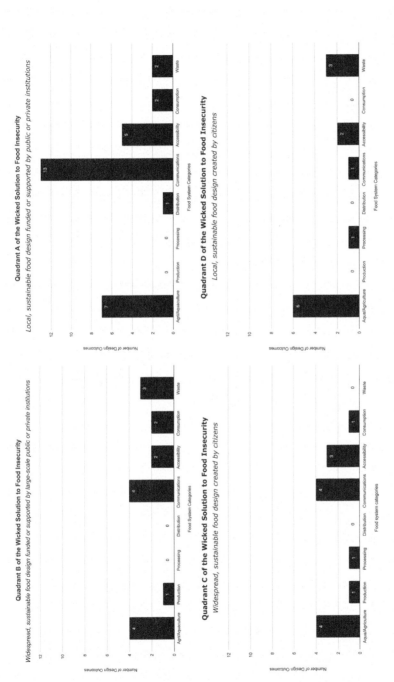

Figure 1.10 Proof of concept of the wicked solution to food insecurity critically mapped. Each actor or layer comprises DOs or activities across a spectra—top-down (policy-driven) to bottom-up (individual-driven or engendered agency) and localized (affecting a limited amount of people) to memetic or widespread (affecting many)—that contribute to the wicked solution to the wicked problem of food insecurity. Image courtesy of Audrey G. Bennett.

- Objects: single- and multi-purposed, multi- and intersensory, three-dimensional objects (e.g., a saltshaker, refrigerator, or a farming tool) encountered in private and public spaces that function in some capacity that is intuitive or learned (56).
- Communications: two-dimensional imagery accompanied by text (e.g., hashtags, package designs, a logo, an interface, or an app) that can evoke an array of emotions and actions and influence cognition and behavior (82).
- Environments: frameworks that facilitate activities, patterns of use, behavior, and expectations within living, learning, and working spaces (102).
- Identities: any strategic combination of objects, communications, and environments that expresses meaning intended to shape, even pre-empt, what others perceive or understand (125).
- Systems: interacting, interrelated, or interdependent elements that form a collective and functioning entity (145).
- Contexts: the professional organization and management of the knowledge set, scope, conduct, and playing field of a specialized activity, including but not limited to a program, professional organization, or governing policy (166).

In addition, recent scholarship in design extends Heskett's categories to include the following *actions* as design forms:

- Futures: a series of speculative or imaginary activities directed towards a desired outcome (e.g., a campaign or movement). See Taylor (2019) for other definitions.
- Service: a mindset, process, toolset, cross-disciplinary language, or management approach that improves a service or creates a new one (Stickdorn et al. 2018).
- Interaction: the shaping of use-oriented qualities of digital artifacts (Löwgren and Stolterman 2004) for a satisfactory or improved experience.
- Experience: the strategic orchestration of an engagement with something that is functional, engaging, purposeful, compelling, memorable, and enjoyable (McLellan 2000).

In assessing fit with sustainable food design as previously operationalized, for each article we asked the following questions:

1. Is there a DO that fits one of the design categories (i.e., object, communication, environment, identity, system, context, future, service, interaction, or experience)?
2. Is the DO effectuated and discussed as effective?
3. Does the DO align with one or more of the other 8Es of sustainability criteria?
4. Does the DO address a part of the food system (i.e., aqua/agriculture, production, processing, distribution, communication, accessibility, consumption, or waste)?

From this review of the original articles we eliminated those that fell outside the qualitative scope of our research agenda to compile effective and sustainable food

DOs that address the wicked problem of food insecurity through the lenses of equity and justice. Appendix I lists the 49 peer-reviewed publications from which we gleaned 73 sustainable DOs to critically map a proof of concept of the wicked solution to food insecurity.

Step 3: Plotting sustainable design outcomes onto a wicked solution grid

In the introduction to the "GLIDE 2012: Global Interaction in Design Education" conference's proceedings, Bennett (2012) argues that the global food problem epitomizes a wicked problem that is an ill-defined and confounding challenge because it exists within an evolving and complex system of smaller, context-specific, and cross-cultural challenges. Thus, it is improbable that any single communication design solution can solve it. Moreover, as no single solution can address the wicked problem of food, no single discipline can address it either. Thus, Bennett (2012, 2–10) posits the need for a wicked solution—an equally complex system of independent solutions derived from transdisciplinary inquiry inclusive of design perspectives—that systemically, over time, can address a wicked problem. In confirming the relationship between food studies and design studies, design historian Victor Margolin supports this proposition when encouraging consideration of:

> both food and design as embedded in systems and to initiate a mapping process to define the scope of each system and identify points of connection between the two. In this way, we can expand the conceptual space of each field and consequently discover themes and issues that may result in new methodological, narrative, and activist approaches by scholars in both of them.
>
> (2013)

To this end, applying Bennett's model of a wicked solution to the food system in Figure I.1, we depict the wicked solution to food insecurity as the visualization illustrated in Figure 1.10 onto which sustainable DOs are organized by two sets of dimensions: top-down or bottom-up and localized or memetic. Along the vertical axis we group sustainable food DOs that emerge bottom-up by individuals and communities (quadrants C and D) impacted by the wicked problem versus top-down from a status of economically funded or otherwise supported by public or private institutions (quadrants A and B). Along the horizontal axis we group sustainable food DOs that range from memetic (quadrants B and C) to localized (quadrants A and B), that is, from being replicated globally to situated locally.

Returning to the question of where designers *should* intervene in the food system to create a more sustainable food future that is secure, equitable, and just, we integrated Bennett's model of a wicked solution visualization from the introduction of this book with the food system's categories in Figure 1.6 to depict the wicked solution applied to food insecurity in Figure 1.9.

Next, we compiled all 73 DOs culled from the integrative literature review phase and organized them using a spreadsheet (see Appendix II) with four separate tables, where each table represents a quadrant in the wicked solution. Within each table we grouped the sustainable DOs gleaned from the literature review according to the categories of food and design that each addresses. We found 30 DOs that fit quadrant A, 16 DOs that fit quadrant B, 14 DOs that fit quadrant C, and 13 DOs that fit quadrant D.

We determined the primary food category to which each DO contributes. We also determined a primary design category that each DO represents. It is important to note that though a DO may arguably contribute to multiple food and design categories, we selected a primary food and design category for each DO. For each DO we noted the year of creation, place of use or implementation, and the in-text citation for peer-review publication from which it came.

Quadrant A's 30 sustainable food DOs are funded or supported by public or private institutions for implementation within local geographic contexts. Figure 1.10 shows the quantity of DOs that addresses each category of food in quadrant A. As shown, we found:

- 7 DOs that address the agricultural/aquacultural phase of the food system.
- 0 DOs that address the production phase of the food system.
- 0 DOs that address the processing phase of the food system.
- 1 DO that addresses the distribution phase of the food system.
- 13 DOs that address the communications phase of the food system.
- 5 DOs that address the accessibility phase of the food system.
- 2 DOs that address the consumption phase of the food system.
- 2 DOs that address the waste phase of the food system.

Quadrant B's 16 sustainable food DOs are also funded or supported by public or private institutions for implementation on a more widespread scale. As Figure 1.10 shows, we found:

- 4 DOs that address the agricultural/aquacultural phase of the food system.
- 1 DO that addresses the production phase of the food system.
- 0 DOs that address the processing phase of the food system.
- 0 DOs that address the distribution phase of the food system.
- 4 DOs that address the communications phase of the food system.
- 2 DOs that address the accessibility phase of the food system.
- 2 DOs that address the consumption phase of the food system.
- 3 DOs that address the waste phase of the food system.

Quadrant C's 14 sustainable food DOs are designed by citizens for implementation on a more widespread scale. As Figure 1.10 shows, we found:

- 4 DOs that address the agricultural/aquacultural phase of the food system.
- 1 DO that addresses the production phase of the food system.

- 1 DO that addresses the processing phase of the food system.
- 0 DOs that address the distribution phase of the food system.
- 4 DOs that address the communications phase of the food system.
- 3 DOs that address the accessibility phase of the food system.
- 1 DO that addresses the consumption phase of the food system.
- 0 DOs that address the waste phase of the food system.

Quadrant D's 13 sustainable food DOs are designed by citizens for implementation in a local context. As Figure 1.10 shows, we found:

- 6 DOs that address the agricultural/aquacultural phase of the food system.
- 0 DOs that address the production phase of the food system.
- 1 DO that addresses the processing phase of the food system.
- 0 DOs that address the distribution phase of the food system.
- 1 DO that addresses the communications phase of the food system.
- 2 DOs that address the accessibility phase of the food system.
- 0 DOs that address the consumption phase of the food system.
- 3 DOs that address the waste phase of the food system.

The sustainable food DOs all together represent a proof of concept of food insecurity's wicked solution and what Vokoun (2018) describes as socially responsive design and art that democratize food. The solutions, categorized by bar charts and plotted to the field of four quadrants, neither represent all existing solutions in use in present-day society nor do they solve the food insecurity problem. However, they contribute to a proof of concept for a wicked solution to food insecurity that arguably has the potential to contribute to solving (at the very least addressing more strategically) the food problem as the gaps in the diagram are filled and quantities balanced.

Step 4: Finding places to intervene in the system to attain a more sustainable food future

The question that remains—where *should* designers intervene in the food system to create a more sustainable food future that is secure, equitable, and just?—can now be addressed. Delineating food problems that design should address to create a better food future requires analyzing the evolving food insecurity's wicked solution in Figure 1.10 to understand and identify what Meadows (1999) calls "leverage points," that is, "places within the system where a small shift in one thing can produce big changes in everything." Similarly, Hamdi (2013) examines design solutions from a global perspective and notes that imagination and creativity are valued as the impetus for generating an idea, while reason and planning can carry an idea through. Hamdi's work in participatory planning is relevant, as we examine the food system as a key component of a community, both on a local and global level. Like Meadows's "leverage points," Hamdi (2010) advocates for looking for starting points, looking where to intervene, likening it to urban acupuncture, finding a way to release the energy of a place, and creating positive ripples of change. Note that Meadows (1999) acknowledges that we have no direct influence on the system and cannot change the system directly, but we can act on the variables around it. A leverage point in the food system derives from an experience of perceiving the state of the system as unbalanced and determining the activity or set of activities within the spectrum producing it; then, in turn, applying goal-oriented tweaking that produces a discrepancy in inflow or outflow to attain a more desired state. Meadows's (1999) model of using leverage points to address complex systems change works on any system, large or small.

Finding leverage points for design intervention in the food system, we argue, entails critically analyzing the wicked solution. For instance, the evolving wicked solution to food insecurity in Figure 1.10, while not exhaustive and inclusive of all the activities of all stakeholders, reflects a probable need for a range of more top-down and bottom-up innovation or appropriation. Perceiving this state in the food system, based on visual analysis, can inform one's design goal. However, the critical mapping we propose also involves deriving design goals based on a participatory analysis of research-generated knowledge that comes from scholarly and/or lay expertises. For instance, as noted earlier, Nelson et al. (2018) implore that future research priorities should emphasize nutritional quality by increasing the availability and affordability of nutrient-dense foods and improving dietary diversity. Using this scholarly finding, a design researcher conducting transdisciplinary research on food can conduct primary research to derive appropriation plans or additional sustainable food DOs to balance the wicked solution. As boundaries of traditional academic disciplines have expanded (Hadorn et al. 2008), transdisciplinary research has emerged with varied definitions. The *Handbook of Transdisciplinary Research* identifies four core concerns found in definitions of "transdisciplinarity" (29). The first is a "focus on life-world problems" (29); the second, "transcending and integrating of disciplinary paradigms" (29); the third, "participatory research" (29); and finally, "the search for unity of knowledge beyond disciplines" (29). While there is general agreement on the first two core concerns, the third and fourth are oft debated (29). For the purposes of this book, transdisciplinary research includes the idea of participatory research and the unifying of knowledge beyond disciplines, and we use Klein's description based on the European transdisciplinary movement: "trans-sector, problem-oriented research involving a wider range of stakeholders in society" (2008, S117). Through this lens, participatory analysis of the wicked solution might derive goals that center on the activities in the food system related to food availability, affordability, and improved dietary diversity. Accessibility and consumption, then, may be places in the food system where designers can intervene to create better food futures based on that goal.

Conclusion

In this chapter, we identified some of the existing sustainable DOs in the food system that are contributing to the wicked solution to food insecurity, and the current leverage points or gaps that exist to design a more sustainable food future.

We used critical mapping, a problematizing and reflective framework, to visualize the food system as an interdependent network of actors and activities engaged in systemic interaction to communicate: 1) the places—leverage points—where designers should intervene to create a more sustainable food future, and 2) the analysis needed at those places to impact the state of the food system more sustainably. In the next four chapters, we discuss the sustainable food DOs giving a general sense of the actors and activities occurring in each phase of the food system. One will find that not all phases are included in each quadrant. If a phase of the food system is missing it is because there were no sustainable food DOs that emerged from the integrative literature review of peer-reviewed publications. The sustainable food DOs come from peer-reviewed sources published after 2009—the founding year of the International Food Design Society—though some of them may have an earlier creation or effectuation date. We discuss each DO generally in terms of 1) the challenge it addresses and why the challenge is significant, 2) which global or local context/community the challenge impacts, 3) how the DO addresses the challenge, 4) how the DO works or functions and what it comprises, 5) when and where it was effectuated, tested, or implemented, and found to be effective, and 6) who the stakeholders are and what their activities are. We conclude each chapter by analyzing that quadrant of the wicked solution and gleaning leverage points to intervene with further design innovation or appropriation.

Notes

1 See United States Department of Agriculture Economic Research Service, n.d., "Interactive Charts and Highlights," accessed [February 22, 2023], https://www.ers.usda.gov/topics/food-nutrition-assistance/food-security-in-the-u-s/interactive-charts-and-highlights/.
2 As income increases, people consume more meat and high-calorie, processed foods that lack the micronutrients needed to sustain good health and contribute to obesity.
3 Agency and sustainability were "proposed by the High Level Panel of Experts (HLPE) of the Committee on World Food Security (CFS)" in their publication titled "Food Security and nutrition: Building a global narrative towards 2030" available at https://www.fao.org/3/ca9731en/ca9731en.pdf (FAO 2021, 53).
4 Named after Gro Harlem Brundtland, former prime minister of Norway, and chair of the Brundtland Commission, formerly the World Commission on Environment and Development, a sub-organization of the United Nations.
5 See: https://afhvs.wildapricot.org/Past-Conferences
6 While no longer active, the development of the International Food Design Society was a significant step forward for the field.
7 See: https://phd-design.jlscmall.ac.narkive.com/aXKeP4zX/1st-international-symposium-on-food-experience-design.
8 See: https://www.core77.com/posts/22865/International-Conference-on-Food-Design-2012-Food-from-Waste-and-Wall-mounted-Bread.
9 See: https://www.theicod.org/en/resources/publications/iridescent/iridescent-vol-2-issue-3.
10 See: https://www.lafooddesign.org.
11 See: https://www.foodesignmanifesto.org/1st-european-conference-on-understanding-food-design/.

12 The first FDxE was held in Colombia in 2014. While the website for FDxE is no longer
    active, the organization hosted symposiums around the world centered on developing
    didactics and pedagogy for food design education.
13 See: https://thisismold.com/event/conferences/the-designers-role-in-food-systems
    -and-hospitality-the-2nd-annual-food-design-conference.
14 See: http://labcom-ifp.ubi.pt/files/experiencing-food/.
15 See: https://viacampesina.org/en/.
16 One of the most successful special issues of *Visible Language*, a flagship journal in visual
    communication design, focused on design failure. It generated content to populate
    three journal issues between 2009 and 2010.

Bibliography

Abson, David J., Joern Fischer, Julia Leventon, Jens Newig, Thomas Schomerus, Ulli
    Vilsmaier, Henrik von Wehrden, Paivi Abernathy, Christopher D. Ives, Nicolas W.
    Jager, and Daniel J. Lang. 2016. "Leverage Points for Sustainability Transformation."
    Ambio 46, no. 1: 30–39. https://doi.org/10.1007/s13280-016-0800-y.

Agyeman, Julian. 2008. "Toward a 'Just' Sustainability?" *Continuum* 22, no. 6: 751–756.

Agyeman, Julian, Robert Doyle Bullard, and Bob Evans, eds. 2003. *Just Sustainabilities:
    Development in an Unequal World*. Cambridge, MA: MIT Press.

Alhaddi, Hanan. 2015. "Triple Bottom Line and Sustainability: A Literature Review."
    Business and Management Studies 1, no. 2: 6–10. http://dx.doi.org/10.11114/bms.v1i2.752.

Alkon, Alison Hope, and Julian Agyeman. 2011. *Cultivating Food Justice: Race, Class, and
    Sustainability*. Cambridge, MA: MIT Press.

Artmann, Martina, Katharina Sartison, and Jan Vávra. 2020. "The Role of Edible
    Cities Supporting Sustainability Transformation–A Conceptual Multidimensional
    Framework Tested on a Case Study in Germany." *Journal of Cleaner Production* 255:
    120220. https://doi.org/10.1016/j.jclepro.2020.120220.

Ballantyne-Brodie, Emily, and Ida Telalbasic. 2017. "Designing Local Food Systems in
    Everyday Life through Service Design Strategies." *The Design Journal* 20, no. sup1:
    S3079–S3095. https://doi.org/10.1080/14606925.2017.1352816.

Barthes, Roland. 2018. "Toward a Psychosociology of Contemporary Food Consumption."
    In *Food and Culture: A Reader, Fourth Edition*, edited by Carole Counihan, Penny Van
    Esterik, and Alice Julier, 13–20. London: Routledge.

Béné, Christophe, Peter Oosterveer, Lea Lamotte, Inge D. Brouwer, Stef de Haan, Steve
    D. Prager, Elise F. Talsma, and Colin K. Khoury. 2019. "When Food Systems Meet
    Sustainability – Current Narratives and Implications for Actions." *World Development*
    113: 116–130. https://doi.org/10.1016/j.worlddev.2018.08.011.

Bennett, A. 2012. "Good Design is Good Social Change: Envisioning an Age of
    Accountability in Communication Design Education." *Visible Language* 46, no. 2: 66–78.

Berman, David B. 2008. *Do Good Design: How Design Can Change Our World*. Berkeley,
    CA: Peachpit Press.

Bhamra, Tracy, and Ricardo J. Hernandez. 2021. "Thirty Years of Design for Sustainability:
    An Evolution of Research, Policy and Practice." *Design Science* 7: e2. https://doi.org/10
    .1017/dsj.2021.2.

Bonacho, Ricardo, Maria José Pires, and Elsa Cristina Carona de Sousa Lamy, eds.
    2021. *Experiencing Food: Designing Sustainable and Social Practices: Proceedings of the
    2nd International Conference on Food Design and Food Studies (EFOOD 2019), 28–30
    November 2019, Lisbon, Portugal*. London: CRC Press.

Bordewijk, Marielle, and Hendrik N. J. Schifferstein. 2020. "The Specifics of Food Design: Insights from Professional Design Practice." *International Journal of Food Design* 4, no. 2: 101–138. http://dx.doi.org/10.1386/ijfd_00001_1.

Buchanan, Richard. 1992. "Wicked Problems in Design Thinking." *Design Issues* 8, no. 2: 5–21.

Buchanan, Richard. 2019. "Systems thinking and design thinking: The search for principles in the world we are making." *She Ji: The Journal of Design, Economics, and Innovation* 5, no. 2: 85–104.

Ceschin, Fabrizio, and Idil Gaziulusoy. 2016. "Evolution of Design for Sustainability: From Product Design to Design for System Innovations and Transitions." *Design Studies* 47: 118–163. https://doi.org/10.1016/j.destud.2016.09.002.

Chambers, Robert, and Gordon Conway. 1992. *Sustainable Rural Livelihoods: Practical Concepts for the 21st Century*. Brighton, UK: Institute of Development Studies.

Chase, Lisa, and Vern Grubinger. 2014. *Food, Farms, and Community: Exploring Food Systems*. Durham, NH: University of New Hampshire Press.

Choi, Jaz Hee-Jeong, and Eli Blevis. 2010. "HCI & Sustainable Food Culture: A Design Framework for Engagement." In *Proceedings of the 6th Nordic Conference on Human-computer Interaction: Extending Boundaries*, edited by Ebba Þóra Hvannberg, Marta Kristín Lárusdóttir, Ann Blandford, and Jan Gulliksen, 112–117. Reykjavik, Iceland.

Clendenning, Jessica, Wolfram H. Dressler, and Carol Richards. 2016. "Food Jjustice or Food Sovereignty? Understanding the Rise of Uban Food Movements in the USA." *Agriculture and Human Values* 33, no. 1: 165–177. https://doi.org/10.1007/s10460-015-9625-8.

Cockrall-King, Jennifer. 2012. *Food and the City: Urban Agriculture and the New Food Revolution*. Amherst, NY: Prometheus Books. https://play.google.com/store/books/details?id=d7d1DwAAQBAJ.

Coleman-Jensen, Alisha, Matthew P. Rabbitt, Christian A. Gregory, and Anita Singh. 2021a. "Household Food Security in the United States in 2020." U.S. Department of Agriculture, September 2021.

———. 2021b. "Overview." USDA Economic Research Service-food Security in the U.S., September 2021. https://www.ers.usda.gov/topics/food-nutrition-assistance/food-security-in-the-us/.

Comber, Rob, Jaz Choi, Hoonhout Jettie, and Kenton O'Hara. 2014. "Designing for Human-food Interaction: An Introduction to the Special Issue on 'Food and Interaction Design'." *International Journal of Human-Computer Studies* 72, no. 2: 181–184. http://dx.doi.org/10.1016/j.ijhcs.2013.09.001.

"Conference Program - Afhvs.wildapricot.org." Accessed August 12, 2022. https://afhvs.wildapricot.org/resources/Documents/Conference%20programs/2005-AFHVS-ASFS-Program.pdf.

Costanza-Chock, Sasha. 2020. *Design Justice: Community-led Practices to Build the Worlds We Need*. Cambridge, MA: MIT Press.

Cross, Nigel. 1982. "Designerly Ways of Knowing," *Design Studies* 3, no. 4: 221–227.

Dolejšová, Markéta, Sjef Van Gaalen, Danielle Wilde, Paul Graham Raven, Sara Heitlinger, and Ann Light. 2020. "Designing with More-than-human Food Practices for Climate-resilience." In *Companion Publication of the 2020 ACM Designing Interactive Systems Conference*, edited by Ron Wakkary, Kristina Andersen, Will Odom, Audrey Desjardins, and Marianne Graves Petersen, 381–384. https://doi.org/10.1145/3393914.3395909.

Dorninger, Christian, David J. Abson, Cristina I. Apetrei, Pim Derwort, Christopher D. Ives, Kathleen Klaniecki, David P. M. Lam, Maria Langsenlehner, Maraja Riechers, Nathalie Spittler, and Henrik von Wehrden. 2020. "Leverage Points for Sustainability Transformation: A Review on Interventions in Food and Energy Systems." *Ecological Economics* 171: 106570. https://doi.org/10.1016/j.ecolecon.2019.106570.

Dorst, Kees. 2019. "Co-evolution and Emergence in Design." *Design Studies* 65: 60–77. https://doi.org/10.1016/j.destud.2019.10.005.

Du Pisani, Jacobus A. 2007. "Sustainable Development–Historical Roots of the Concept." *Environmental Sciences* 3, no. 2: 83–96. https://doi.org/10.1080/15693430600688831.

Eden, Colin. 2004. "Analyzing Cognitive Maps to Help Structure Issues or Problems." *European Journal of Operational Research* 159, no. 3: 673–686. https://doi.org/10.1016/S0377-2217(03)00431-4.

Edwards, Ferne, and Dave Mercer. 2010. "Meals in Metropolis: Mapping the Urban Foodscape in Melbourne, Australia." *Local Environment* 15, no. 2: 153–168. https://doi.org/10.1080/13549830903527662.

Eglash, Ron. 2016. "An Introduction to Generative Justice." *Revista Teknokultura* 13, no. 2: 369–404. http://doi.org/10.5209/rev_TEKN.2016.v13.n2.52847.

Eizenberg, Efrat, and Yosef Jabareen. 2017. "Social Sustainability: A New Conceptual Framework." *Sustainability* 9, no. 1: 68. https://doi.org/10.3390/su9010068.

El Bilali, Hamid, and Mohammad Sadegh Allahyari. 2018. "Transition Towards Sustainability in Agriculture and Food Systems: Role of Information and Communication Technologies." *Information Processing in Agriculture* 5, no. 4: 456–464. https://doi.org/10.1016/j.inpa.2018.06.006.

Elkington, John. 2008. "The Triple Bottom Line: Sustainability's Accountants." In *Environmental Management, Second Edition*, edited by Michael V. Russo, 49–66. Los Angeles, CA: Sage Publications, Inc.

Elmqvist, Thomas, Erik Andersson, Niki Frantzeskaki, Timon McPhearson, Per Olsson, Owen Gaffney, Kazuhiko Takeuchi, and Carl Folke. 2019. "Sustainability and Resilience for Transformation in the Urban Century." *Nature Sustainability* 2, no. 4: 267–273. https://doi.org/10.1038/s41893-019-0250-1.

Ericksen, Polly J. 2008. "Conceptualizing Food Systems for Global Environmental Change Research." *Global Environmental Change* 18, no. 1: 234–245. https://doi.org/10.1016/j.gloenvcha.2007.09.002.

Flood, Catherine, and May Rosenthal Sloan, eds. 2019. *Food: Bigger than the Plate*. London: V&A.

Food and Agriculture Organization of the United Nations (FAO). 2008. "Food Security Information for Action: An Introduction to the Basic Concepts of Food Security." EC - FAO Food Security Programme. https://www.fao.org/3/al936e/al936e00.pdf.

Food and Agricultural Organization of the United Nations (FAO). 2018. *The State of Food Security and Nutrition in the World 2018: Building Climate Resilience for Food Security and Nutrition*. Rome: FAO. https://www.fao.org/3/I9553EN/i9553en.pdf#page=28.

Food and Agricultural Organization of the United Nations (FAO). 2021. *The State of Food Security and Nutrition in the World 2021: Transforming Food Systems for Food Security, Improved Nutrition and Affordable Healthy Diets for All*. Rome: FAO. https://doi.org/10.4060/cb4474en.

Foster, Phillips Wayne. 1992. *The World Food Problem: Tackling the Causes of Undernutrition in the Third World*. Boulder, CO: Lynne Rienne Publishers.

Friedman, Ken, Deirdre Barron, Silvana Ferlazzo, Tania Ivanka, Gavin Melles, and Jeremy Yuille. 2008. "Design Research Journal Ranking Study: Preliminary Results." https:// researchbank.swinburne.edu.au/items/cdc86f43-a015-495a-9162-f46f25a98f6a/1/.

Frerichs, Leah, Tiffany L. Young, Gaurav Dave, Doris Stith, Giselle Corbie-Smith, and Kristen Hassmiller Lich. 2018. "Mind Maps and Network Analysis to Evaluate Conceptualization of Complex Issues: A Case Example Evaluating Systems Science Workshops for Childhood Obesity Prevention." *Evaluation and Program Planning* 68: 135–147. https://doi.org/10.1016/j.evalprogplan.2018.03.003.

Gaitán-Cremaschi, Daniel, Laurens Klerkx, Jessica Duncan, Jacques H. Trienekens, Carlos Huenchuleo, Santiago Dogliotti, María E. Contesse, and Walter A. H. Rossing. 2019. "Characterizing Diversity of Food Systems in View of Sustainability Transitions. A Review." *Agronomy for Sustainable Development* 39, no. 1: 1–22. https://doi.org/10 .1007/s13593-018-0550-2.

Gaziulusoy, İdil, and Elif Erdoğan Öztekin. 2019. "Design for Sustainability Transitions: Origins, Attitudes and Future Directions." *Sustainability* 11, no. 13: 3601. https://doi .org/10.3390/su11133601.

Goel, Puneeta. 2010. "Triple Bottom Line Reporting: An Analytical Approach for Corporate Sustainability." *Journal of Finance, Accounting & Management* 1, no. 1: 27–42.

Gottlieb, Robert, and Anupama Joshi. 2010 *Food Justice*. Cambridge, MA: MIT Press.

Granvik, Madeleine, Sofie Joosse, Alan Hunt, and Ingela Hallberg. 2017. "Confusion and Misunderstanding—Interpretations and Definitions of Local Food." *Sustainability* 9, no. 11: 1981.

Grubinger, Vern, Linda Berlin, Elizabeth Berman, Naomi Fukagawa, D. N. Kolodinsky, B. Parsons, A. Trubek, et al. 2010. "Proposal for a Food Systems Spire of Excellence at the University of Vermont." *UVM Extension Faculty Publications*. https://scholarworks .uvm.edu/extfac/3/.

Guixe, Marti, Octavi Rofes, Inga Knölke, and Jeffrey Swartz. 2010. *Food Designing, Second Edition*. Mantova: Corraini Edizioni.

Hadorn, Gertrude Hirsch, Holger Hoffmann-Riem, Susette Biber-Klemm, Walter Grossenbacher-Mansuy, Dominique Joye, Christian Pohl, Urs Wiesmann, and Elisabeth Zemp, eds. 2008. *Handbook of Transdisciplinary Research*. Vol. 10. Dordrecht: Springer.

Hamdi, Nabeel. 2010. *The Placemaker's Guide to Building Community*. London: Routledge. https://www.taylorfrancis.com/books/mono/10.4324/9781849775175/placemaker -guide-building-community-nabeel-hamdi.

———. 2013. *Small Change: About the Art of Practice and the Limits of Planning in Cities*. London: Earthscan. https://play.google.com/store/books/details?id=-JB4JYQjawgC.

Haysom, Gareth, E. Gunilla Almered Olsson, Mirek Dymitrow, Paul Opiyo, Nick Taylor Buck, Michael Oloko, Charlotte Spring, Kristina Fermskog, Karin Ingelhag, Shelley Kotze, and Stephen Gaya Agong. 2019. "Food Systems Sustainability: An Examination of Different Viewpoints on Food System Change." *Sustainability* 11, no. 12: 3337. https://doi.org/10.3390/su11123337.

Heskett, John. 2005. *Design: A Very Short Introduction*. Vol. 136. Oxford: Oxford University Press.

HLPE. 2020. *Food Security and Nutrition: Building a Global Narrative towards 2030: A Report by the High Level Panel of Experts on Food Security and Nutrition of the Committee on World Food Security*. Rome, Italy. https://www.fao.org/3/ca9731en/ca9731en.pdf.

Holt-Giménez, Eric. 2015. "Racism and Capitalism: Dual Challenges for the Food Movement." *Journal of Agriculture, Food Systems, and Community Development* 5, no. 2: 23–25. https://doi.org/10.5304/jafscd.2015.052.014.

Jacobi, Johanna, Grace Wambugu, Mariah Ngutu, Horacio Augstburger, Veronica Mwangi, Aymara Llanque Zonta, Stephen Otieno, Boniface P. Kiteme, José M. F. Delgado Burgoa, and Stephan Rist. 2019. "Mapping Food Systems: A Participatory Research Tool Tested in Kenya and Bolivia." *Mountain Research and Development* 39, no. 1: R1–R11. https://doi.org/10.1659/MRD-JOURNAL-D-18-00024.1.

Jones, Peter, and Jeremy Bowes. 2017. "Rendering Systems Visible for Design: Synthesis Maps as Constructivist Design Narratives." *She Ji: The Journal of Design, Economics, and Innovation* 3, no. 3: 229–248. https://doi.org/10.1016/j.sheji.2017.12.001.

Juri, Silvana, Sonia Massari, and Pedro Reissig. 2022. "Editorial: Food+Design - Transformations via Transversal and Transdisciplinary Approaches." In *DRS2022: Bilbao*, edited by D. Lockton, S. Lenzi, P. Hekkert, A. Oak, J. Sádaba, and P. Lloyd, 25. https://doi.org/10.21606/drs.2022.1060.

Klein, Julie T. 2008. "Evaluation of Interdisciplinary and Transdisciplinary Research: A Literature Review." *American Journal of Preventive Medicine* 35, no. 2: S116–S123.

Knutsson, Per. 2006. "The Sustainable Livelihoods Approach: A Framework for Knowledge Integration Assessment." *Human Ecology Review* 13, no. 1: 90–99.

Köhler, Jonathan, Frank W. Geels, Florian Kern, Jochen Markard, Elsie Onsongo, Anna Wieczorek, Floortje Alkemade, Flor Avelino, Anna Bergek, Frank Boons, Lea Fünfschilling, David Hess, Georg Holtz, Sampsa Hyysalo, Kirsten Jenkins, Paula Kivimaa, Mari Martiskainen, Andrew McMeekin, Marie Susan Mühlemeier, Bjorn Nykvist, Bonno Pel, Rob Raven, Harald Rohracher, Björn Sandén, Johan Schot, Benjamin Sovacool, Bruno Turnheim, Dan Welch, and Peter Wells. 2019. "An Agenda for Sustainability Transitions Research: State of the Art and Future Directions." *Environmental Innovation and Societal Transitions* 31: 1–32. https://doi.org/10.1016/j.eist.2019.01.004.

Kokotovich, Vasilije. 2008. "Problem Analysis and Thinking Tools: An Empirical Study of Non-hierarchical Mind Mapping." *Design Studies* 29, no. 1: 49–69. https://doi.org/10.1016/j.destud.2007.09.001.

Leathers, Howard D., and Phillips Foster. 2004. *The World Food Problem: Tackling the Causes of Undernutrition in the Third World: Third Edition.* Boulder, CO: Lynne Rienner Publishers.

Lees-Maffei, Grace. 2016. "Design History: The State of the Art." *CAA Reviews.* https://doi.org/10.3202/caa.reviews.2016.153.

Loo, Clement. 2014. "Towards a More Participative Definition of Food Justice." *Journal of Agricultural & Environmental Ethics* 27, no. 5: 787–809. https://doi.org/10.1007/s10806-014-9490-2.

Löwgren, Jonas, and Erik Stolterman. 2004. *Thoughtful Interaction Design: A Design Perspective on Information Technology.* Cambridge, MA: MIT Press.

Margolin, Victor. 2013. "Design Studies and Food Studies: Parallels and Intersections." *Design and Culture* 5, no. 3: 375–392. https://doi.org/10.2752/175470813X13705953612327.

Maher, Mary Lou, Josiah Poon, and Sylvie Boulanger. 1996. "Formalising Design Exploration as Co-evolution." In *Advances in Formal Design Methods for CAD: Proceedings of the IFIP WG5.2 Workshop on Formal Design Methods for Computer-aided Design, June 1995*, edited by John S. Gero, and Fay Sudeweeks, 3–30. New York: Springer New York. https://link.springer.com/book/10.1007/978-0-387-34925-1.

Mansfield, Neil J. 2016. "Ranking of Design Journals Based on Results of the UK Research Excellence Framework: Using REF as Referee." *The Design Journal* 19, no. 6: 903–919. https://doi.org/10.1080/14606925.2016.1216212.

Manzini, Ezio. 2015. *Design, When Everybody Designs: An Introduction to Design for Social Innovation*. Translated by Rachel Coad. Cambridge, MA: MIT Press.

Markard, Jochen, Rob Raven, and Bernhard Truffer. 2012. "Sustainability Transitions: An Emerging Field of Research and Its Prospects." *Research Policy* 41, no. 6: 955–967. https://doi.org/10.1016/j.respol.2012.02.013.

Massari, Sonia. 2012. "Introducing food experience design in the food studies curriculum." In *GLIDE' 12 Conference Proceedings* 7.

Massari, Sonia. 2017. "Food Design and Food Studies: Discussing Creative and Critical Thinking in Food System Education and Research." *International Journal of Food Design* 2, no. 1: 117–133. https://doi.org/10.1386/ijfd.2.1.117_1.

Massari, Sonia. 2020. "Design Methods to Inspire the New Decade. Agency-centered Design. Toward 2030." In *Experiencing Food: Designing Sustainable and Social Practices: Proceedings of the 2nd International Conference on Food Design and Food Studies (EFOOD 2019), 28–30 November 2019, Lisbon, Portugal*, edited by Ricardo Bonacho, Maria José Pires, and Elsa Carona de Sousa Lamy, 13–35. London: CRC Press.

McLellan, Hilary. 2000. "Experience Design." *Cyberpsychology and Behavior* 3, no. 1: 59–69. https://doi.org/10.1089/109493100316238.

Meadows, Donella H. 1999. *Leverage Points: Places to Intervene in a System*. Hartland, VT: The Sustainability Institute. https://donellameadows.org/wp-content/userfiles/Leverage_Points.pdf.

Miller, Ethan. 2014. "Economization and Beyond: (Re)Composing Livelihoods in Maine, USA." *Environment and Planning A: Economy and Space* 46, no. 11: 2735–2751. https://doi.org/10.1068%2Fa130172p.

Mourad, Marie. 2016. "Recycling, Recovering and Preventing 'Food Waste': Competing Solutions for Food Systems Sustainability in the United States and France." *Journal of Cleaner Production* 126: 461–477. https://doi.org/10.1016/j.jclepro.2016.03.084.

Nelson, Gerald, Jessica Bogard, Keith Lividini, Joanne Arsenault, Malcolm Riley, Timothy B. Sulser, Daniel Mason-D'Croz, Brendan Power, David Gustafson, Mario Herrero, Keith Wiebe, Karen Cooper, Roseline Remans, and Mark Rosegrant. 2018. "Income Growth and Climate Change Effects on Global Nutrition Security to Mid-century." *Nature Sustainability* 1, no. 12: 773–781. https://doi.org/10.1038/s41893-018-0192-z.

Nyéléni. 2007. "Declaration of Nyéléni." Accessed February 27, 2007. https://nyeleni.org/en/declaration-of-nyeleni/.

Office of Assistant Director-General (Forestry Department). 2006. *Forests for Improved Nutrition and Food Security*. Food and Agriculture Organization of the United Nations. http://www.fao.org/3/a-i2011e.pdf.

Orenstein, Daniel E., and Dalit Shach-Pinsley. 2017. "A Comparative Framework for Assessing Sustainability Initiatives at the Regional Scale." *World Development* 98: 245–256. https://doi.org/10.1016/j.worlddev.2017.04.030.

Papanek, Victor. 1985. *Design for the Real World: Human Ecology and Social Change*. London: Thames & Hudson.

Penniman, Leah. 2018. *Farming While Black: Soul Fire Farm's Practical Guide to Liberation on the Land*. White River Junction, VT: Chelsea Green Publishing.

Pillay, Thundathil Velayudhan Ramakrishna, and Methil Narayanan Kutty. 2005. *Aquaculture: Principles and Practices, 2nd Edition*. Oxford: Blackwell Publishing.

Plain, Craig. 2007. "Build an Affinity for KJ Method." *Quality Progress* 40, no. 3: 88.

Poggenpohl, Sharon, and Dietmar R. Winkler. 2009. "Celebrating Failure." *Visible Language* 43, no. 2/3: 104–111.

Reissig, Pedro. 2017. "Food Design Education." *International Journal of Food Design* 2 no. 1: 3–13. https://doi.org/10.1386/ijfd.2.1.3_2.

Reynolds, Kristin. 2017. "Designing Urban Agriculture Education for Social Justice: Radical Innovation Through Farm School NYC." *International Journal of Food Design* 2, no. 1: 45–63. https://doi.org/10.1386/ijfd.2.1.45_1.

Rocha, Cristina Sousa, Paula Antunes, and Paulo Partidário. 2019. "Design for Sustainability Models: A Multiperspective Review." *Journal of Cleaner Production* 234: 1428–1445. https://doi.org/10.1016/j.jclepro.2019.06.108.

Rockström, Johan, and Pavan Sukhdev. 2016. "Keynote Speech at the EAT Stockholm Food Forum." Accessed June 20, 2016. https://eatforum.org/learn-and-discover/keynote-speech-prof-johan-rockstrom-ceo-pavan-sukhdev/.

Schouwenburg, Louise, and Marije Vogelzang. 2011. *Eat Love: Food Concepts by Eating-designer Marije Vogelzang*. Amsterdam: BIS Publishers.

Sedlacko, Michal, Andre Martinuzzi, Inge Røpke, Nuno Videira, and Paula Antunes. 2014. "Participatory Systems Mapping for Sustainable Consumption: Discussion of a Method Promoting Systemic Insights." *Ecological Economics* 106: 234. https://doi.org/10.1016/j.ecolecon.2014.07.002.

Sevaldson, Birger. 2011. "GIGA-mapping: Visualisation for Complexity and Systems Thinking in Design." *Nordes* 4. http://nordes.org/opj/index.php/n13/article/view/104.

Sherriff, Graeme. 2009. "Towards Healthy Local Food: Issues in Achieving Just Sustainability." *Local Environment* 14, no. 1: 73–92. https://doi.org/10.1080/13549830802522566.

Snyder, Hannah. 2019. "Literature Review as a Research Methodology: An Overview and Guidelines." *Journal of Business Research* 104: 333–339. https://doi.org/10.1016/j.jbusres.2019.07.039.

Spangenberg, Joachim H., Alastair Fuad-Luke, and Karen Blincoe. 2010. "Design for Sustainability (DfS): The interface of sustainable production and consumption." *Journal of Cleaner Production* 18, no. 15: 1485–1493. https://doi.org/10.1016/j.jclepro.2010.06.002.

Stickdorn, Marc, Markus Edgar Hormess, Adam Lawrence, and Jakob Schneider. 2018. *This is Service Design Doing: Applying Service Design Thinking in the Real World*. Sebastopol, CA: O'Reilly Media, Inc.

Suoheimo, Mari, Rosana Vasques, and Piia Rytilahti. 2021. "Deep Diving into Service Design Problems: Visualizing the Iceberg Model of Design Problems through a Literature Review on the Relation and Role of Service Design with Wicked Problems." *The Design Journal* 24, no. 2: 231–251. https://doi.org/10.1080/14606925.2020.1838696.

Taylor, Damon. 2019. "Design Futures." In *A Companion to Contemporary Design Since 1945*, edited by Anne Massey, and Dana Arnold, 51–71. Oxford: Blackwell.

Torraco, Richard J. 2005. "Writing Integrative Literature Reviews: Guidelines and Examples." *Human Resource Development Review* 4, no. 3: 356–367.

United Health Foundation. n.d. "Explore Obesity in Michigan: 2021 Annual Report." Accessed August 13, 2022. https://www.americashealthrankings.org/explore/annual/measure/Obesity/population/Obesity_Hispanic/state/MI.

United Nations. 2015. "The 17 Goals | Sustainable Development." Accessed August 13, 2022. https://sdgs.un.org/goals#history.

United States Census Bureau. n.d. "Quickfacts: United States." Accessed May 24, 2022. https://www.census.gov/quickfacts/US.

Urban Omnibus. 2010. "Food and the Shape of Cities." February 24, 2010. Accessed July 29, 2022. https://urbanomnibus.net/2010/02/food-and-the-shape-of-cities/.

Vallance, Suzanne, Harvey C. Perkins, and Jennifer E. Dixon. 2011. "What is Social Sustainability? A Clarification of Concepts." *Geoforum* 42, no. 3: 342–348. http://dx .doi.org/10.1016/j.geoforum.2011.01.002.

van Hinte, Ed. 2016. *Katja Gruiters: Food Design. Exploring the Future of Food.* Amsterdam: TerraLannoo Publishers.

Vokoun, Jennifer A. 2018. "Food Democracy: Critical Lessons in Food, Communication, Design and Art." *Design and Culture* 10, no. 2: 227–229. https://doi.org/10.1080 /17547075.2018.1469964.

von Braun, Joachim, Kaosar Afsana, Louise Ottilie Fresco, Mohamed Hassan, and Maximo Torero. 2021. "Food System Concepts and Definitions for Science and Political Action." *Nature Food* 2, no. 10: 748–750. https://doi.org/10.1038/s43016-021-00361-2.

Weber, Hanna, Karoline Poeggel, Hallie Eakin, Daniel Fischer, Daniel J. Lang, Henrik Von Wehrden, and Arnim Wiek. 2020. "What Are the Ingredients for Food Systems Change Towards Sustainability?—Insights from the Literature." *Environmental Research Letters* 15, no. 11: 113001. https://doi.org/10.1088/1748-9326/ab99fd.

Winkler, Dietmar R. 2009. "Failure? Isn't It Time to Slay the Design-dragon?" *Visible Language* 43, no. 2/3: 253.

Winne, Mark. 2008. *Closing the Food Gap: Resetting the Table in the Land of Plenty.* Boston, MA: Beacon Press.

World Commission on Environment and Development. 1987. *Report of the World Commission on Environment and Development: Our Common Future towards Sustainable Development 2. Part II. Common Challenges Population and Human Resources.* New York: United Nations. https://sustainabledevelopment.un.org/content/documents/5987our -common-future.pdf.

World Health Organization. 2017. "The Double Burden of Malnutrition: Policy Brief." Accessed May 17, 2017. https://www.who.int/publications/i/item/WHO-NMH-NHD -17.3.

Zahedi, Mithra, and Lorna Heaton. 2016. "Mind Mapping as a Tool, as a Process, as a Problem Solution Space." In *DS 83: Proceedings of the 18th International Conference on Engineering and Product Design Education (E&PDE16), Design Education: Collaboration and Cross-disciplinarity, Aalborg, Denmark, 8th–9th September 2016, 166–71, 2016,* edited by Erik Bohemia, Ahmed Kovacevic, Lundon Buck, Christian Tollestrup, Kaare Eriksen, and Nis Ovesen. Aalborg, Denmark.

Zampollo, Francesca. 2016. "Welcome to Food Design." *International Journal of Food Design* 1, no. 1: 3–9. https://doi.org/10.1386/ijfd.1.1.3_2.

Zampollo, Francesca, and Matthew Peacock. 2016. "Food Design Thinking: A Branch of Design Thinking Specific to Food Design." *The Journal of Creative Behavior* 50, no. 3: 203–210. https://doi.org/10.1002/jocb.148.

Zampollo, Francesca. 2013. "Food and Design: Space, Place and Experience." *Hospitality & Society* 3, no. 3: 181–187. https://doi.org/10.1386/hosp.3.3.181_2.

Zhang, Wei, Jessica Paula Rose Thorn, John Gowdy, Andrea Bassi, Monica Santamaria, Fabrice DeClerck, Adebiyi Adegboyega, et al. 2018. "Systems Thinking: An Approach for Understanding 'Eco-Agri-Food Systems'." In *TEEBAgriFood "Scientific and Economic Foundations" Report,* 37. TEEB for Agriculture and Food "Scientific and Economic Foundations" Report. Geneva: The Economics of Ecosystems and Biodiversity. https:// eprints.whiterose.ac.uk/164950/.

2 Quadrant A

Local, sustainable food design funded or supported by public or private institutions

The number of sustainable food design outcomes (DOs) funded or supported by public and private institutions since 2009 for local impact is relatively high. Quadrant A of the wicked solution to food insecurity includes 30 DOs[1] created for a limited spatial designation that may be a small geographic region, city, local community, or household. The organizations within quadrant A may receive funding from private or public sources, or they are otherwise using resources from public or private institutions, such that they may abide by policies and regulations in their day-to-day operations. The relationship between these top-down resources and local communities, in their best form, constitutes what the literature often calls a "researcher-practitioner partnership" or RPP (e.g., Hellman and Shandas 2022). The RPP disrupts what might otherwise be strict divisions between designers and community members and allows local voices to have influence at every level from conception to research. While quadrant A's stakeholders receive funding or resources from public or private sources, they are often well embedded in communities and include educational institutions, non-profit organizations, community-supported agriculture farms, grassroots agricultural associations, food hubs, food cooperatives, and other kinds of community-based non-governmental organizations. Thus, the DOs in this quadrant emerge at the intersection of these localized stakeholders and the actors with direct access to economic or political resources. This chapter's DOs are organized according to the part of the food system that they address, including agriculture, distribution, communications, accessibility, consumption, and waste. They are equally varied in their design form, including objects, communications, environments, systems, contexts, futures, and experiences.

As illustrated in Figure 2.1, the bulk of the DOs we examined were in US locations (a spurious consequence of our literature review, not meant to reflect the actual density globally), with over a dozen educational institutions, non-profit organizations, and for-profit companies using resources to develop and implement programs, deploy participatory design methods in community-engaged research, and create products for local impact.[2] Top-down, sustainable food design activity and actors in quadrant A include:

1. **3-step solution**: Smallholder farming organizations in Cameroon contributing a subsistence farming strategy.

DOI: 10.4324/9781003222026-3

Figure 2.1 Quadrant A's DOs impact different parts of the world including the continents of North America, South America, Africa, Australia, Asia, and Europe. The shading indicates the density of sustainable food DOs we examined for that geographic region. Image courtesy of Audrey G. Bennett.

2. **Brazilian Mandala System**: An academic institution collaborating with a non-governmental organization (NGO) and local households in Brazil to design a family farming system.
3. **Feeding Milan**: Organizations collaborating with the largest agricultural park in Europe to develop new sustainable business models for production in Milan through participatory design.
4. **Food Access 3.0**: A network of organizations in New Orleans, Louisiana, providing food access resources and support to marginalized communities towards yielding food justice.
5. **Rainforest preservation**: A non-profit organization in Indonesia protecting rainforests in Borneo by facilitating local community members to harvest wild food from the forest.
6. **Seed to Kitchen Collaborative**: An educational institution in Wisconsin, using a participatory design approach with local farmers to breed plants for food sovereignty and justice.
7. **Speculative and participatory design approach for facilitating bottom-up, smart urban food-growing futures**: Academic researchers collaboratively designing food production with urban food growers in Britain.
8. **Pot-in-pot cooler**: A for-profit company in Nigeria innovates an energy efficient food and drug cooling device.

9. **Communicating food recall information to consumers**: Strategies developed to communicate food recall information to millennials in Texas, United States.
10. **EMERGE CT**: A non-profit organization in New Haven, Connecticut, fights food insecurity while assisting previously incarcerated people by providing training in sustainable agriculture, culinary arts, and other food-related skills, many times in partnership with other local organizations and stakeholders.
11. **Farm School NYC**: An educational institution in New York City with key stakeholders in the local community providing urban agriculture training to low-income community members.
12. **Food design cards**: Food design educators in the Netherlands develop a set of cards that teach about the food design process starting with the graduate students at the educational institution where they teach.
13. **Food packaging**: A university in Sweden conducts research with local families on the development of a visualization strategy for package designs that better communicate to consumers how to separate and sort household waste for material recovery.
14. **FoodPlanCNY**: An educational institution, as part of a college-level curriculum, conducts community-engaged research using an asset-based approach to improve the food system across different counties in Central New York.
15. **Instock**: A pop-up shop turned restaurant in the Netherlands that uses design thinking to rescue food waste that is still consumable from a local supermarket chain in Amsterdam and transforms it into prepared food for local communities or redistributes it to local producers and suppliers like food banks.
16. **Neqa Elicarvigmun**: An Indigenous community in Alaska developing curriculum and community activities to encourage consumption of salmon.
17. **Project Daire**: A primary school curriculum involving multiple stakeholders including principals, teachers, food producers, and caterers that educates children in Ireland on healthy food choices.
18. **Project SoL**: An educational institution collaborating with health organizations in Denmark to develop a community intervention program to improve health.
19. **Reactivate Mobile App**: A hospital in Ireland develops an obesity management intervention tool for adolescents.
20. **Yumbox**: Constituents of a for-profit company in New Jersey that designs a lunchbox to help children consume a healthy diet with the recommended daily quantity of vegetables and other types of nutritious food.
21. **Sustainable food tourism**: An academic field trip for a Nordic Culinary Cultures course where tertiary students in Denmark practice and experience sustainability as it relates to the production, preparation, and consumption of food.
22. **Co-creating solutions in food deserts**: An eclectic group of stakeholders from government, academia, and business involved in food, faith, and social

entrepreneurship are sponsored by the US-based design research firm known as IDEO to use design thinking to innovate a solution to food access in Indiana.

23. **Obesity Prevention Tailored for Health II**: A team of educational researchers develops an intervention tool for two medical institutions in Los Angeles to aid patients in maintaining a healthy body mass index (BMI), eating a healthy diet, and exercising.

24. **Slow Food University of Wisconsin**: Constituents of a non-profit organization emerging from an educational project in Wisconsin that collaborates with a local church to facilitate community-engaged food acquisition, preparation, and consumption for marginalized community members.

25. **Urban farms GUI**: A research project that engages Black-owned urban farms in Detroit, Michigan, in the development of an online grocery shopping community for low-income and Black community members to share recipes and get assistance with accessing food.

26. **Free Food on Campus!**: An approach to address food insecurity and food waste with an existing content learning management system at La Salle University in Philadelphia in the United States.

27. **Implementation of school gardens through the Healthy Hunger-Free Kids Act**: An academic study with primary and secondary school gardens in low-income cities in New Jersey after the implementation of a federal statute in 2010.

28. **Umamification of vegetable dishes for sustainable eating**: An educational research team in Denmark with foundation support develops a set of ingredients that make vegetables satisfy the craving for the taste of meat.

29. **Egg of Columbus**: An educational institution in Italy collaborating with a professional chef to develop a design thinking approach to food waste prevention.

30. **Fresh boxes**: A for-profit company packaging fresh meals to decrease food waste in the Netherlands.

In the next section of this chapter, DOs are organized according to the food system phases: aquaculture/agriculture, communication, accessibility, consumption, and waste. Each food category begins with a summary of the challenges within the phase of the food system that existing DOs address, followed by descriptions of each DO that provide more information about the actors and activities involved in their functionality, the type of design form they manifest, the year and geographical place designers effectuated them, and the literature source that provides the evidence that they are effective. This information includes: 1) the food insecurity, inequity, or injustice challenge the DO addresses and why it is a significant sustainability issue, 2) the global or local context/community the challenge impacts, 3) how the DO addresses the challenge, 4) how the DO works or functions and what qualities or components it comprises, 5) when and where the DO was effectuated, tested, or implemented, and found to be effective, and 6) who the stakeholders are and their activities. Sometimes, we rely on supplemental sources to tell a more detailed story of the sustainable food DO. From this discussion, the chapter concludes with an analysis of the places the data suggests to intervene with further design innovation or appropriation by citizens towards sustainable food security, equity, and justice in local contexts.

Agriculture

Within the vast literature on food production, only a subset is focused on sustainability, and much of that is devoted to critique, analysis, policy debates, and so on. Thus, the specific literature that frames sustainable food production as a design process with assessed DOs is relatively much smaller. Nonetheless, it is a powerful means of developing a body of publications addressing food challenges like environmental damage, poverty, and hunger. For instance, in Africa, environmental, social, and economic factors—many due to colonial legacies—have contributed to a yield gap in staple food crops, particularly cereal. That is to say there are population, land, and water resources capable of providing food security, and the gap between this potential yield and the current yield is one way of framing food insecurity. Since the insecurity itself is often addressed by stopgap measures such as food imports, it creates a cycle of crises involving soil, labor, economy, and other factors. Reversing this cycle requires rehabilitating the land to reduce poverty, and reducing poverty to improve rehabilitating the land. Leakey (2018) introduces a 3-step solution process used in Cameroon to address the challenge of yield gap by working with farmers in poor regions to improve their soil and develop and market Indigenous food and non-food cash crops.

Food insecurity caused by social, economic, and environmental factors is an inequity that also contributes inequitably to a range of chronic illnesses related to malnutrition. For instance, after Hurricane Katrina in New Orleans, Louisiana, food disparity increased. As a result, the first locally directed healthy food retail incentive program was developed utilizing federal disaster funds. This program was transformative for food access efforts around food insecurity. Historical efforts to address food insecurity like that of post-Katrina New Orleans included the Food Stamp Program that mostly attributed food insecurity to a lack of adequate household income as the underlying problem. Rose and O'Malley (2020) refer to programs and other DOs aimed at addressing low household income for food security as Food Access 1.0. Subsequently, the challenge evolved to be more about attaining food access for the food deserts in marginalized communities with low household incomes—what became known as Food Access 2.0 (Rose and O'Malley 2020). The next iteration of food access—Food Access 3.0—identifies the structural inequities contributing to food inaccessibility and responds with more innovative and participatory interventions that involve many stakeholders from low-income communities and operate at different points in the food system to empower those impacted.

As the world population increases, and climate change degrades current farming practices, more sustainable sources of nutritious food are needed along with strategies to eradicate hunger and poverty sustainably. The Brazilian Mandala

System, a household farming system, provides a model of how individual families can obtain nourishment and economic sustenance in a culturally relevant way. As well, Healy and Dawson (2019) argue for the use of participatory research to connect agricultural activity with community-based food system reform efforts using plant breeding as an example of a type of participatory research activity to address seed development to promote food sovereignty and food justice initiatives. In addition, the participatory design model was used with the largest agricultural park in Europe to develop design initiatives to connect fresh produce grown nearby to the city of Milan (Manzini 2014).

The DOs in this section address these food security, equity, and justice issues in wide-ranging ways, from the facilitation of household agriculture to collaborative design methods for growing food (e.g., participatory design, design thinking) that fit within futures, experience, context, and systems design.

1. 3-step solution

Subsistence farming strategy in Cameroon
Food category: Agriculture
Design category: Experience
Year of creation: n.d.
Source: Leakey 2018

One solution proposed by Leakey (2018) to address the yield gap involves a three-step process. First, supporting farmers in extreme poverty requires a low-cost solution to improve soil health. Research has shown that planting trees and shrubs can contribute to replenishing nitrogen in the soil. This agroecological approach, planting crops in an array of configurations and densities, is only Step 1, as this step alone still produces a yield gap due to other soil deficiencies that cannot be replaced biologically and require artificial fertilizers. Due to the prohibitive cost of such, Step 2 is income generation through a cash crop.

In Cameroon, smallholder farmers indicated the desire to cultivate Indigenous tree species that represented their traditions and cultures through non-food and food items, often very nutritious and healthy (Leakey 2018). While some refer to these foods as "famine foods," locals in Cameroon recognize their value in their diets, even if some have a stigma associated with them. However, in Kenya, Indigenous crops have a less desirable impression. In 1994, to assist farmers in Cameroon in the cultivation of food and non-food products from the Indigenous trees, a participatory approach was initiated. This approach has since moved to an up-scaled and out-scaled community approach, with researchers contributing from around the world to help develop socially modified crops. In the community, participatory domestication hubs were used to train farmers in the necessary skills to cultivate the wild woody perennials and make their own products for household consumption and to generate income. Since little may be known of these emerging crops external to the community that produces them, the final step, Step 3, is to market the new crop products (Leakey 2018). Locals are aware of the value of their products, and recognize the economic values of unique variations that occur tree-to-tree; however, when selling regionally, wholesale trade prices are based on bulk samples even if it includes samples of more valuable crop products (Waruhiu et al. 2004). A uniformity of product is needed, as is better processing and packaging to lengthen shelf life (Leakey 2018).

2. Brazilian Mandala System

Family farming system in João Pessoa and Cuité, Brazil
Food category: Agriculture
Design category: System
Year of creation: 2000
Source: Nobre and Biscaia 2015

In 2003, 15 multidisciplinary undergraduate students from a range of different academic disciplines collaborated with an entrepreneur, Willy Pessoa Rodrigues, on the development of Agência Mandala (or Mandala Agency), a non-governmental organization (NGO) in Paraiba, Brazil, with the aim to eradicate hunger and poverty in that locale in a sustainable way. They wanted to educate members of low-income families on how their fields could be used to cultivate food that can provide both nourishment and income. Then, in turn, the students, through the NGO, collaborated with low-income families in rural areas of João Pessoa and Cuité to innovate solutions to hunger and poverty. Their collaborative process was informed by design thinking and also by the solar system. The latter is particularly inspiring through its structure. As the sun lies in the center of the solar system with eight planets revolving around it, they conceived of a similarly structured family farming system called the Brazilian Mandala System (BMS). BMS is a family farming space that reflects the structure of the solar system. Research was conducted on the BMS from a longitudinal perspective from 2000 to 2012 (Nobre and Biscaia 2015).

In the center of the BMS illustrated in Figure 2.2 is a water reservoir and around it are nine concentric circles. Then, six hoses are stretched in equal distance from each other from the center of the water reservoir to the outer edge of

Figure 2.2 Brazilian Mandala System (DO #2). Image courtesy of Farley Nobre.

the ninth circle. These hoses enable a drip or sprinkler system to distribute water to all of the nine circles. The first three circles of the BMS provide food security for the family. The next five circles of the BMS can be used for generating family income. The ninth circle of the BMS can be used to sustain the environment by cultivating native crops. Each Brazilian Mandala System is a family farming system designed for sustainable interaction between an NGO, a family, consumers, and animals.

3. Feeding Milan

Participatory design with the largest agricultural park in Italy
Food category: Agriculture
Design category: Experience
Year of creation: 2010
Source: Manzini 2014

In Milan, Italy, the demand for fresh quality food exceeded availability, despite the presence of the Agricultural Park South Milan, the largest agricultural park in Europe (Simeone and Cantù, 457). The goal of this research project was to innovate with the park by developing new sustainable business models to increase production through a metro-agricultural regional model (Manzini 2014, 63).

Figure 2.3 Mandala irrigation system in Brazil. This image by LeRoc is licensed under the Creative Commons Attribution-Share Alike 3.0 Unported license: https://creativecommons.org/licenses/by-sa/3.0/deed.en.

Designers and researchers from Politecnico di Milano-INDACO department, University of Gastronomic Sciences, and Slow Food Italy gathered stakeholders including community members, farmers, designers, and food experts, to implement a framework for the project (Simeone and Cantù, 457).

Tools including storyboards, mock-ups, moodboards, and videos were utilized by the design researchers in workshops to facilitate the building of scenarios with the stakeholders to guide a co-designed vision of regional food development in Milan focused on multifunctionality and de-mediation (Manzini 2014). The resulting Feeding Milan promoted design initiatives and brought solutions to life, including a series of events that were promoted digitally including 1) the Earth Market of Milan, selling the farmers' produce in the city; 2) Veggies for the City, a project focused on production and distribution of fresh vegetables in the city; and 3) the Local Bread Chain, seeking restoration of the process for fresh bread, from crop to consumer.

4. Food Access 3.0

A food access intervention in New Orleans, Louisiana, United States
Food category: Agriculture
Design categories: Context
Year of creation: 1993
Source: Rose and O'Malley 2020

Food Access 1.0 refers to the Food Stamp Program, which addressed food insecurity through increased purchasing power due to low income. Food Access 2.0 refers to the next wave of interventions including increased access to groceries in underserved areas. The impact of Hurricane Katrina in New Orleans led to the rise of Food Access 3.0, which refers to a movement comprised of a network of organizations in New Orleans that responds to the recognized social-determinant inequities through collaboration and participatory design to address systemic issues. Food Access 3.0's interventions include:

- Grow Dat Youth Farm, an urban agriculture and youth development organization that supplies food to the community.
- Sankofa Community Development Corporation, which hosts classes on healthy cooking and gardening, and has a mobile market and fresh produce markets.
- Liberty's Kitchen, which focuses on food preparation and service, employing youth from the community, running a restaurant, catering school meals, and providing warehouse space for a local corner store.

Boxes of discounted foods are distributed by Top Box Foods, who also provide fresh produce to local corner stores, a project by Propeller: A Force for Social Innovation. Propeller provides community education on food and health. While not a new approach, grassroots food organizations face many challenges including significant turnover (Rose and O'Malley 2020).

5. Rainforest preservation

Social enterprise to preserve rainforests in Indonesia
Food category: Agriculture
Design category: Environment
Year of creation: 2020
Source: Bordewijk and Schifferstein 2020

To protect the remaining rainforest in Indonesia, the social enterprise Forestwise was founded to empower local inhabitants to stop tropical deforestation in Borneo. The organization supports local residents to sustainably harvest wild products from the rainforests including arenga sugar, virgin coconut oil, kemiri oil, and illipe butter. By helping to facilitate the process and production of these authentic local forest products, residents are empowered to protect the forest (Bordewijk and Schifferstein 2020). Food products are harvested from the forest and marketed to consumers. Utilizing the naturally produced items found in the forest provides income for local communities and preserves the forest. The whole value chain from harvesting to the consumer product is controlled by the organization with small-scale production facilities that allow the local community to generate a basic income. In February 2020, Forestwise was able to open its first factory, employing a majority of local residents. They have recently acquired illipe and kemiri nuts from 700 farmers, preserving large areas of the rainforest (Bordewijk and Schifferstein 2020).

6. Seed to Kitchen Collaborative to promote food sovereignty and food justice

A participatory plant-breeding method in Wisconsin, United States
Food category: Agriculture
Design category: Experience
Year of creation: 2013
Source: Healy and Dawson 2019

The Seed to Kitchen Collaborative, established in 2013, is a participatory design project on plant breeding. The process of plant breeding is relatively accessible to those without formal training. The challenge is to connect with farmers who have insights on needed plant varieties and understand how this impacts the overall food system and stakeholders in participatory plant breeding (PPB). The PPB process entails plant breeders connecting to the local food system, including farmers and other stakeholders, to gain input on seed development to promote food sovereignty and food justice initiatives (Healy and Dawson 2019).

The Seed to Kitchen Collaborative project was conducted by the University of Wisconsin-Madison in the Upper Midwest of the United States, impacting the communities in those regions and across the country. In 2014, the collaboration began with five local farmers and five chefs, along with seven UW-Madison plant breeders. At the time of publication of the article, the expanded network included ten core chefs from Madison, and over 70 other connected individuals representing farmers, plant breeders, and independent stakeholders from across the country (Healy and Dawson 2019).

The stakeholders including farmers, gardeners, plant breeders, chefs, and food advocates work together to plan, reviewing in January what happened in the previous year, and creating implementation plans for the upcoming year. Farmers and chefs identify trends and needs for quality and taste. Vegetables have been the primary test, though expansion has included trials for bread wheat and apple cider (Healy and Dawson 2019).

This DO was developed and tested through the University of Wisconsin-Madison. The impact has been primarily on the market-based seed system, with slower results in collaborating community systems on seed and food sovereignty and food justice. This DO may be useful to breeders, farmers, researchers, and those invested in seed and food sovereignty, and food justice in the Midwest and across the country in the United States (Healy and Dawson 2019).

7. Speculative and participatory design approach for facilitating bottom-up, smart urban food-growing futures

An approach for co-designing with urban food growers in Newcastle upon Tyne, Britain
Food category: Agriculture
Design category: Futures
Year of creation: 2018
Source: Heitlinger et al. 2019

Top-down, smart city, sustainability initiatives are gaining momentum in the United Kingdom (Heitlinger et al. 2019). However, Heitlinger et al. (2019) argue that these envisioned designs tend to focus primarily on the integration of high technologies (e.g., embedded networked sensing, cloud computing, and automation) instead of on the sustenance of the human beings that will occupy and interact in these high-tech spaces. Smart city designs have a limited definition of sustainability geared towards increased productivity and efficiency (Heitlinger et al. 2019). However, what about the other dimensions of sustainability like the socio-cultural and economic sustenance of grassroots communities? Heitlinger et al. (2019) argue that even when citizens are engaged in the development of top-down, smart cities, shared control over ownership and management of resources is vague in its legislation.

In a four-month inquiry, Heitlinger et al., researchers in Britain, investigated the design of a bottom-up, smart future for urban food growers in Newcastle upon

Tyne in the United Kingdom using a speculative participatory design (SPD) approach that the researchers developed.

In a nutshell, SPD facilitates dialogic interaction between citizens and small business stakeholders (Heitlinger et al. 2019).

Heitlinger et al. (2019) tested SPD between March and June 2018 in four iterative workshops engaging "grassroots food growing communities in the co-design of sustainable urban futures, through experimentation and creative exploration" (115). The geographic and socio-cultural context in which these workshops occurred Heitlinger et al. describe the following way:

> The geographical area we worked with sits on the outskirts of Newcastle upon Tyne city centre in the north of England. Residents experience a number of challenges associated with social and economic deprivation, poor health, also transitory student and migrant populations. Alongside this there is a rich history of diverse cultural and food heritage, accompanied by high density living, poor waste management facilities, a limited growing season due to its northernly location attracting Baltic weather systems, and limited food growing spaces.
>
> (2019, 115)

Community members with an interest in urban agriculture collaborated in a series of workshops on participatory mapping, walking through neighborhoods and then creating a speculative food future scenarios board game. In the last workshop participants built a model of a fictional food future. Each workshop was developed based on insights gained in the previous sessions. Participants shared skills and received incentives (free lunch and seeds), and researchers managed the design process and conducted the workshops, provided incentives, and recorded and coded audio recordings. Mark Ridsdill Smith of Vertical Veg, a community partner, facilitated skill sharing, shared expertise on growing food in small spaces, assisted with recruitment, participated in activities, and served as a trainer (Heitlinger et al. 2019).

Distribution

Research shows minimal design activity within the food category of distribution. The sole DO, an object, concerns Nigeria and similar areas that may lack access to electric refrigeration.

8. *Pot-in-pot cooler*

An energy-efficient food and drug cooling device in Nigeria
Food category: Distribution
Design category: Object
Year of creation: 2018
Source: Yahaya and Akande 2018

The pot-in-pot, invented in Africa, is an energy-efficient food and drug cooling device beneficial in developing nations where access to mechanical refrigeration may be unavailable or too expensive. It is built on the principle of evaporative cooling and is most effective in areas of low humidity and high sun ray reception (Yahaya and Akande 2018). The outer part of the pot-in-pot cooler is made of a porous earthenware with wet sand or other materials, and has an inner pot that can store 12kg of vegetables for about 20 days (Yahaya and Akande 2018). The outer liquid evaporates, drawing heat from the inner pot, keeping it cool. The pot-in-pot cooler is economical, quiet, and operates without fuel, resulting in zero fumes or pollution. These coolers are sold in Nigerian markets in a wide variety of shapes and sizes. While the pots are not refrigerators, they do help to keep food longer, and serve to reduce food-borne illnesses (Yahaya and Akande 2018).

Continued evaluation of ways to increase the rate of evaporation is necessary to maximize the pot-in-pot cooling effectiveness. This is done through quantifying the effects of relative humidity, air flow, and area for evaporation (Yahaya and Akande 2018). While sand is often used as the inner lining, research has shown that charcoal can be an effective lining to keep pot-in-pot items cool (Yahaya and Akande 2018).

Figure 2.4 Pot-in-pot cooler (DO #8). This image by James Emery is licensed under the Creative Commons Attribution 2.0 Generic (CC BY 2.0): https:// creativecommons.org/licenses/by/2.0/

Communications

Design has historically played a pivotal role in food communications, with a variety of DOs including conventional forms that top-down and bottom-up designers traditionally create, like marketing materials, along with more contemporary forms like apps and food recall that takes multiple modes—a crucial component to a functioning food system and also to humanity and the environment, the latter through the reduction of waste. The advent of digital communication technologies has contributed to digital solutions that address food systems issues including distribution, consumption, and waste (Michelini et al. 2018). Food waste mobile apps, like Too Good to Go and YWaste, have been created to prevent waste by distributing discounted foods (Apostolidis et al. 2021). An early app developed to promote healthy eating is Reactivate Mobile App in Ireland. Designers have also typically played a crucial role in food communication through the design of packages, and sustainability of packaging is a critical aspect of this practice, as evidenced in the DO from Sweden. Assisting parents to provide fun and nutritional lunches for children is addressed with the design of the product Yumbox that communicates nutritious portions and food type through its novel redesign of the lunchbox.

Unconventional forms of design for food communication include EMERGE CT, a restorative justice program that aims to mitigate the effects of food insecurity for those previously incarcerated (Santino 2021). High incarceration rates in the United States significantly impact communities of color and low-income communities. These individuals face many hurdles when released from prison, including limited employment assistance, barriers on job applications, and bans on food stamps contributing to their lack of access to healthy and affordable food.

Design's role in food communication has expanded to include systems and integrate design methods in their design. For instance, towards the former, several DOs highlight curriculum development and implementation that showcase the unique aspects of curricula and interventional programs to benefit local Indigenous and small-scale farming communities, including *Neqa Elicarvigmum* in Alaska, Project Daire in Ireland, and Project SoL in Denmark. Many DOs in the category of food communications emphasize participatory design processes to address food systems issues including restorative justice, education, and food waste. These include EMERGE in Connecticut, Farm School in New York City, Fleet Farming in Florida, Food Plan in Central New York State, and Instock market in the Netherlands. Finally, as the field of food design emerges, food design cards represent a unique DO created to guide those interested in working in the field.

9. *Communicating food recall information to consumers*

Strategies for communicating food recall information to millennials in Texas, United States

Food category: Communications

Design category: Communications
Year of creation: 2012
Source: Carlson and Peake 2012

The United States food recall system facilitates consumers' awareness of what they are consuming and in helping them to make the right food choices during periods of food recall. When food is determined to be unsafe by companies that produce them, the process of notifying consumers can be slow and ineffective, thus creating a life-threatening and environmentally unsafe situation. To determine how best to communicate food recall to consumers, Carlson and Peake (2012) designed an instrument to survey millennial college students from two university campuses on how they would prefer to receive food recall information and from whom (15). They found that food recall information communicated during point of purchase (i.e., inside stores near the recalled product) is most effective for these consumers (19). They also found that millennials would prefer to receive this information from federal agencies (19) like the Food and Drug Administration (FDA) and the United States Department of Agriculture (USDA) (18).

10. EMERGE CT, *United States*

A restorative food justice program in New Haven, Connecticut
Food category: Communications
Design category: Communications
Year of creation: 2020
Source. Santino 2021

EMERGE CT in New Haven, Connecticut, is a non-profit organization and a certified home improvement contractor. They provide skills training, education, mentorship, and personal development services to those previously incarcerated. Stakeholders worked with EMERGE CT to mitigate the effects of food insecurity for those previously incarcerated through a restorative justice program (Santino 2021).

Santino (2021) first created an exploratory survey for EMERGE participants to develop a food systems curriculum. The questions revolved around participants' favorite foods, where they got their food, and how they got there, their thoughts on prison food, their favorite foods since being released, and what they would like to see out of a food project. Then, more information was gained on EMERGE to get a sense of the organization's mission and values. Partnerships were also developed with BIPOC working in food justice in New Haven. In response to the diverse learning styles of the returning citizens, courses were developed in non-didactic ways on food systems, safety, culinary arts, and sustainable agriculture that included participatory approaches including photovoice and share-outs.

Unique protective factors of this population were assessed through the survey results, including "self-efficacy, stress response, communal reliance, and cultural connectivity" (45). The food access issues of New Haven were researched through city mapping tools and available government data. Without resources to address policy, the main goals were to:

1. Increase food access (healthy, sustainable, culturally appropriate) for return-ing citizens.
2. Utilize a hands-on food systems curriculum to heal from the damages of incarceration.
3. Confront social trauma perpetuated in both the food and prison systems by amplifying voices.
4. Provide foundational training for economic opportunities (Santino 2021).

Financial, technical, and stakeholder resources were needed to create a holistic program built on racial and class equality. While some wanted the program to rely on unpaid labor, the stakeholders fundraised at a grassroots level, recognizing that unlivable wages in restaurants, farming, and other general work perpetuate income inequality (Santino 2021).

Santino (2021) adds that "food justice necessitates the linkage of economic, racial, environmental, and restorative justice practices that help integrate, reha-bilitate, and heal returning citizens" (46). According to Santino (2021) further research might include:

1. Examination of prison food policies and programs through case studies, and advocacy recommendations for sustainable, safe, and culturally appropriate food in prison.
2. Longitudinal studies on the relationship between food security, incarcera-tion, and "banning the box" on job applications.
3. Researching the farm-to-school movement effects on abolishing the school-to-prison pipeline.

11. *Farm School NYC*

an urban-situated, educational program in New York City, United States
Food category: Communications
Design category: Environment
Year of creation: 2010
Source: Reynolds 2017

Even with the rise in development of urban agriculture in New York City, there remains perennial inequity in access among its marginalized communities to food and agricultural education (Reynolds 2017). Due to its success in contrib-uting to multi-sustainability aims including food security, the state government supports and nurtures the further development of urban agriculture in its com-munities through amended zoning to support food production and livestock husbandry and benefits for commercial urban farms through tax incentives

(Reynolds 2017). Yet, low-income communities in New York, particularly those of people of color, still continue to experience "structural inequity" in their local food system (Reynolds 2017). Farm School is a DO that addresses this challenge and exemplifies sustainable food design both through its functionality as an anti-racism, agricultural, educational program and through its design.

Founded in 2010, Farm School NYC is a research-generated, not-for-profit, community-based urban agriculture educational program and project of Just Food, a non-profit food justice organization (Reynolds 2017). Its mission is to "train local residents in urban agriculture in order to build self-reliant communities and inspire positive local action around food access and social, economic, and racial justice issues" (Farm School NYC). Reynolds (2017) argues that the design of Farm School NYC epitomizes the radical design innovation of designer Ezio Manzini and the educational theories of Paolo Freire (57). That is, on the one hand, Farm School NYC operates through a broad network of stakeholders with non-degree-based training in urban agriculture and related pedagogical topics. As such, its stakeholders include teachers and students from the NYC communities who have lived experiences that have nurtured their expertise in urban agriculture rather than formal, degree-based education. Thus, Farm School NYC's stakeholders epitomize what Manzini (2014) describes as "everyday designers." There are a range of actors and activities involved in Farm School NYC that facilitate it contributing to multi-sustainability goals. The founders of Farm School NYC participated in an apprenticeship at The University of California's Center for Agroecology and Sustainable Food Systems in Santa Cruz to learn how to adapt their model of teaching urban agriculture in a dense area (Reynolds 2017). The USDA provided grant funding.

On the other hand, Farm School NYC's curriculum "is designed to help students understand the social and political structures that give rise to food injustices, as well as how they may use both the theoretical and practical knowledge that they develop through the program to make changes in these systems" (56). Thus, student participants of Farm School NYC can expect to take diverse courses ranging from how to grow and even preserve food to how to recognize racism and dismantle it in the food system. Farm School NYC's radical apprenticeship training epitomizes the well-known radical pedagogical perspectives of educational theorist Paolo Freire (1996).

12. *Food design cards*

A food design process tool in Delft, Netherlands
Food category: Communications
Design category: Communications
Year of creation: n/a
Source: Lee et al. 2020

As food design emerges as a new sub-discipline of design, and with few programs specializing in food design in existence, designers need to become familiar with the food system, particularly as it relates to agriculture, hospitality, and culinary processes.

The food design cards were developed as a tool and resource to support innovation and idea development in the emerging field of food design both within food businesses and in schools. They can be utilized throughout the design process and are based on the spectrum of the food system activities, that is, agriculture, industrial processing, distribution and marketing, kitchen management, eater characteristics, consumption situation, and policy and legislation. These 7 categories, with 5 cards each, form the basis for the 35 total color-coded cards that pose topic-specific questions, with examples of answers listed on the back. These cards inspire and promote awareness and expansive thinking (Lee et al. 2020).

Prototypes of the food design cards were tested with graduate students in two workshops. Based on feedback, general instructions were devised, and six games were developed to aid in the use of the cards. Additional user testing was conducted in three contexts, with students and professional designers, then with Master's level students, and finally with Master's level students through an elective course on food design (Lee et al. 2020).

The stakeholders included student and professional designers working to innovate in the emerging field of food design. These food design cards focus on the key components of a project to provide an overview, and were designed and tested in the Netherlands, but could be used across the globe by those working in food design. Different cultures may necessitate different translated versions or adaptations (Lee et al. 2020).

13. Food packaging

A visualization strategy to enable material recovery in Karlskrona, Sweden
Food category: Communications
Design category: Communications
Year of creation: 2019
Source: Nemat et al. 2020

In 2020, it was estimated that, globally, 60% of all packaging was for food products (Nemat et al. 2020, 9–11). Packaging waste accounted for over 30% of all municipal solid waste (7–9). In Sweden, packaging waste was 21% of the municipal solid waste in 2017 (6). In fact, a large amount of materials like plastic are used in food packaging annually (1). Yet, the recycle rate is less than 5% (12–13). To curtail these alarming statistics, Sweden decided to increase the recycling rate for packaging waste from 65% by 20% per year (14).

However, Nemat et al. (2020) argue that more bottom-up waste management strategies that engender agency among citizens to recycle food waste are still needed. Thus, prior to 2020, a user-centered design research study was conducted in Karlskrona, Sweden, with 15 families that included 37 different people of varied demographics in which their research team sought to "understand consumer behavioral problems and demands during the separating and sorting of food packaging waste, and how food packaging attributes can influence them" (6). They found that proper design of food packaging has the potential to enhance consumer decision-making when separating and sorting packaging waste, and that current food packaging design does not communicate this information adequately (16). Specifically, the packaging of yogurt and cream should be especially targeted for redesign as these products are purchased often and are the most sorted by household members (16). Specifically focusing on the "package's visual attributes, the material selection, and the package's waste sorting related functions" can have transformational effects on household waste sorting practices (1). These findings are significant because of the potential "improved material recovery" that could result and the positive impact on environmental sustainability (1).

14. FoodPlanCNY

A participatory food system planning in Onondaga County, New York, United States
Food category: Communications
Design category: Experience
Year of creation: 2012
Source: Weissman and Potteiger 2018

The Onondaga County Agriculture Council was developed in 2012 to strengthen the county food system and connect its farms and agricultural regions to its urban center, Syracuse. The Council acknowledged it needed a greater understanding of the Central New York (CNY) food system and how it functioned to support its overall goals.

This project specifically focused on Onondaga County in New York with the ability to shape and guide others in participatory food system planning (Weissman and Potteiger 2018).

To address the need to understand the current state of the Central New York food system, the project FoodPlanCNY was developed by the authors, Weissman and Potteiger, with support from the Onondaga County Agriculture Council. This participatory food system planning project was

> a project designed to assess, coordinate, educate and make recommendations to improve the food system of CNY to achieve the goals of (1) inclusive economic development, (2) enhanced environmental sustainability and (3) improved public health outcomes.
>
> (Weissman and Potteiger 2018)

The FoodPlanCNY project utilized mixed-methods, engaging diverse stakeholders in community-engaged research. Along with utilizing an assets-based approach, which promotes community change by identifying and leveraging assets, the researchers, along with undergraduate and graduate students, utilized existing secondary data from state and federal sources, as well as existing community resources like interviews, surveys, and reports. Land use was explored utilizing a graphic information system, as well as archival data from historical documents. Interviews were conducted with key stakeholders and actors in the food system from across the region. Market basket surveys were also conducted in the community. The information collected was shared via a website to communicate transparency and ongoing project updates (Weissman and Potteiger 2018).

As of the publication of the article, data was still being contextualized and analyzed. Preliminary results revealed that many involved in the food system lacked a full understanding of the framework of a food system or their role within it. Additionally, the diverse stakeholders sought real-time data to understand what was happening in the food system at any given time (Weissman and Potteiger 2018).

In this study, the stakeholders are the communities and key actors in the Central New York food system; specifically cited are the counties of Onondaga, Cayuga, Cortland, Madison, and Oswego.

15. Instock

A former restaurant, now market, rescuing food to address food waste in Amsterdam, Netherlands
Food category: Communications
Design category: Communications
Year of creation: 2014
Source: Massari et al. 2021

With nearly a third of all food being wasted, Instock approaches the issue of food waste through innovation (Massari et al. 2021). Supported by the local Dutch supermarket chain, Albert Heijn, Instock started as a pop-up shop in 2014 and then converted to a restaurant, rescuing food in the community that would have gone to waste due to unappealing appearance or a near expiration date (Daniel 2016). Recently, the restaurant has closed, and their focus has shifted to repurposing food waste for Instock Market, in addition to producing other products including Instock beers, with varieties made from rescued potatoes, bread, and raspberries. Additional items include Instock granola and a cookbook ("Instock" 2022).

Instock rescues usable food waste from around the community from stores, packaging companies, growers, and producers. Usable food waste is food that is discarded but considered still safe for consumption. The rescued food is inspected for quality and safety in their Food Rescue Center and follows all regulations of the Food and Consumer Product Safety Authority. The food is then repackaged and distributed at a discount to area restaurants and caterers. This helps to support both the producers and area caterers ("Instock" 2022).

Instock is also committed to bringing awareness to the issue of food waste through their entrepreneurial efforts. Instock's innovative work shows "how design methods can generate impact and sustainability on creative capacity building" through consumer awareness (Massari et al. 2021, 3). Their iterative process of design evident in moving from a pop-up shop, to restaurant, to now market, highlights the need to adapt to the ever-changing world to remain viable and sustainable.

16. Neqa Elicarvigmun

Curriculum and community activities to encourage consumption of salmon in Alaska, United States
Food category: Communications
Design category: Communications
Year of creation: n/a
Source: Nu and Bersamin 2017

Neqa Elicarvigmun or Fish-to-School (F2S) Program is a nutrition intervention in Southwest Alaska, in the Yup'ik community of the Yukon Kuskowim Delta designed to address the increasing gap that area youth had to the traditional fish-based diet. The program was designed to provide middle school and high school students in Indigenous communities with a connection to their local food system by reconnecting salmon as a nutritious, local, and culturally significant food. As a traditional food that is harvested, processed, and distributed locally, salmon met the required regulations for serving at school, which has a universal free lunch program. These lunches meet the national nutrition standards, but the food provided contributes to the disconnect students have to their local, traditional food system (Nu and Bersamin 2017).

While Western dietary interventions typically address how food impacts health, in Indigenous communities, food is connected to place, and is viewed holistically through a spiritual, social, cultural, and economic lens (Nu and Bersamin 2017). In these communities, it is vital that nutrition interventions integrate local and cultural considerations through a collaborative and iterative process with the community (Nu and Bersamin 2017). A community work group consisting of an elder, tribal council members, city government officials, teachers, parents, students, and business and community leaders was established to work with researchers (Nu and Bersamin 2017). Nine major themes emerged from a series of focus groups that examined the relationship between salmon and well-being. The identified themes were: family, traditional life skills, *neqpik* or "real food," supporting local livelihoods, pride, hard work, connection to the environment, social connection, and gratitude (Nu and Bersamin 2017). Three core interventions were then established. The first was to serve local salmon, utilizing local recipes, in school lunches about once a week. The second was to deliver food system lessons to students showcasing the benefits of traditional foods, including for personal and community health, culturally, and economically. The final intervention was to host free community activities open to the public in celebration of salmon, and this included a scavenger hunt, film festival, cooking classes, and a community celebration (Nu and Bersamin 2017).

Connecting place, culture, and empowering the Indigenous community to connect salmon, a local food, to students as part of a nutrition intervention contributed to a solution that went beyond traditional Western approaches that focus solely on food's nutritional value (Nu and Bersamin 2017).

17. Project Daire

A school-aged curriculum intervention on the food system in Northern Ireland
Food category: Communications
Design category: Communications
Year of creation: 2018
Source: Brennan et al. 2021

Childhood nutrition is critical for a child's physical and mental health, and often varies based on the socio-economic status of a child's family (Brennan et al. 2021). Addressing these issues through school-based programs can help to reach all children. The Health Promoting Schools (HPS) framework is an international "whole-school" approach that promotes healthy lifestyles, but a lack of awareness of the program has hindered its implementation. In Northern Ireland, Project Daire was tested in 2018–19 as a method to improve primary school children's understanding and knowledge of healthy food and choices utilizing a multi-stake-holder approach. This program approached the whole school and all food groups in schools in socio-economic disadvantaged areas (Brennan et al. 2021).

Project Daire was a four-arm multi-component randomized controlled facto-rial design trial study evaluating two interventions with four 6-month interven-tion arms: nourish, engage, nourish and engage, and control (delayed) with data collected at pre- and post-intervention. Schools received nourish, engage, nour-ish and engage, or the control. Stakeholders involved in the study included pri-mary schools and teachers, principals, school caterers, and local food producers (Brennan et al. 2021).

The nourish intervention for 6–7-year-olds and 10–11-year-olds focused on awareness of a balanced diet based on the four major food groups, and introduc-tion and encouragement of eating and cooking new and local foods. Nourish included healthy snacks; information on the presentation of food, cooking, and equipment; educational materials; discussions on effective implementation of food policies; and area tasting days to taste local food (Brennan et al. 2021).

The engage intervention crossed curricula to provide age-appropriate educa-tion on all food groups, agriculture, food and nutrition science, and career oppor-tunities in food. This intervention included food system–related topics including food chain, product development, and others connected to subjects including literacy, mathematics, and physical activity in the Northern Ireland Curriculum (Brennan et al. 2021).

Results of the study suggest that making modifications through these interventions in the primary schools positively impacted the well-being and food knowledge of students in an economically disadvantaged area of need in the short term. More studies are needed to assess the long-term sustainability (Brennan et al. 2021).

18. Project SoL

A community intervention program to improve health in the Regional Municipality of Bornholm and Odsherred, Denmark
Food category: Communications
Design category: Communications
Year of creation: 2012–15
Source: Mikkelsen et al. 2018; Toft et al. 2018

Project SoL was carried out in Denmark from 2012 to 2015 and was designed to promote healthier lifestyles among Danish families and their children ages 3 to 8. The project tested a new participatory approach, supersetting, in three local communities in the Regional Municipality of Bornholm, and implementing and coordinating in everyday locations including schools, childcare, supermarkets, and local media, for maximum impact and sustainability. Three communities in the Odsherred municipality served as non-intervention control communities for the quasi-experimental study (Toft et al. 2018). The supersetting approach includes five principles:

1. Integration, to implement activities across specific areas.
2. Participation, to motivate and empower people to own the process of developing and implementing activities.
3. Action competence, helping people gain the skills and competencies needed to act on their ideas and visions.
4. Context, to respect the challenges that all citizens and professionals face when considering activities.
5. Knowledge, to inform decisions and action from scientific knowledge, and that this knowledge is a result of action.

In supersetting, the community serves as the driver of change by utilizing the resources that already exist to address a common goal. This approach recognizes the complexities of the interactions within communities and the need for a holistic perspective. "It also calls for multi-component interventions addressing multiple settings and levels in a whole-systems perspective" (Toft et al. 2018, 4).

Multiple stakeholders assisted with the development and implementation of the designed activities that were meant to create a combination of interventions over a single intervention approach to strengthen the solution. These activities included local teachers; leaders; professionals; and experts in nutrition, cooking, recreation, and physical activity (Toft et al. 2018). Formal research partners included Aalborg University, Steno Diabetes Center, and the Research Centre for

Prevention and Health. Additional stakeholders included government officials, a local NGO, supermarket chains, and a local television station. Three local action groups consisting of teachers, fitness instructors, and local business owners were also involved (Toft et al. 2018).

The main goals of the program were to increase healthy eating, decrease poor food choices, and increase overall physical activity through empowerment of the community with participatory approaches to help sustain the intervention (Toft et al. 2018). The program was developed based on existing scientific evidence and chosen activities considered:

1. The needs and ideas of the community and stakeholders.
2. The broader priorities and agendas for development of the community.
3. The researchers' evidence-based knowledge and experience.

An action research approach was used to develop the interventions and a balance was sought between what was known to have been tried and successful elsewhere, and activities that already existed within the community.

> The project implemented iterative cycles of participatory intervention development, assessment, and adjustment in which ideas were generated and knowledge was shared among researchers, local professional stakeholders, and citizens in the continued search for ways to improve health promotion in the local community.
>
> (Toft et al. 2018, 6)

The program was branded for visibility and connection in the community. Interventions included the distribution of healthy eating materials throughout the communities where families regularly congregated, including schools and stores, as well as promotion of fun outdoor activities in nature. Themes to support the activities were selected based on the local communities and varied including "taste and senses," "fish," and "nature as a pantry" (Toft et al. 2018).

A local coordinator was employed to assist with the sustainability of the project, recognizing the need to empower the local community and all the participatory stakeholders to take ownership of the project to secure long-term implementation of the interventions. Project SoL was the "first study to use the supersetting approach as the overall theoretical framework of the intervention" (Toft et al. 2018, 12).

19. Reactivate Mobile App

An intervention for adolescent obesity management in Dublin, Ireland
Food category: Communications
Design category: Communications
Year of creation: 2014
Source: O'Malley et al. 2014

Addressing obesity in adolescence is critical to minimize comorbidities and prevent future diseases. The Reactivate mobile app was designed for adolescent obesity management at a time when few evidence-based apps existed for obesity interventions for adolescents. It was developed in 2014 for use in the Temple Street W82GO Healthy Lifestyles Program, Ireland's only obesity treatment for children and adolescents, at Temple Street Children's University Hospital (O'Malley et al. 2014).

Semi-structured interviews and focus groups identified key features to consider in the app: design, benefits of app for treatment, data protection, and privacy (O'Malley et al. 2014). The evidence-based app was developed based on social cognitive theory, the theory of planned behavior, and the COM-B framework (capability, opportunity, motivation). It included behavioral tools to self-monitor, set goals, earn rewards, and receive support from peers. It also included tips and education based on evidence on subjects such as the importance of sleep. Texts, videos, and images are sent as a form of engagement for meeting goals (O'Malley et al. 2014).

While thousands of apps exist related to health and fitness, little evidence exists on their best-practice guidelines, or the user-experience design for both technical and clinical effectiveness. Kushniruk et al. (1997) and Shneiderman's (2016) usability testing methods utilize a 3-stage test plan, assessing:

1. The technical effectiveness of the app.
2. Relative user efficiency of the app.
3. User satisfaction of the app.

Reactivate was installed on ten Android mobiles, and a usability testing book was developed for participants and testers (developed by University College Cork – National University of Ireland, Cork, Ireland). The testing was done at the Vodafone user experience center in Dublin, with both the adolescent and tester. Each was reminded that the study was focused on the app, not the participant (O'Malley et al. 2014).

Each participant was given a series of eight tasks to complete to test the technical effectiveness. Relative user efficiency measured the time taken to complete a task, when compared to an expert user of the app (O'Malley et al. 2014).

Finally, participants completed the standardized Software Usability Measurement Inventory (SUMI) at the end of testing to measure user satisfaction. SUMI is a standardized questionnaire with five main factors: efficiency, affect, helpfulness, controllability, and learnability. Usability testing is critical to test mobile apps for health and clinical issues.

20. Yumbox

A healthy eating tool in New Jersey, United States
Food category: Communications

Design category: Object
Year of creation: n/a
Source: Shukaitis and Elnakib 2021

Studies have shown that preschoolers fail to consume the recommended amount of vegetables for a healthy diet. Increased intake of empty calories in sugar and fats contributes to childhood obesity and other health issues (Shukaitis and Elnakib 2021). Even though parents and caregivers may be aware of what comprises a healthy diet, lunches packed at home often are less nutritious, with more calories, fat, and sugar than those served at school (Shukaitis and Elnakib 2021).

Research in behavioral economics indicates that a behavior can be influenced by changes to the environment. Putting more healthy foods in front of students increases the chances that they will eat them (Shukaitis and Elnakib 2021). Adding sections, or images, on plates and trays accentuates this idea.

Yumbox is a bento-style lunchbox that reflects USDA's MyPlate[3] recommended food groups and quantities with five corresponding labeled compartments, including vegetable, fruit, dairy, grain, and protein. Yumbox is designed for caregivers of preschoolers to help guide them in packing lunches according to the MyPlate recommendations, guided by the visual cues in the box.

Figure 2.5 Yumbox (DO #20). Image courtesy of Maia Neumann/Yumbox.

A pilot program testing the Yumbox was conducted over three days with private Montessori preschool students in the United States, in the state of New Jersey. Results indicated that the use of the Yumbox increased the variety of foods to at least three of the five MyPlate components. Caregivers packing the lunch were more likely to include fruits and vegetables, indicating an increased awareness. Administrators considered utilizing Yumbox as an official lunchbox in the classroom as an educational component on nutrition (Shukaitis and Elnakib 2021). The visual cues in the Yumbox provide the opportunity to make packing a nutritional lunch a habit.

21. *Sustainable food tourism*

An academic field trip from Denmark to the Faroe Islands
Food category: Communications
Design category: Experience
Year of creation: 2019
Source: Leer 2020

Despite the negative impacts of tourism on the environment, sustainable food tourism can be developed through well-designed sustainable food experiences that inspire more sustainable lifestyles. Foodie tourists have been visiting the Nordic region to experience innovative culinary experiences with local food and sustainability since the early 2000s. However, the carbon emissions involved in travel can have a negative impact causing a dilemma for sustainably minded individuals. Sustainable food tourism, despite the negative impacts, has the potential to inspire more sustainable lives beyond the travel experience. This DO focuses on the design of sustainable food tourism experiences. It uses as a case study the Nolsoy Experience in the Faroe Islands, a self-governing region of the Kingdom of Denmark, where the gastronomic scene has erupted since 2010 due to marketing initiatives. Faroese cuisine is distinct with fermented produce. The case study is based on a summer class, Nordic Culinary Cultures, taught in 2019, which spent a week on the Faroe Islands. Rather than discuss sustainability, the students experienced it. The trip demanded shared participation in procuring ingredients, cooking, and working in the garden. Eating and cooking overlapped with creating a shared informal experience that combined both familiar foods with the unfamiliar, making new tastes and flavors accessible, leading to future opportunities to think about sustainability. The act of gardening contributed to the community and exchange experience, emphasizing the need to have the sustainable food tourist actively participate as a co-creator of the social and environmental value (Leer 2020, 69).

Accessibility

Within the food category of accessibility, research shows design activity around the food insecurity challenges of climate change, lack of access to healthy food due to economic inequity and environmental injustice, and the negative health consequences of this inaccessibility.

For instance, a food desert is a community that lacks convenient access to healthy and affordable food and is not able to economically sustain a supermarket (Fernhaber et al. 2018). Poor eating habits can result from residing in a food desert that can lead to malnutrition and high mortality rates for members of the community affected. According to Fernhaber et al. (2018), Indianapolis, Indiana, has historically been "ranked the worst city in the United States for food deserts" with most of its residents beyond a five-minute walk of a grocery store. And, as we pen this book in 2021, the Indiana Division of Nutrition and Physical Activity food access webpage shows food access as a major problem in the state affecting mostly people of color and low-income people, a problem likely exacerbated by the COVID-19 pandemic.

Johnson and Eglash (2021, 1) note that the current food distribution chain is one that is clearly dominated by top-down actors like industrial agriculture and large corporations. They argue that the resulting economic impact of such a phenomenon has been devastating to food access for low-income communities like those in Detroit that experience a decrease in community connection and an increase in dependency on external suppliers who do not return food and economic value to those communities (1–2). They argue further that a "generative production network (GPN)" facilitated by an online marketing and purchasing GUI (graphical user interface) can create new opportunities for these communities, though its effectiveness may be thwarted somewhat by barriers related to race and class (1). A generative production network is grounded on the concept of "generative justice" (Eglash 2016) defined as:

> the universal right to generate unalienated value and directly participate in its benefits; the rights of value generators to create their own conditions of production; and the rights of communities of value generation to nurture self-sustaining paths for its circulation.
>
> (https://generativejustice.org/)

A generative production network operates counter to existing corporate-based production networks that extract value from these communities. Instead, it aims to provide "unalienated value return" to them through online consumption (Johnson and Eglash 2021).

The DOs in the category of food accessibility include a co-creation approach; a nutrition-sensitive agriculture intervention; an obesity-prevention app; a community-engagement, educational program; and a GUI. These DOs span the categories of design objects, experiences, environments, and systems.

22. Co-creating solutions in food deserts

A design thinking approach to food access in Indiana, United States
Food category: Accessibility

Design category: Experience
Year of creation: 2018
Source: Fernhaber et al. 2018

From February to May 2017, communityINNOVATE, a constituent of IDEO and OpenIDEO, recruited 30 local participants from "government and health, business, academic institutions, design experts, community organizations, food organizations, social entrepreneurship experts, and faith-based organizations" named "challenge champions" to participate in an Indy Healthy Food Access Challenge campaign consisting first of training on their respective roles in the process (Fernhaber et al. 2018, 5–6). communityINNOVATE then formed a lead team composed of representatives from its own enterprise, an Indianapolis design consultancy called Collabo Creative, and the Indianapolis City Food Policy and Program Coordinator. This lead team provided oversight for the design thinking (DT) process using an open digital platform that they co-created to market, organize, and generate community buy-in for the campaign.

The DT process began in February 2017 and consisted of four timed phases of one month. The first phase, inquire, aimed to understand the problem. A group of participants representing both the lead team and members of the community came together in this initial phase to respond to given prompts developed by the lead team. The community's responses to the prompts were subsequently shared on the open platform. Towards the end of the inquire phase, the lead team analyzed the responses to identify issues. They engaged members of the community face-to-face in an issue prioritization session and via an email survey to prioritize and update the issues identified by the lead team. Finally, they synthesized the responses and developed challenge questions including:

1. How might we start and sustain more urban farms?
2. How might we empower youth to inspire healthy eating in their homes?
3. How might we make transportation convenient and affordable in getting people to existing grocery stores?
4. How might we create affordable ways for people to buy healthy food in the areas where they live?

In the second phase, ideate, that started in March 2017, the lead team engaged members of the community in generating ideas to address the four challenge questions. The lead team facilitated both community participation through an open digital platform as well as through an in-person brainstorming event. The lead team then analyzed the 271 ideas submitted to create an idea map (Fernhaber et al. 2018, 7). The idea map was used in the third phase, investigate, to inspire participants to "make" things to address the questions from the inquire phase. Through a "daylong make-a-thon" Collabo Creative in collaboration with Do Tank, another consultancy, and community members made solutions, practiced empathy mapping, created experience prototypes, solicited peer feedback, and developed business models (7).

In the final impact phase starting in May 2017, the lead team exhibited the made solutions at local community centers allowing the community makers to solicit further feedback and resources for their respective solution. Then, they offered "Do Something" micro-grants to 20 makers that totaled $10,000. Six months later, the lead team queried the 20 makers that received micro-grants requesting a summary of their progress and insights gained regarding food access. The lead team then posted their comments via the open digital platform.

23. Obesity prevention tailored for Health II

An online obesity intervention tool in Los Angeles, California, United States
Food category: Accessibility
Design category: Experience
Year of creation: n.d.
Source: Su 2015

Obesity is an ongoing health issue in the United States with significant consequences for both adults and children. Lack of access to healthy, nutritious foods, and increased intake of processed foods has contributed to this issue. Compounding this issue is a lack of physical activity, which can be linked directly to obesity and other diseases (Su 2015). Addressing both diet and activity levels is critical to decreasing obesity levels. The Obesity Prevention Tailored (OPT) for Health II project developed strategies to limit increase in BMI, increase the intake of fruit and vegetables, reduce saturated fat consumption, increase physical activity, and reduce sedentary lifestyle choices. This was done through interviews, in-person meetings, and individualized printed materials. While this was manageable with a small number of participants, challenges arose when scaling up due to the lack of connection within the health system (Su 2015).

To address this, an online obesity intervention tool was developed utilizing Google Maps to implement OPT II to serve two medical centers in the Los Angeles metropolitan area. The intervention tool located neighborhood healthy food stores and markets, area parks and recreation sites, licensed healthcare facilities, and helped to navigate active transportation, with an emphasis on bicycling and walking, calculating calories burned (Su 2015). Through Google Maps the tool allowed participants to choose personalized routes that evaluate safety, distance, elevation gain, air quality, and areas with vegetation and trees. It included elements like air quality, so that those with asthma can avoid areas of high pollution, and traffic accident incidences, guiding participants safely through their communities. This tool differed from primary weight intervention tools that are delivered in a healthcare setting by encouraging walking or biking to destinations; the program helps to reduce greenhouse gas, carbon dioxide, and air pollution caused by car emissions. The Obesity Prevention Tailored for Health II was beneficial because it could be accessed by a large number of participants, including anyone who is seeking a healthier lifestyle, at any time (Su 2015).

24. *Slow Food University*

Social innovation for food democracy in Wisconsin, United States
Food category: Accessibility
Design category: Environment
Year of creation: 2013
Source: Zepeda and Reznickova 2017

Zepeda and Reznickova (2017) argue that food insecurity contributes to social, health, and environmental problems, particularly for the poor who due to their economic status are more vulnerable to food-related diseases like diabetes (167). The food system undoubtedly needs to change. But how? Zepeda and Reznickova (2017) discuss the role of the alternative food movement (AFM) in bringing about change in the food system through fair trade products, organic methods, farmers markets, and community supported agriculture (167). AFM activities emphasize production and distribution strategies that bring production and consumption closer together (168). Slow Food International (SFI) is an example of an actor within the alternative food movement. Slow Food is an international movement created in Italy by Carlo Petrini in 1986. However, SFI was officially formed in Paris in 1989. Its mascot is a snail and its motto is "Good, Clean, Fair Food" (169). While the slow food movement mission advocates that food be sustainable and just, it has been critiqued as being elitist (Tam 2008). Recognizing this need to make food good, clean, fair, and more affordable, in 2007, two graduate students at the University of Wisconsin founded a chapter of SFI called Slow Food University of Wisconsin-Madison (SFUW). It is a student-run, all-volunteer organization that practices a democratic form of community-engaged "food procurement, cooking, and eating" (Zepeda and Reznickova 2017, 167). SFUW is dedicated to making "sustainable, fairly produced food accessible" by serving around "500 locally sourced and affordable meals a week" (167–8).

SFUW established itself with 501c3 status for fundraising purposes through tax deductible donations. It also created an advisory board with external members to oversee its activities and inform its successful evolution. As a student-run organization, it offers internships for academic credit to students of the University of Wisconsin-Madison. Then, it partners with a local church that provides the physical space that includes a kitchen for cooking fresh meals *slowly*. SFUW organizes various collaborative activities that feed and educate the public. For instance, a family dinner night event provides the public with affordable meals ($5) from a fixed menu.

25. *Urban farms GUI*

A generative production network facilitated by an online marketing and purchasing GUI in Detroit, Michigan, United States
Food category: Accessibility
Design category: Context

Year of creation: 2021
Source: Johnson and Eglash 2021

In the development of the urban farms GUI to provide a proof of concept for GPNs, Johnson and Eglash (2021) ask: "Can we link unalienated forms of production, such as the Blacked owned urban farms of Detroit, with unalienated forms of consumption, as we see in the Black food justice movement? Can an online system be designed that facilitates this value flow" (26)?

Working with D-Town Urban Farm and Oakland Avenue Urban Farm, Keesa Johnson, a graduate student enrolled in the Master of Integrative Design program at the Penny W. Stamps School of Art and Design at the University of Michigan, conducted field research gathering data from "online surveys, in-person interviews, rapid prototyping, a wall board, and a focus group" for each farm (30). Johnson identified the current state of online grocery shopping, particularly within the context of the COVID-19 pandemic that created a high demand for online grocery shopping, particularly for seniors (29). Within this online community there are food-related activities including the sharing of heritage recipes and grocery delivery managed by North West Initiative, a non-profit organization.

26. *Free Food on Campus!*

Utilizing existing instructional technology to address food insecurity and food waste in Philadelphia, Pennsylvania, United States
Food category: Accessibility
Design category: Experience
Year of creation: n.d.
Source: Frank et al. 2021

Food insecurity on college campuses is a widespread issue. Students' academic achievement can be negatively impacted when also dealing with food insecurity on college campuses, and it is often these students who are working significant hours in addition to attending classes. College campuses also often contribute significantly to food waste. Some students and organizations have addressed this by collecting leftover food and distributing it to those in need in the community. Technology has been created to facilitate this, including the Food Rescue Hero app, created in Pittsburgh, Pennsylvania, to alert volunteers to pick up food from retail venues and distribute to community partners in an effort to address local food insecurity. In the 1990s MIT was at the forefront of this kind of service creating FoodCam to take pictures of leftover food and send them to a designated email list as notification. Other apps include Titan Bites by California State University at Fullerton, which notifies students when food leftovers from campus events are available, and PittGrub from the University of Pittsburgh, which through an algorithm system determines which of its large student population will receive notices of food availability (Frank et al. 2021).

Researchers from La Salle University in Philadelphia, Pennsylvania, utilized the university's content learning management system to launch Free Food on Campus! (FFOC). The content learning management system, Canvas, notified students of available leftover food after events. The familiar system created an easy-to-use platform to address both food insecurity and food waste on campus. Faculty and staff were trained as Food Rescue Champions who volunteered to post announcements about available free food. To reduce stigma, announcements to students omitted words referring to need or hunger. Students enrolled as "Food Rescuers." Additional on-campus events promoted the system and awareness of food waste. Because the program utilized the existing content learning management system to send out notifications, this program may be easy to implement at other smaller-size universities (Frank et al. 2021).

Consumption

The consumption of healthy and nutritious foods is critical to address rising rates of health-related illnesses including malnutrition, obesity, diabetes, and heart disease. Consumption is directly tied to food access. Location, transportation, affordability, limited access to education, and lack of tools or resources for preparing food all impact consumption. One of the DOs in this category speaks to both the development of policy, the Healthy Hunger-Free Kids Act of 2010, and the impact of that policy on consumption of healthy foods through the implementation of school gardens in New Jersey. The other explores the sustainable protein of edible insects to address food insecurity.

27. *Implementation of school gardens through the Healthy Hunger-Free Kids Act*

A school garden in New Jersey, United States
Food category: Consumption
Design category: Context
Year of creation: 2010
Source: Reyes and Ohri-Vachaspati 2021

The Healthy Hunger-Free Kids Act of 2010 (HHFKA) promoted the consumption of healthy fruits and vegetables by supporting the implementation of school gardens. This study examines the impact before and after the implementation of school gardens in four New Jersey cities.

The study analyzes the prevalence in school gardens at 97 elementary schools and 51 middle/school levels from 2013 to 2018 after the passing of the HHFKA.

The HHFKA was a federal statute signed in 2010 to address childhood nutrition and establish new standards for nutrition in schools in an effort to combat rising rates in childhood obesity. While the legislation primarily addressed changes to school lunch programs, it also provided resources for schools on gardens to grow and distribute produce.

This study examined data on four low-income New Jersey cities from the New Jersey Child Health Study (NJCHS). Data on gardens at the schools was collected between 2010 and 2018. The results indicate that there was an increase in school gardens following the HHFKA, but expressed a need to examine the differences in prevalence found in the racially and ethnically diverse student enrollment, with majority Hispanic student populations less likely to have a school garden compared to schools with a majority Black student enrollment. As federal legislation, the stakeholders impacted by the HHFKA include all school-aged children and their families. This study examines the stakeholders in four New Jersey cities at 148 schools (Reyes and Ohri-Vachaspati 2021).

28. *Umamification of vegetable dishes for sustainable eating*

A taste rack of ingredients for vegetable umamification, Denmark
Food category: Consumption
Design category: Experience
Year of creation: n.d.
Source: Mouristen and Styrbæk 2020

Sustainable, healthy eating, which involves eating a plant-based diet, is one way to address food waste. However, humans have been eating a carnivorous diet throughout time. How can plant-based diets be adapted to address the craving of the umami taste, a taste common to prepared meat? Changes in the way we eat, particularly our overconsumption of meat, are needed to address Earth's changing ecosystem (Mouristen and Styrbæk 2020). The design outcome addressing this challenge is a taste rack of spices to enhance vegetables by umamification. Based on science and culinary insights, green vegetables were umamified to create a taste that satiated in a way similar to meat. This can be done with engineered flavoring, adding in umami or kokumi substances as is done in much Asian cooking, or using marine food sources, especially in fermented form. A taste rack of ingredients and condiments was established to contribute to umami, kokumi, and or crispness of vegetables. Each is described and its taste and aroma, as well as its texture, are noted. One case study highlights how to use the taste rack to prepare dishes of the Brassica genus, including broccoli and cabbage, and the Raphanus genus, including the Chinese radish. Another case study reveals how to use the taste rack to add crunch to vegetables (Mouristen and Styrbæk 2020). The authors' work was supported by the Nordea Foundation through a center grant for Taste for Life.

Waste

The COVID-19 pandemic that spread to the United States in early 2020 has devastated the country to historic proportions and further splintered an already struggling democracy by fueling political divisiveness. Worldwide, COVID-19 has caused nearly 6.5 million deaths (thus far). In the United States, it has claimed the lives of over 1 million people (WHO Coronavirus Dashboard).[4] However, there is hope for humanity with the development of vaccines and for the earth regarding environmental sustainability. Massari et al. (2021) observe that as a result of COVID-19 and the measurements taken to curb the spread of the disease through social distancing, food consumption has led to arguably less food waste; thus, there has been a positive impact on consumption and production that leads to food waste.

These DOs in the food waste category address challenges in Italy and Australia. CEASE-DT is a design thinking food program in Rome, Italy; and Egg of Columbus is a participatory design workshop that works to transform food and storage processing for people who are homeless in Turin, Italy. SecondBite, also in Australia, is a food rescue program that implements nutrition education and advocacy programs related to more sustainable waste management.

29. Egg of Columbus

A participatory workshop on food transformation and storage process in Turin, Italy
Food category: Waste
Design category: Experience
Year of creation: 2015
Source: Campagnaro and Ceraolo 2017

How might we appropriate still-edible fruit and vegetable waste to feed homeless people? Two design educators, a chef, and 18 multidisciplinary students set out to address this question between 2015 and 2016 in Turin, Italy. Their project, called Egg of Columbus (EC), occurring from February to March of 2016, engaged visual communication design students (tutored by a chef and university design faculty), the Alimenta network of community partners, and homeless people in developing enticing recipes using still-edible fruit and vegetable waste that could nourish homeless people and keep them from getting bored with the redundancy of food provided to them; the latter, in turn, hurts their health. They used a design-led, participatory approach to design anthropology in which they co-designed recipes. The DO comprised recipe cards for the homeless people and the shelters they occupy in Turin, that transform the consistency of the still-edible vegetable and food waste provided by wholesale suppliers into more aesthetic eating experiences that sustain the homeless people's health, "ease the tense atmosphere in the unstable and depersonalized conditions of the shelters," and sustain the environment (Campagnaro and Ceraolo 2017, 105). The two-month workshop took place within the Turin community at a university dormitory that also hosts an "interdisciplinary laboratory for social inclusion and empowerment of homeless people" (Campagnaro and Ceraolo 2017, 106).

EC is part of a larger framework called Alimenta initiated by the Universita degli Studi di Torino's departments of architecture and philosophy and education sciences (104). Among the aims of Alimenta is the promotion of food access for people who are homeless. Alimenta has a broad network of partners that support and contribute to the EC project in various ways—from funding to project management.

30. Fresh boxes

Food design to limit food waste in the Netherlands
Food category: Waste
Design category: Object
Year of creation: 2016
Source: Bordewijk and Schifferstein 2020

A challenge of food insecurity is to create a less wasteful, easy-to-prepare, healthy meal for consumers. In the Netherlands, shelf-stable easy-to-prepare meals have been available since the 1980s, often including rice or pasta, with international flavors including tacos, tandoori, and lasagna. However, as the desire for more vegetables increased, the sales in these meal boxes declined (Bordewijk and Schifferstein 2020). To address this issue, the fresh box (*verspakket*) was created in 2016, which included fresh vegetables and sauces by Bakker Barendrecht, a supplier affiliated with the Dutch retailer Albert Heijn. The idea was copied by competitors Lidl and Jumbo. The fresh box contains a recipe as well as the needed ingredients to prepare the meal. To encourage sustainability by consuming less meat, all meals are vegetarian, and adding meat is optional. The fresh vegetables are visible in the packaging so consumers can see them. Designing a package with foods combined in unique ways can have a major impact on healthy food consumption and

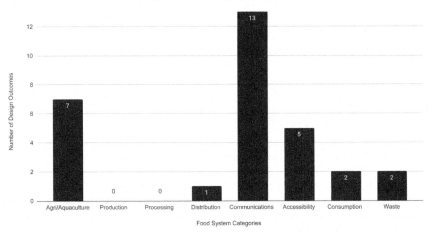

Figure 2.6 Quadrant A's DOs mapped according to the food system category to which they contribute. Image courtesy of Audrey G. Bennett.

the reduction of waste. Nearly 25% of Dutch households bought one or more of these fresh boxes in 2018 with Albert Heijn's product being the market leader (Bordewijk and Schifferstein 2020). The stakeholders are Dutch food consumers.

Places to intervene

The DOs in this quadrant show a high amount of top-down design activity to address food insecurity with sustainable food DOs that address local contexts that may be an individual, household, community, region, city, state, or country. As Figure 2.6 shows, most of the sustainable food DOs that are top-down, local, and funded or supported by public or private institutions and have been peer-reviewed address agri/aquaculture, communications, and accessibility with minimal activity in the food supply phases of consumption, waste, and distribution. There are clear gaps in the food system's phases of production and processing. Each gap is a leverage point or place where designers can intervene and contribute to balancing the system towards food security in ways that are equitable and just.

Notes

1 Note that the DOs in this quadrant come from peer-reviewed sources published after 2009—the founding of the International Food Design Society—though some of the DOs within the publications may have earlier creation or effectuation dates.
2 Based on peer-reviewed sources in English.
3 See: https://www.myplate.gov/.
4 In December 2020, COVID had claimed over 800,000 people in the United States and over 5 million deaths worldwide (Massari et al. 2021).

Bibliography

Apostolidis, Chrysostomos, David Brown, Dinuka Wijetunga, and Eranjana Kathriarachchi. 2021. "Sustainable Value Co-creation at the Bottom of the Pyramid: Using Mobile Applications to Reduce Food Waste and Improve Food Security." *Journal of Marketing Management* 37, no. 9–10: 856–886. https://doi.org/10.1080/0267257X.2020.1863448.

Bordewijk, Marielle, and Hendrik N. J. Schifferstein. 2020. "The Specifics of Food Design: Insights from Professional Design Practice." *International Journal of Food Design* 4 no. 2: 101–138. https://doi.org/10.1386/ijfd_00001_1.

Brennan, Sarah F., Fiona Lavelle, Sarah E. Moore, Moira Dean, Michelle C. McKinley, Patrick McCole, Ruth F. Hunter, Laura Dunne, Niamh E. O'Connell, Chris R. Caldwell, Chris T. Elliott, Danielle McCarthy, and Jayne V. Woodside. 2021. "Food Environment Intervention Improves Food Knowledge, Wellbeing and Dietary Habits in Primary School Children: Project Daire, a Randomised-controlled, Factorial Design Cluster Trial." *The International Journal of Behavioral Nutrition and Physical Activity* 18: 23. https://doi.org/10.1186/s12966-021-01086-y.

Campagnaro, Cristian, and Sara Ceraolo. 2017. "Fighting Food Waste towards a New Social Food Chain: The Egg of Columbus Workshop." *International Journal of Food Design* 2, no. 1: 103–116. http://dx.doi.org/10.1386/ijfd.2.1.103_1.

Carlson, Clinton C., and Whitney O. Peake. 2012. "Rethinking Food Recall Communications for Consumers." *Iridescent* 2, no. 3: 11–23.

Daniel, Diane. 2016. "Amsterdam Restaurant Takes Food from Wasted to Tasted." *The New York Times*, June 10, 2016. https://www.nytimes.com/2016/06/12/travel/instock -amsterdam-restaurant-review.html.

Eglash, R. 2016. "An Introduction to Generative Justice." *Teknokultura* 13, no. 2: 369–404.

Fernhaber, Stephanie A., Terri Wada, Pamela Napier, and Shellye Suttles. 2018. "Engaging Diverse Community Stakeholders to Co-create Solutions in Food Deserts: A Design-thinking Approach." *Journal of Public Affairs* 13, no. 3: e1874. https://doi.org /10.1002/pa.1874.

Frank, Laura B., Emily M. Finkbinder, and Virginia S. Powell. 2021. "'Free Food on Campus!': A Novel Use of Instructional Technology to Reduce University Food Waste and Feed Hungry Students." *Journal of Hunger and Environmental Nutrition* 16, no. 5: 706–724. https://doi.org/10.1080/19320248.2020.1850389.

Freire, Paulo. 1996. "Pedagogy of the oppressed (revised)." *New York: Continuum* 356: 357–358.

Healy, G. K., and J. C. Dawson. 2019. "Participatory Plant Breeding and Social Change in the Midwestern United States: Perspectives from the Seed to Kitchen Collaborative." *Agriculture and Human Values; Dordrecht* 36: 879–889. https://doi.org/10.1007/s10460 -019-09973-8.

Heitlinger, Sara, Rachel Clarke, Adrian K. Clear, Simran Chopra, and Özge Dilaver. 2019. "Co-creating 'Smart' Sustainable Food Futures with Urban Food Growers." In *Proceedings of the 9th International Conference on Communities & Technologies - Transforming Communities (C&T '19)*, edited by Hilda Tellioglu, Maurizio Teli, and Lisa Nathan, 114–120. New York: Association for Computing Machinery. https://doi .org/10.1145/3328320.3328399.

Hellman, Dana, and Vivek Shandas. 2022. "An Introduction to Researcher–Practitioner Partnerships for Climate Equity." Essay. In *Collaborating for Climate Equity: Researcher Practitioner Partnerships in the Americas*, edited by Vivek Shandas and Dana Hellman, 1–16. England, UK: Routledge.

"Instock Turns Food Surplus into Delicious Meals." *Instock*, May 2, 2022. https://www .instock.nl/en/.

Johnson, Keesa V., and Ron Eglash. 2021. "Redesigning On-line Food Consumption to Enhance Racial and Social Inclusion through Generative Production Networks." *New Design Ideas* 5, no. 1: 21–40. http://jomardpublishing.com/UploadFiles/Files/journals/ NDI/V5N1/Johnson_%20Eglash.pdf.

Kushniruk, Andre W., Vimla L. Patel, and James J. Cimino. 1997. "Usability Testing in Medical Informatics: Cognitive Approaches to Evaluation of Information Systems and User Interfaces." In *Proceedings of the AMIA Annual Fall Symposium*, edited by Daniel R. Masys, 218–222. Philadelphia, PA: Hanley & Belfus, Inc. https://www.ncbi.nlm.nih .gov/pmc/articles/PMC2233486/.

Leakey, Roger R. B. 2018. "Converting 'Trade-offs' to 'Trade-ons' for Greatly Enhanced Food Security in Africa: Multiple Environmental, Economic and Social Benefits from 'Socially Modified Crops'." *Food Security* 10, no. 3: 505–524.

Lee, Youngsil, Carola Breuer, and Hendrik N. J. Schifferstein. 2020. "Supporting Food Design Processes: Development of Food Design Cards." *International Journal of Design* 14, no. 2: 51–64. http://www.ijdesign.org/index.php/IJDesign/article/view/3467/909.

Leer, Jonatan. 2020. "Designing Sustainable Food Experiences: Rethinking Sustainable Food Tourism." *International Journal of Food Design* 5 no. 1–2: 65–82. https://doi.org/10 .1386/ijfd_00010_1.

Manzini, Ezio. 2014. "Making Things Happen: Social Innovation and Design." *Design Issues* 30, no. 1: 57–66. http://dx.doi.org/10.1162/DESI_a_00248.

Massari, Sonia, Ludovica Principato, Marta Antonelli, and Carlo Alberto Pratesi. 2021. "Learning from and Designing after Pandemics. CEASE: A Design Thinking Approach to Maintaining Food Consumer Behaviour and Achieving Zero Waste." *Socio-Economic Planning Sciences* 82, no. part A: 101143. https://doi.org/10.1016/j.seps.2021.101143.

Michelini, Laura, Ludovica Principato, and Gennaro Iasevoli. 2018. "Understanding Food Sharing Models to Tackle Sustainability Challenges." *Ecological Economics* 145: 205–217. https://doi.org/10.1016/j.ecolecon.2017.09.009.

Mikkelsen, Bent Egberg, Paul Bloch, Helene Christine Reinbach, Tine Buch-Andersen, Lise Lawaetz Winkler, Ulla Toft, Charlotte Glümer, Bjarne Bruun Jensen, and Jens Aagaard-Hansen. 2018. "Project SoL—A Community-based, Multi-component Health Promotion Intervention to Improve Healthy Eating and Physical Activity Practices among Danish Families with Young Children Part 2: Evaluation." *International Journal of Environmental Research and Public Health* 15, no. 7: 1513. https://doi.org/10.3390/ijerph15071513.

Mouritsen, Ole G., and Styrbæk, Klavs. 2020. "Design and 'Umamification' of Vegetable Dishes for Sustainable Eating." *International Journal of Food Design* 5, no. 1–2: 9–42. https://doi.org/10.1386/ijfd_00008_1.

Nemat, Babak, Mohammad Razzaghi, Kim Bolton, and Kamran Rousta. 2020. "The Potential of Food Packaging Attributes to Influence Consumers' Decisions to Sort Waste." *Sustainability* 12, no. 6: 2234. https://doi.org/10.3390/su12062234.

Nobre, Farley Simon, and Heloisa G. Biscaia. 2015. "Design Thinking for Sustainability: Fighting Against Hunger and Poverty." In *Proceedings of the XXVI ISPIM Conference—Shaping the Frontiers of Innovation Management, Budapest, Hungary, 14–17 June 2015*, edited by Eelko Huizingh, Steffen Conn, Marko Torkkeli, and Iain Bitran. Budapest, Hungary: ISPIM. https://doi.org/10.13140/RG.2.1.4266.3844

Nu, Jennifer, and Andrea Bersamin. 2017. "Collaborating with Alaska Native Communities to Design a Cultural Food Intervention to Address Nutrition Transition." *Progress in Community Health Partnerships: Research, Education, and Action* 11, no. 1: 71–80. https://doi.org/10.1353/cpr.2017.0009.

O'Malley, Grace, Grainne Dowdall, Amanda Burls, Ivan J. Perry, and Noirin Curran. 2014. "Exploring the Usability of a Mobile App for Adolescent Obesity Management." *JMIR mHealth and uHealth* 2, no. 2: e29. https://doi.org/10.2196/mhealth.3262.

Reyes, Naomi, and Punam Ohri-Vachaspati. 2021. "P42 A Longitudinal Analysis of School Garden Prevalence Across 4 New Jersey Cities." *Journal of Nutrition Education and Behavior* 53, no. 7: S43. https://doi.org/10.1016/j.jneb.2021.04.434.

Reynolds, Kristin. 2017. "Designing Urban Agriculture Education for Social Justice: Radical Innovation through Farm School NYC." *International Journal of Food Design* 2, no. 1: 45–63.

Rose, Donald, and Keelia O'Malley. 2020. "Food Access 3.0: Insights From Post-Katrina New Orleans on an Evolving Approach to Food Inequities." *American Journal of Public Health* 110, no. 10: 1495–1497. https://doi.org/10.2105/AJPH.2020.305779.

Santino, Cara. 2021. "Recipes for Resistance: Practical Applications of Restorative Food Justice in New Haven, Connecticut." *Journal of Agriculture, Food Systems, and Community Development* 10, no. 4: 43–46. https://doi.org/10.5304/jafscd.2021.104.025.

Shneiderman, Ben, Catherine Plaisant, Maxine S. Cohen, Steven Jacobs, Niklas Elmqvist, and Nicholas Diakopoulos. 2016. *Designing the User Interface: Strategies for Effective Human-computer Interaction*. Boston, MA: Pearson.

Shukaitis, Jennifer, Sara Elnakib, and Cuite Cara. 2021. "P41 Yumbox: Bringing MyPlate to Preschoolers' Lunches." *Journal of Nutrition Education and Behavior* 53, no. 7: S43. https://doi.org/10.1016/j.jneb.2021.04.433.

Simeone, Giulia, and Daria Cantù. 2010. "Feeding Milan: Energies for Change ('Nutrire Milano. Energie per il cambiamento')." In *Cumulus Proceedings Shanghai: Young Creators for Better City Better Life 2010*, edited by Yongqi Lou and Xiaocun Zhu, 457–463. Helsinki, Finland: School of Art and Design, Aalto University.

Su, Jason G. 2015. "An Online Tool for Obesity Intervention and Public Health." *BMC Public Health* 16: 136. https://doi.org/10.1186/s12889-016-2797-3.

Tam, Daisy. 2008. "Slow Journeys: What Does it Mean to Go Slow?" *Food, Culture & Society* 11, no. 2: 207–218. https://doi.org/10.2752/175174408X317570.

Toft, Ulla, Paul Bloch, Helene C. Reinbach, Lise L. Winkler, Tine Buch-Andersen, Jens Aagaard-Hansen, Bent Egberg Mikkelsen, Bjarne Bruun Jensen, and Charlotte Glümer. 2018. "Project SoL—A Community-Based, Multi-Component Health Promotion Intervention to Improve Eating Habits and Physical Activity among Danish Families with Young Children. Part 1: Intervention Development and Implementation." *International Journal of Environmental Research and Public Health* 15, no. 6: 1097. https://doi.org/10.3390/ijerph15061097.

Waruhiu, Annabelle N., Joseph Kengue, Alain R. Atangana, Zac Tchoundjeu, and Roger R. B. Leakey. 2004. "Domestication of Dacryodes edulis. 2. Phenotypic Variation of Fruit Traits in 200 Trees from Four Populations in the Humid Lowlands of Cameroon." *Journal of Food Agriculture and Environment* 2: 340–346.

Weissman, Evan, and Matthew Potteiger. 2018. "Collaboration and Diverse Stakeholder Participation in Food System Planning: A Case Study from Central New York." *Renewable Agriculture and Food Systems* 35, no. 2: 115–119. https://doi.org/10.1017/S1742170518000431.

World Health Organization. n.d. "WHO Coronavirus (COVID-19) Dashboard." Accessed August 4, 2022. https://covid19.who.int/.

Yahaya, Suleiman Abimbola, and Kareem Adeyemi Akande. 2018. "Development and Performance Evaluation of Pot-in-pot Cooling Device for Ilorin and Its Environ." *USEP: Journal of Research Information in Civil Engineering* 15, no. 1: 2045–2060.

Zepeda, Lydia, and Anna Reznickova. 2017. "Innovative Millennial Snails: The Story of Slow Food University of Wisconsin." *Agriculture and Human Values* 34, no. 1: 167–178. https://doi.org/10.1007/s10460-016-9701-8.

3 Quadrant B

Widespread, sustainable food design funded or supported by large-scale public or private institutions

Sustainable food design emerging since 2009 and funded or supported by public and private institutions are few in number but far in reach. Quadrant B of the wicked solution to food insecurity shows peer-reviewed design outcomes[1] (DOs) funded or supported by public and private institutions for a wider geographic region that may include adoption or appropriation by multiple countries, states, regions, cities, communities, or households. Quadrant B's stakeholders include educational institutions, non-profit organizations, community-supported agriculture farms, grassroots agricultural associations, food hubs, food cooperatives, non-governmental organizations, among other types of entities. The DOs in this quadrant emerge primarily from actors or stakeholders with access to economic or political resources. Some DOs may have a place of origin before widespread production, adoption, or appropriation; whereas others seemingly self-replicate in multiple places. These DOs are also organized according to the part of the food system that they address including agriculture, production, communications, accessibility, consumption and waste, and they are equally varied in their design form including objects, communications, environments, contexts, futures, and experiences.

As Figure 3.1 shows, according to our literature review, the United States and Canada have the most sustainable food design activity generated by public and private institutions worldwide participating in a global effort to annihilate food insecurity, inequity, and injustice.[2] Top-down, sustainable food design activity and actors in Quadrant B include:

31. **Carrot City**: Canadian educational institutions teaming up with other professional stakeholders around the world to create a digital archive of urban agriculture models situated in local contexts worldwide.
32. **Circular bioeconomy intervention**: A non-profit organization using a circular bioeconomy approach to design sustainable agricultural outcomes in various countries in sub-Saharan Africa.
33. **Community-supported agriculture farm**: Farms in Japan and the United States that localize food production and distribution for economic and social sustenance.
34. **Grassroots rural producer movement**: A network of grassroots non-profit organizations in Bolivia, the Netherlands, Peru, Brazil, and Canada

DOI: 10.4324/9781003222026-4

Figure 3.1 Quadrant B's DOs originate in or propagate in various locales around the world including the continents of North America, South America, Africa, Australia, Asia, and Europe. The shading indicates the density of sustainable food DOs we examined for that geographic region. Image courtesy of Audrey G. Bennett.

contributing to the rural producer movement and providing support to small-scale farms.

35. **Urban rooftop farm**: Academic, hotel, and food industry organizations conducting zero-acre agricultural farming in the United States, Canada, Spain, Germany, Switzerland, Singapore, India, and other countries around the world.

36. **Food safety infosheets**: Academic researchers design communication flyers to teach food safety to food handlers in Michigan and Kansas.

37. **Great food street**: Architects in collaboration with local communities and other governmental stakeholders in various countries around the world (e.g., Canada, the United States, France, and Italy) design streets that are walkable, and provide aesthetically pleasing food experiences among other qualities that qualify them as "great food streets."

38. **Why Cheap Art?**: A theatre and publishing press in Vermont use the design of a poster to advocate through creative typesetting that food is art.

39. **Memefest**: A collection of writing, art, and design interventions from the Memefest Festival in Slovenia and Australia that counter mainstream forms of the food system with practical and creative interventions.

40. **Food hub**: Community members around the world collaborate with multidisciplinary experts to form food cooperatives that serve their marginalized communities in ways that are more ecologically and economically sustainable.

41. **International Potato Center**: A Peruvian research-for-development organization collaborating with smallholder farming organizations in Ethiopia to implement a nutrition-sensitive agriculture intervention.
42. **Edible insects**: For-profit companies in Finland, Austria, Benin, and the DRC market alternative protein farming kits for household use around the world.
43. **Edible mushroom**: Farmers grow and harvest mushrooms in Benin and DRC to counter food insecurity.
44. **CEASE-DT**: An academic researcher in Italy extends design thinking beyond the context of business to sustainability particularly in regard to waste management.
45. **High-quality cassava peels (HQCP)**: Representatives of two organizations in Benin and Rwanda collaborate to upcycle and transform cassava peels from waste into animal feed.
46. **SecondBite**: A non-profit organization in Australia redistributing excess food from restaurants and other food businesses to those in need.

In the next section of this chapter, DOs are organized according to the food system phases they address: aquaculture/agriculture, production, processing, distribution, communication, accessibility, consumption, and waste. Our integrative review of peer-reviewed literature shows sustainable food design activity in the food system for quadrant B specifically in the phases of agriculture, production, communication, accessibility, consumption, and waste. Each food category begins with a summary of the challenges within the phase of the food system that existing DOs address, followed by descriptions of each DO. These descriptions provide more information about the actors and activities involved in their functionality, the type of design form they manifest, the year and geographical place where they were effectuated, and the literature source that provides the evidence that they are effective. Our aim in each food category is to provide a brief summary overview gleaned from the respective peer-reviewed publication. This information includes: 1) the food insecurity, inequity, or injustice challenge the DO addresses and why it is a significant sustainability issue, 2) the global or local context/community the challenge impacts, 3) how the DO addresses the challenge, 4) how the DO works or functions and what qualities or components it comprises, 5) when and where the DO was effectuated, tested, or implemented, and found to be effective, and 6) who the stakeholders are and their activities. Sometimes, we rely on supplemental and credible gray sources to tell a more detailed story of the sustainable food DO. From this discussion, the chapter concludes with an analysis of the places the data suggests to intervene with further design innovation or appropriation by public or private institutions and other organizations towards sustainable food security, equity, and justice for widespread impact.

Agriculture

Within the food category of agriculture, research shows design activity related to addressing food insecurity, inequity, and injustice challenges like the long distances that food travels, supply and demand challenges due to rising populations, government-regulated multi-purpose land management, and the interrelatedness of climate change, food access, and chronic diseases.

Industrial agricultural production continues to dominate conceptualizations of how to address food insecurity and malnutrition around the world; and this dominant globalization model of the food supply chain from farm to plate has food traveling long distances around the world. Foodwise, formerly known as the Center for Urban Education and Sustainable Agriculture (CUESA) ("How Far" 2018) estimates that meals in the United States travel on average about 1,500 miles to get from where they were produced to where they are consumed. Transporting food over these long distances contributes to the "carbon footprint" or carbon emissions and results in environmental damage. According to Gorgolewski et al. (2011), when there is a long distance between the food's origin, that is, where it is produced, and where it is consumed, the environment and humanity suffer; that is, the high energy usage that is required to transport processed food long distances damages the natural environment, and the consumers' access to high-quality food for good health is compromised. This challenge is particularly significant to cities' lack of agricultural and food-production means. Carrot City,[3] an analog and digital multimodal DO, provides models of urban agriculture in different cities around the world that shorten the distance from the food's origin to where it is consumed.

Another impending food insecurity crisis relates to food supply shortages anticipated in the next few decades. "With over 140 million children born every year, the global population…is projected to increase to 9.7 billion by 2050," putting an incredible demand on food supply; and the anticipated huge gap between demand and supply will lead to food price increases that disproportionately affect the poor like the impoverished communities in sub-Saharan Africa (Feleke et al. 2021, 2). In the countries that make up sub-Saharan Africa, there is already this pressure today from a rapidly growing population that is motivating farmers to cultivate more land; however, due to excessive environmental degradation, they are unable to do so (2). This makes sustainable food supply a life-threatening challenge in sub-Saharan Africa that will prevail in the future unless successful interventions emerge. Intertwined with environmental degradation are other challenges specific to the region of the African continent including climate change and low economic growth (2). However, a circular bioeconomy addresses this issue in its use of resources more efficiently and sustainably.

There are also the negative ramifications of climate change with which we must contend. Communities in rural areas of Bolivia, Peru, Canada, and the Netherlands that are experiencing the impact of climate change ranging from frosts to droughts, which are caused in part by their agricultural practices, are regulated heavily by their governments. For instance, the United Nations' Department of Economic and Social Affairs (UN DESA) may advise governments and assist in the implementation of UN policies related to economic, social, and environmental goals.[4] To address these kinds of multi-functional land management requirements and challenges, grassroots producer movements provide assistance through on-farm agroecological training along with off-farm guidance on how to sustain natural ecosystems and farming economies (Hart et al. 2016, 305).

31. Carrot City

An urban agriculture digital archive with accompanying book developed in Toronto, Canada
Food category: Agriculture
Design category: Environment
Year of creation: 2011
Source: Gorgolewski et al. 2011

The Carrot City digital archive and the accompanying book were created by university researchers in Canada who aim to shorten distances between where food is produced and where it is consumed in cities. They've compiled models of urban agriculture in cities and on rooftops worldwide. Both the Carrot City's online archive and its accompanying book include case studies from the Netherlands, Germany, Ecuador, Brazil, Switzerland, Nicaragua, Britain, and the United States, among other countries around the world. From this tremendous open-source resource, one can deduce that anyone anywhere in the world with at least internet access can peruse this online archive or read the accompanying book and adapt one of the case studies to a similar urban environment in their local community. Urbanites worldwide can glean ideas for adoption or appropriation in their communities, and they can use the case studies to locate healthy food. The Carrot City digital archive includes the following effectuated urban agriculture projects:

Edible Estates Regional Prototype Garden, the United States

a food art installation by Fritz Haeg propagated throughout the world including England, Italy, Turkey, Hungary, Israel, and Denmark

Artist Fritz Haeg's wide-ranging oeuvre includes edible gardens in which his art media comprise lawn, seeds, and the natural and man-made tools for gardening. For an art installation series titled "Regional Prototype Gardens" he received commissions to create "lush, aesthetically pleasing, climate-appropriate, edible landscapes" around the world featuring sites in North America and Europe (Gorgolewski et al. 2011, 132). For this series, he received commissions from institutions including the Salina Art Center in Kansas City; the Tate Modern in London; Arthouse in Austin, Texas; and The Contemporary Museum in Baltimore, Maryland. His edible gardens can be found on suburban and urban residential properties along with public properties (e.g., a park) in Salina, Kansas; Lakewood, California; Maplewood, New Jersey; Southwark, London; Austin, Texas; Baltimore, Maryland; New York City, New York; and La Cañada Flintridge, California, among other sites around the world.

The Edible Schoolyard

an urban agriculture program for school children in Brooklyn, New York

In 1995, the first Edible Schoolyard project was started in Berkeley, California, at the Martin Luther King, Jr. Middle School (Gorgolewski et al. 2011, 90). Since then, the project has spread widely within the United States. The Edible Schoolyard in Brooklyn, New York, represents a collaboration between Chef Alice Walters, her non-profit organization the Chez Panisse Foundation, Public School (PS) 216, and WORK Architecture Company. It aims to educate children in grades K through 5 on how to grow their own food sustainably (and the impact of growing on the environment and their health), improve the quality of their school lunches, meet the state's learning standards, and integrate food into the standard academic subjects. WORK Architecture Company designed the Edible Schoolyard at PS 216 to include an organic produce garden accompanied by three separate learning, growing, and cooking spaces that engage school children along with their teachers, family, and the community in active learning about food production (90).

Wood Street Urban Farm

a certified organic farm in Chicago, Illinois

Since 2008, Growing Home, a non-profit organization, and Shed Studio, an architecture firm, have collaborated on the award-winning Wood Street Urban Farm that is run in a marginalized Chicago community known as Englewood. Englewood is also a food desert. This organic farm runs a transitional employment program for residents of Chicago who may be having difficulty entering the job market after being homeless or previously incarcerated, or recovering from substance abuse (98). The program trains its enrollees in the work of farming. The Wood Street Urban Farm includes three hoop house greenhouses and a multipurpose building that includes "a permanent attached greenhouse, processing and storage space, and rooms for offices and meetings" (98). The farm yields over 4,500 kg of produce a year, half of which it sells to the community (98). Over the years, the collaboration has expanded to include legal experts who assist the "production assistants" in sealing and expunging their records (Growing Home n.d.).

32. Circular bioeconomy intervention

An approach to alternative food supply in Nigeria, Ghana, Kenya, Benin, Mali, and Ethiopia
Food category: Agriculture, Consumption, Waste
Design categories: Object and context
Year of creation: 2004–21
Source: Feleke et al. 2021

Feleke et al. (2021) provide an evidence-based argument that a circular bioeconomy approach can produce interventions to address the multifaceted challenge of food supply not meeting the growing demand for food due to population increases that countries in sub-Saharan Africa face now and will continue to face in the near future. A circular bioeconomy uses resources efficiently through nutrient recycling, sustainable biomass for biofuel production, value addition, minimization of the use of toxic chemicals (i.e., chemical fertilizers and pesticides), and post-harvest losses through breeding improved varieties using gene editing (3). Over the past decade, the International Institute of Tropical Agriculture (IITA) has tested the circular bioeconomy approach in sub-Saharan Africa to address "natural resource degradation, climate change, hunger, and poverty" (3). IITA designed interventions applied to the concept of circular bioeconomy and this led to the development of the following:

- Aflasafe (bio-control of aflatoxin), Nigeria: Aflasafe, a bio-control innovation product to be used against aflatoxin contamination in maize and groundnuts. Aflatoxin poses a food safety risk, as contaminated products that are eaten can lead to serious sickness and death. It also impacts farmers' income when the crop is contaminated. Aflasafe is an all-natural product that reduces aflatoxin. It was developed in collaboration with the United States Department of Agriculture (USDA) Agricultural Research Service (ARS). This process included incubation for commercialization, awareness, certification, dissemination, and finally adoption, highlighting to small-holder farmers in Nigeria and Kenya Aflasafe's potential to reduce aflatoxin in maize and groundnuts. Changes were identified and tracked through a backward tracking approach, starting with the farmers who were using Aflasafe.
- Biochar, Ghana and Kenya: Developed in collaboration with the International Institute of Tropical Agriculture (IITA) and the Swedish University of Agricultural Sciences (SLU), biochar from crop residue is a bio-based product used in Ghana. It is a bio-ecological approach, being developed to sequester carbon, utilizing different feedstock, to improve soil quality in Kenya, as well as fight climate change.
- Biodiesel, Benin and Mali: Another bio-based technological innovation product is second-generation biofuel development, biodiesel. The International Institute of Tropical Agriculture (IITA), in collaboration with the Center for Information, Research & Action for the Promotion of Farmers Initiatives (CIRAPIP), is developing biodiesel fuel in Benin and Mali. This jatropha-based fuel utilizes jatropha oil to replace diesel fossil fuel, and the byproduct is used as a substitute for inorganic fertilizer. This bio-enterprise was under development at the time the research was written.
- Edible insects, Benin and the Democratic Republic of Congo: See the description in the Consumption category.
- Edible mushrooms, Benin and the Democratic Republic of Congo: See the description in the Consumption category.

- Genetically modified cassava, Nigeria: Another IITA biotechnology intervention to address food insecurity and natural resource efficiency is genetically modified cassava, developed to address postharvest physiological deterioration (PPD), which is vulnerable for two days after harvesting, impacting its starch quality. Cassava varieties that can be stored longer are being tested in field trials in Nigeria with the Swiss Federal Institute of Technology (ETH-Zurich).[5] They have set up a platform for PPD-tolerant cassava varieties that are preferred by farmers. Reducing food loss requires less land and other resources. However, cassava-producing countries are missing regulatory guidelines for genetically modified crops.
- HQCP (Animal Feed), Benin and Rwanda: See summary in the Waste category below.
- Insect-based feed, Benin and Rwanda: Another intervention developed by IITA in collaboration with the International Center of Insect Physiology and Ecology (ICIPE) is the development of insect-based animal feed to address food insecurity and climate change. Raised-and-fed black soldier fly larvae are being used to develop chicken feed to replace the need for land required for traditional animal feed crops like soybean, impacting the reduction of greenhouse gas (GHG) emissions.
- NoduMax, bio-fertilizer, Nigeria: The soybean inoculant NoduMax is a bio-fertilizer developed with rhizobium. It was produced at the IITA headquarters in Nigeria by the Business Innovation Platform (BIP). It works by adding beneficial bacteria to the soil and can increase soybean yields and enhance the soybean's ability to facilitate biological nitrogen fixation. NoduMax increases crop productivity and has received regulatory approval in Nigeria. Sub-Saharan Africa, the Democratic Republic of Congo, Ethiopia, Rwanda, and South Africa IITA, in collaboration with the public research institute ETH Zurich, have developed a bio-ecological approach to organic fertilizer through urban-rural nexus. Targeting urban centers, this nutrient recycling effort replaces or reduces the use of chemical fertilizers. The waste from urban households from food produced in rural areas is collected and composted in rural dumpsites to produce organic fertilizer that is then sold to the farmers, increasing crop productivity, creating jobs, and reducing GHG emissions. This has been adopted by smallholder farmers.

33. *Community-supported agriculture farm*

Food production and distribution localization in Japan and the United States
Food category: Agriculture
Design category: Experience
Year of creation: 1960
Source: Hartling 2019

Local farms and communities are negatively impacted socially and economically by the dominance of the global food supply chain. Hartling (2019) analyzes the existing food localization model of "community-supported agriculture (CSA)" as an opportunity to address the challenges created by the globalization model of food distribution and supply.

There are three types of CSA. The first type is:

> the farm who owns the land and the equipment does all of the farming and harvesting work. The only involvement of members is purchasing a share. In the second type, CSA members work on the farm as part of their payment for produce. The third type, there is no single proprietor but a community form of ownership with multiple owners and workers with a stake.
>
> (Hartling 2019, 3)

According to Hartling (2019), CSA originated in Japan and permeated European boundaries in the 1960s (2). The first CSA was effectuated through an agreement known as "teikei" in Japanese that translates to "food with the farmer's face on it" (Henderson and Van En 2007). The first CSA in the United States can be accounted for in 1985 in Massachusetts (Henderson and Van En 2007). Since 2015, according to the U.S. Department of Agriculture there are 7,398 CSA farms in the United States.[6]

34. Grassroots rural producer movement

A grassroots producer movement in Boliva, Netherlands, Peru, Brazil, and Canada
Source: Hart et al. 2016
ANAPQUI a grassroots producer movement in Altiplano, Bolivia
Food category: Agriculture
Design category: Futures
Year of creation: 1983

The southern Altiplano of Bolivia grapples perennially with the dual climate conditions of frost and drought. Yet, it's home to a farming community that supplies the world with quinoa, a seed whose global demand has increased since the late twentieth century when Bolivia's government reverted to democracy (Hart et al. 2016). ANAPQUI is a grassroots producer movement situated in Altiplano, Bolivia. It stands for *Asociación Nacional de Productores de Quinua* (ANAPQUI) translated as The National Association of Quinoa Producers. ANAPQUI is a movement characterized by a network of stakeholders engaged in activities to yield sustainability. ANAPQUI functions as a global network of activities by stakeholders including the United Nations, Western alternative trade organizations, and a community of Bolivian producers that aim to cultivate environmental, ecological, and economic sustainability in Bolivia's agricultural community.

Northern Friesian Woodlands

an environmental cooperative in Friesland, the Netherlands
Food category: Agriculture

Design category: Context
Year of creation: 1992

Another type of producer movement in the world contributing to sustainability through multi-functional land management is the environmental cooperative (Hart et al. 2016). An example of such is the Northern Friesian Woodlands Association (NFW) in the Netherlands. As the story goes:

> In the early nineties, following growing concerns around groundwater pollution and acid rain, The Hague imposed new regulations on farmers to protect the landscape and reduce emissions of ammonia and nitrogen. These regulations posed a serious threat to small peasant farms. Injecting manure into the soil instead of spreading it on top would not only bring an increased cost, but more importantly, some farmers suspected the heavy machines necessary would have a detrimental effect on the condition of the soil and the quality of groundwater. In 1992 four men in the northern part of Friesland came together to fight for their farms and their way of life. They were Fokke Benedictus, Pieter de Jong, Geale Atsma and Taeke Hoeksma. Their message to The Hague was "we want to take care of the environment – you have to help us".
>
> (The Bond Project n.d.)

The NFW manages the land in a multi-functional manner towards multi-sustainability with a varied set of stakeholders. They work in agreement with the government (i.e., The Hague) and in consultation with agricultural experts to create policies for farmers that sustain biodiversity and provide economic sustenance. The NFW represents local farmers who hold paid memberships with them. They create policies to which farmers who are members must adhere to maintain government support and, in return, the NFW provides the farmers with training and other professional services like managerial assistance.

Potato Park

Ayllu biocultural food management for food sovereignty in Pisac, Peru
Food category: Agriculture
Design category: Futures
Year of creation: 2000

In understanding the role of government-supported grassroots producer movements in the management of multi-functional land in rural parts of the world, in addition to ANAPQUI, Hart et al. (2016) discuss the case of the Ayllu biocultural management in the Potato Park (Potato Park). Located in Peru, Potato Park[7] represents government-approved food sovereignty towards food security through economic, ecological, and social sustainability. In Potato Park, an Indigenous farming community practices agrobiodiversity by relying on their traditional knowledge to cultivate mainly native and some externally provided crops, and to maintain rights to the resources generated. Potato Park comprises around 30,000 acres of multi-functional land managed by Indigenous people of Pisac, Peru who use Ayllu, a form of "Andean social organization based on family ties and kinship" (314). Ayllu is an "endogenous approach to sustainable development" in which the traditional Andean values of *chaninchay* (balance), *ayninakuy* (reciprocity) and *yanantin* (duality) are practiced" (314). That is, with the Ayllu approach, the land is divided into different "ecological zones" in which residents exchange agricultural goods between zones (Hart et al. 2016, 315). Potato Park also serves in part as a tourist attraction that contributes to its economic sustenance.

Rural Landless Workers' Movement

land reform in Pontal do Paranapanema, Brazil
Food category: Agriculture
Design category: Futures
Year of creation: 1984

While improvements have been noted on poverty and development in Brazil, large estate producers, or *latifundos*, continue to maintain control over the land distribution patterns (Hart et al. 2016). The Rural Landless Workers' Movement (MST) or the *Movimento dos Trabalhadores Rurais Sem Terra*, was established in 1984, originally to obtain land for those without, and to stabilize food production. More recently, MST has focused on ecological land reform which is the practice that fosters ecological citizenship and environmental management within the community (Wittma 2010). MST includes more than one million people throughout Brazil, and as of 2000, more than 10,000 families were re-settled on redistributed land (Ashoka 2022). The Agrarian Reform Settlers' Cooperative in the Pontal (COCAMP), or *Cooperativa dos Assentados da Reforma Agrária do Pontal*, settled more than 3,000 of these families in the Reserva do Pontal. This area has a history of significant land-ownership conflicts and deforestation and cattle pasture, contributing to a shrinking of the forests of the Morro do Diabo State Park to 36,000 hectares. The Reserva do Pontal covers 260,000 hectares of the threatened Atlantic Forest ecosystem and was designated a protected area in 1942 (Hart et al. 2016). It is a conservation area critical for its endangered endemic species and as a source of seed for Atlantic forest restoration programs in the area (Cullen et al. 2005). The settlements were originally placed on the lands buffering the Park and the remaining forest fragments to appease the *latifundos* managing large areas of agriculture at the time. This strategy, however, contributed to the conservation community raising concerns that the placement minimized nature conservation efforts (Valladares-Padua et al. 2002).

Having previously worked as farm workers, sharecroppers, or in other urban jobs, many COCAMP and MST members found that the large-scale collective production methods were economically and environmentally unsuitable for the land parcels that they now managed (Holt-Giménez 2009). As a result, MST renamed its "Sector of Production" to the "Sector of Production, Cooperation and Environment" in 2000. It also published *Commitment to Land and Life*, sharing its philosophy and beliefs on nature and the constitutional rights to social production and environmental sustainability (Wittman 2010).

Recognizing the opportunity provided by land reform, since 2003, MST and local organizations in Pontal have developed initiatives in agroforestry and "support rural livelihoods through landscape-level coordination" (Hart et al. 2016, 309).

Through a participatory approach, a wide variety of stakeholders have contributed to environmental education and conservation strategies promoting earlier resolution of conflicts that arise among all the stakeholders. The approach considers the opinions of participants as individuals, and the local and cultural contexts, helping stakeholders to co-create a vision of their land and communities (Valladares-Padua et al. 2002).

Saskatchewan Soil Conservation Association and crop diversification

a rural producer movement in Saskatchewan, Canada
Food category: Agriculture
Design category: Futures
Year of creation: 2010

Traditional farming practices across the southern Canadian prairies contributed to widespread soil erosion and loss of nutrients. This threat on farm sustainability, limited knowledge on best practices, and the need for making farms economically viable led to the creation of producer groups (Hart et al. 2016). ManDak, an organization of producers from Manitoba and North Dakota (since renamed to Northern Prairies Ag Innovation Alliance), hosted the first area meeting in 1978 on conservation tillage. Within a decade, the Saskatchewan farmers formed the Saskatchewan Soil Conservation Association (SSCA) (McClinton and Polegi 2010). SSCA serves as a farmer-led movement, providing education in coordination with farmers, researchers, extension services, and industry on new technologies and promoting change in tillage practices (Hart et al. 2016). The reduction of dust blowing across the plains and the adoption of conservation tillage in the 1990s indicates that efforts have had an impact (Fox et al. 2012).

SSCA utilizes an approach to conservation tillage that is based on the foundation of conservation tillage practices in Canada. To add to farm viability and soil fertility, this has included crop diversification in Saskatchewan and other areas. Due to the improvement of soil fertility and increased economic viability, crop rotations of pulse-oilseed-grain and conservation tillage have become common practice (Hart et al. 2016). While many conservation efforts began with care for the land, increased evidence has made soil conservation move from "the right thing to do, to simply, 'the thing to do'" (McClinton and Polegi 2010).

The Saskatchewan government has used best management practices (BMPs) for multi-functionality of landscapes as an incentive program for farmers.

Emphasis has shifted from the conservation tillage and crop rotation to a list of 18 BMPs promoting the ecosystem through the Canada-Saskatchewan Farmer Stewardship Program (CSFSP) (Government of Sakstachewan 2014).

Since 2005, SSCA has also contributed to climate change mitigation conversations on policies related to agricultural soil carbon. While conservation tillage and crop rotation practices have restored soil and economic viability, they rely on herbicides and crops modified for herbicide resistance. More profitable than oilseeds or grains, pulses are susceptible to weeds (Barr et al. 2009). These issues and pest resistance may have an impact on the long-term sustainability of these agricultural programs (Hart et al. 2016).

Production

As noted previously, food production often takes place a significant distance from the areas where the food is consumed. This long transportation impacts the environment and human health negatively. As a result, urban agriculture has expanded with the goals to address food insecurity and create methods of community connection with zero-acreage farming. Zero-acreage farming (ZFarming) includes backyard gardens, community gardens, and gardens in and on top of buildings. Within these spaces, additional concepts include vertical farming, edible walls, and indoor and rooftop farming (Buehler and Junge 2016). Studies have shown that urban agriculture can contribute to local food sustainability. While urban rooftop gardens may compete for space with solar panels, incorporating both has already been prototyped.

35. *Urban rooftop farm*

Zero-acre agriculture in the United States, Canada, Spain, Germany, Switzerland, Singapore, India et al.
Food category: Production
Design category: Context
Year of creation: 1995–2015
Source: Buehler and Junge 2016

To review current urban rooftop farming (URF), a form of zero-acreage farming, Buehler and Junge (2016) compiled a list based on published case studies found online in English, German, and Dutch. The criteria to be included in the study included having a minimum area of $100m^2$ to farm being located on a roof, growing over 50% vegetables, and operating in 2015, the year of the study. The study resulted in 57 cases that met the criteria from across the world including 40 in North America, 11 in Europe, and 6 in Asia.

In their study New York was a leader in URFs. With nearly 5,000 hectares of rooftop space in 2009, and only 0.23% used, New York's URFs could grow food for more than 30 million people (Caplow 2009). Europe and Asia have also begun to implement URFs. While urban farming and Zfarming case studies were found for Europe, several were not included in the study because they were not

Figure 3.2 Brooklyn Grange Rooftop at Brooklyn Navy Yard. This image by Ian Bartlett | @bartlettville is licensed under the Creative Commons Attribution-Share Alike 4.0 International license: https://creativecommons.org/licenses/by-sa/4.0/deed.en.

located on a roof. In addition, while rooftop gardens in Asia are a traditional form of gardening, few studies written in English were found.

The complete list of urban rooftop farms included in their study in 2015:

- Brooklyn Grange Flagship Farm, New York, United States
- Brooklyn Grange Navy Yard Farm, New York, United States
- Hell's Kitchen, New York, United States
- Eagle Street Rooftop Farm, New York, United States
- Higher Ground Farm, Boston, United States
- HK Farm, Hong Kong, China
- Lufa Farms Ahuntsic, Montreal, Canada
- Lufa Farms Laval, Montreal, Canada
- Gotham Greens Greenpoint, New York, United States
- Gotham Greens Gowanus, New York, United States
- Gotham Greens Hollis, New York, United States
- Gotham Greens Pullman, Chicago, United States
- Rooftop Greenhouse Lab (RTG-Lab), Bellaterra, Spain
- Community Rooftop Garden, Bologna, Italy
- The Vinegar Factory, New York, United States
- Arbor House at Forest Houses, New York, United States
- Rye's Homegrown, Toronto, Canada
- ECF Farmer's Market, Berlin, Germany

- Rooftop Farm Ecco Jäger, Bad Ragaz, Switzerland
- The Science Barge, New York, United States
- School Sustainability Laboratory, New York, United States
- UF001 LokDepot, Basel, Switzerland
- UF002 De Schilde, The Hague, Netherlands
- The Urban Canopy, Chicago, United States
- Fairmont Royal York Hotel, Toronto, Canada
- Fairmont Waterfront Hotel, Vancouver, Canada
- Fenway Farms, Boston, United States
- Whole Food Market, Lynnfield, United States
- Rothenberg Rooftop Garden, Cincinnati, United States
- The Visionaire Penthouse Green Roof, New York, United States
- Khoo Teck Puat Hospital (KTPH), Singapore
- Gary Comer Youth Center Green Roof, Chicago, United States
- Trent University Vegetable Garden, Peterborough, Canada
- Changi General Hospital, Singapore
- Zuidpark, Amsterdam, Netherlands
- Bronxscape, New York, United States
- Carrot Common Green Roof, Toronto, Canada
- Uncommon Ground restaurant, Chicago, United States
- True Nature Foods' Victory Garden, Chicago, United States
- Le Jardin sur le Toît, Paris, France
- 5th Street Farm Project, New York, United States
- RISC Rooftop Forest "Forest Garden," Reading, Britain
- Santropol Roulant, Montreal, Canada
- Gartendeck, Hamburg, Germany
- Via Verde, New York, United States
- Maison Productive, Montreal, Canada
- Dakkaker, Rotterdam, Netherlands
- Florida State University, Tallahassee, United States
- Hôtel du Vieux-Québec, Québec, Canada
- Up Top Acres at Elm and Woodmont, Bethesda, United States
- Shagara at School, Cairo, Egypt
- Mumbai Port Trust Terrace Urban Leaves, Mumbai, India
- Urban Leaves, Mumbai, India
- Food Roof Farm, St. Louis, United States
- Metro Atlanta Task Force Rooftop Garden, Atlanta, United States
- McCormick Palace, Chicago, United States
- Roosevelt University, Chicago, United States

Communications

Addressing the wicked problem of food insecurity will take many disciplines, including art and design, teaming up to collaborate creatively. From the artwork, to the built environment, to tools for food safety, the DOs in this food category of communication represent a scope of communication design that impacts sustainable food.

In the *Food: Bigger than the Plate* exhibition in Britain, one learns that the histories of art and design are intertwined with that of food. For instance, design and food production and processing as we know them today emerged during the Industrial Revolution (Flood and Sloan 2019, 13). Art and design have contributed to food processes through advertising, marketing, branding, and packaging of food products throughout history. Within the DO "Why Cheap Art?" the poster provocatively declares "art is food" (see Figure 3.3).

Then, in examining the DO of great food streets, de la Salle (2019) argues that today's built environment separates food production from food consumption, and that this divergence has been detrimental to humanity's health. Due primarily to industrialization, a small few—located far away from the consumer—control food production, processing, and distribution. de la Salle (2019) also notes that this current separation departs from how food production used to be when it was much more interconnected with the consumer.

An important part of sustainable food design for food security is food safety training. Chapman et al. (2011) argue that "the generic and prescriptive content and school-like delivery methods used in current food safety training may be a barrier to application" (160). Chapman et al. argue further that a more cross-cultural approach to food safety training can likely lead to more hygienic practices among food handlers (162). This argument is supported by culture theorists who agree that dialogue within a peer group allows the individual to determine the validity of the message and how to act on it (Schein 1993) recognizing that collective learning can lead to behavioral changes (Chapman et al. 2011; Ajzen 1991; Dignum et al. 2001). Creating food information sheets based on theory and psychology can help communicate more effectively, as described below (see DO #36).

36. *Food safety infosheets*

A communication design tool for food safety training in Michigan and Kansas, United States
Food category: Communications
Design category: Communications
Year of creation: 2011
Source: Chapman et al. 2011

> *Foodborne diseases impede socioeconomic development by straining health care systems, and harming national economies, tourism, and trade.*
> –World Health Organization

How does one design food safety training that is more sensitive to cultural differences within a peer group? Through a two-part Delphi and pilot posting study, Chapman et al. (2011) propose the design of a food safety infosheet where the

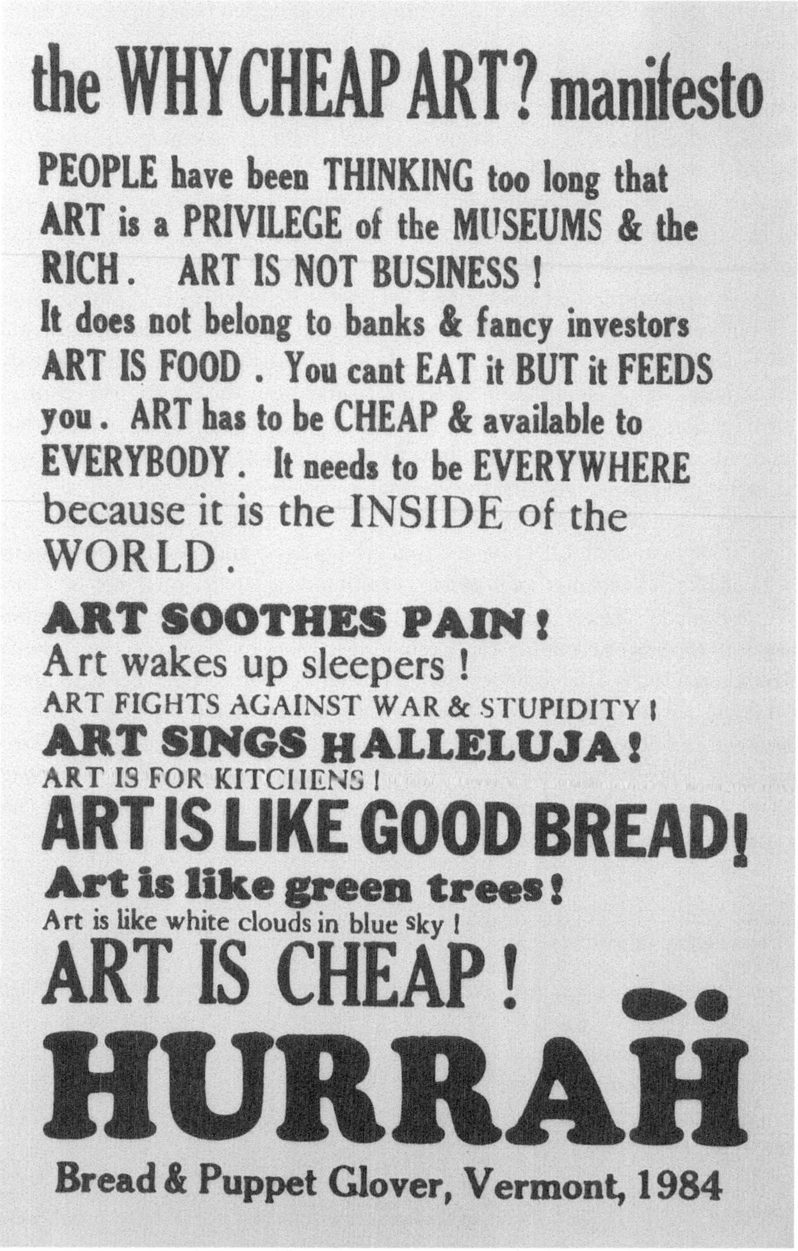

the WHY CHEAP ART? manifesto

PEOPLE have been THINKING too long that
ART is a PRIVILEGE of the MUSEUMS & the
RICH . ART IS NOT BUSINESS !
It does not belong to banks & fancy investors
ART IS FOOD . You cant EAT it BUT it FEEDS
you . ART has to be CHEAP & available to
EVERYBODY . It needs to be EVERYWHERE
because it is the INSIDE of the
WORLD .
ART SOOTHES PAIN !
Art wakes up sleepers !
ART FIGHTS AGAINST WAR & STUPIDITY !
ART SINGS HALLELUJA !
ART IS FOR KITCHENS !
ART IS LIKE GOOD BREAD!
Art is like green trees !
Art is like white clouds in blue sky !
ART IS CHEAP !
HURRAH
Bread & Puppet Glover, Vermont, 1984

Figure 3.3 Why Cheap Art? poster (DO #38). A manifesto by Peter Schumann hand
printed on a letterpress and then reproduced as an offset poster throughout the
years. This text has inspired multitudes to change course and make more art.
Image courtesy of Bread and Puppet.

content is "limited to one specific foodborne illness factor such as handwashing, cross-contamination, sanitation, or temperature control" (177). Guided by communication theory and psychology, their research team designed infosheet prototypes aimed specifically at food safety training and tested them in two rounds with food handlers in Lansing, Michigan, and Manhattan, Kansas. Their findings confirm that effective food safety training through infosheet design may communicate more effectively when designed with an element of surprise (Shannon 1948) that could take aesthetic form as shocking and surprising graphics (Chapman et al. 2011, 175). Additionally, infosheet design for food safety training of food handlers may be more communicatively effective when storytelling (Howard 1991) is infused in the visual/verbal design. Particularly, they found that including stories about real victims of foodborne illness and images of celebrities were effective in creating a personal connection with the food handlers (175). This DO is significant as according to WHO, "Globalization has triggered growing consumer demand for a wider variety of foods, resulting in an increasingly complex and longer global food chain" (World Health Organization 2022).

37. *Great food streets*

An inclusive, public, built environment where commercial food is consumed in Canada, the United States, France, and Italy

Food category: Communications
Design category: Environment
Year of creation: n.d.
Source: de la Salle 2019

The design of "great streets" (Jacobs 1993) is a standard convention within architecture poised to address the challenge of sustainable food design and converge the production and processing of food with inclusive public consumption for better human health. To this end, de la Salle (2019, 119) asks: how can we plan, design, and program a street to facilitate a more inclusive and sustainable food system?

de la Salle posits that a "great food street" (121) has the following qualities:

- It is walkable.
- It provides visibly compelling and sensory food experiences.
- It supports temporary uses.
- It fosters inclusion.
- It includes dynamic features.

Examples of great food streets, according to de la Salle (2019), include Commercial Drive, Gore Street, and Wilder Snail in Vancouver, Canada; Trackside Cantina (where Main Street terminates) in the Town of Smithers, Canada; Eastern Market in Detroit, Michigan; Rue Mouffetard in Paris, France; and Campo de' Fiori in Rome, Italy.

38. Why Cheap Art?

A poster produced in Vermont, United States
Food category: Communications
Design category: Object
Year of creation: 1984
Source: Flood and Sloan 2019

The DO in Figure 3.3 shows that art and design, particularly the design convention of a poster, have not solely been and need not only be in service to commercialize food. The poster's connotated meaning is that food is itself art. This powerful position broadens the scope and media of art and design to include food. Doing so allows contemporary artists and designers entry to creative inquiries involving food. This DO takes the form of a designed manifesto, an artistic object, inspiring future creative inquiry with food as the medium.

39. Memefest

Festival of Socially Responsive Communication, Design, and Art in Slovenia and Australia
Food category: Communications
Design category: Communications
Year of creation: 2013
Source: Vodeb 2017

Memefest is an online international network of academics, activists, and professionals, engaged in art, design, social sciences, and philosophy, collaborating in alternative, non-institutional ways that allow for new possibilities to respond to critical urgent world issues. This public network fosters experimental public research through participatory action, media, and communication. The network consists of the Memefest Collective, a group of curators and editors helping to make decisions. The Festival includes a public forum, multiple types of feedback through the memefest.org website, and work is also posted online for public viewing. Research is generated from this collection of submissions, and these are then used to develop a symposium, an intervention event to develop the research in a local context.

For instance, consumers' knowledge of the journey of the food they consume is often limited, contributing to a limited understanding of the wider food system. Art, design, and communication are often confined to defined roles within their discipline. Memefest addressed the latter topic, food democracy, as part of its Festival of Socially Responsive Communication, Design, and Art in 2013, which aimed to tackle social issues through communication, art, and design.

Food democracy workshops were held in Brisbane, Australia, at Griffith University, Queensland College of Art, and included collaboration with the Aboriginal activist group, The Brisbane Aboriginal Sovereign Embassy (BSAS), which at the time was starting to run a food program in aboriginal communities. Food democracy acknowledges shared responsibility and advocates that "inclusive and dialogic communication, design, and art is at the core of socially responsive strategies and in opposition to the exclusionary delusions of marketing-based communication, design, and art" (Vodeb 2017, 24). The image is crucial for visibility to serve as the impetus for conversation and leading to action.

The collected research from across the globe engages in food democracy, connecting art and design with the social sciences and philosophy. In addition to written research that explores food and democracy, other submissions include visual examples of visual communication and participatory art that address culture, food community building, and projects that explore power in society, all of which culminates into a book titled *Food Democracy: Critical Lessons in Food, Communication, Design and Art* (Vodeb 2017). The book also includes curated works that were submitted to the Memefest competition and deemed to be of high relevance based on the prompts provided, referencing *Stolen Harvest: The Hijacking of the Global Food Supply* by Vandana Shiva as well as Nikolaus Geyrhalter's documentary *Our Daily Bread*. The curated works include public feedback from a diverse set of curators alongside the presented designs. Works include:

- Mohammad Naser's presentation of audio-visual work and photography titled "Seeds of Hope/Destruction" highlighting the impact of hybrid rice introduced in Bangladesh in the 1990s. The introduction of hybrid seeds, while producing higher-yield crops, created environmental, economic, and political hardships on the farmers. This work seeks to raise consumer awareness on the issues behind the food people eat.
- Mariella Bussolati's work, "Orto Diffuso," maps connections of community gardens and neighborhoods. As an activist, Bussolati has spoken on community gardening all over Italy. In addition to a wiki map that allows for community participation to input data on gardens, she has written a book and created a video on the same issues. Her goal is to use gardens strategically to address economic crises and to create common food communities.
- Zayra Dolores developed "Pick Me," a set of color wheels to encourage consumers to choose local, seasonal produce at farmer's markets in Sydney and New South Wales, Australia. The color wheel helps to easily identify what is in season.
- "The Food Trade Apparatus (FTA)" by Thomas Roohan is a piece of cloth with the countries of Australia, United States, Mexico, and China printed on it depicting the commodification of food as it passes through free trade agreements. The design could serve as a tablecloth in restaurants or cafes to promote further conversations on the impact of trade on the food system.

Overall, the artifacts from this instance of Memefest focused on food democracy and highlighted many ways that artists and designers can address sustainable food design in their creative practice.

Accessibility

According to Ballantyne-Brodie et al. (2015):

> the corporate-dominated globalized food system is resulting in detrimental outcomes for food producers and consumers alike; family farmers are struggling to earn a living while, paradoxically, fresh nutritious food is becoming less affordable and thus contributing to increasing rates of poor health and obesity.
>
> (44)

Research shows that within this top-down "corporate food system" (Prost 2019, 142) where the aim is mainly to profit, communities with high socio-economic resources have greater access to healthy food. Even in some bottom-up, locally distributed food systems that may focus on greater access to high-quality food for better health, those communities with high economic resources tend to benefit most. Access to high quality food, whether it is globally or locally sourced, is a serious problem for communities experiencing "socio-economic deprivation" and one that food democracy initiatives aim to address.

Whereas Ballantyne-Brodie et al. (2015) advocate for food sovereignty and implore that "sustainable and equitable food systems are needed to benefit food producers and consumers alike" (44), Prost (2019) advocates for food democracy and defines it as:

> 1) a strong ethical commitment to environmental sustainability, social justice, as well as individual and community health, 2) democratic governance through active participation of food citizens, and 3) a whole system perspective aiming to transform the entire food system.
>
> (142)

An example of a food democracy initiative are civic food networks (CFNs) propagating in Australia, the United States, Britain, and other parts of the world that aim to provide access to food equitably and sustainably to the benefit of socio-economically challenged communities. Then, in Ethiopia, a nutrition-sensitive agriculture intervention program, implemented by its government, provides another great example of food democracy in progress.

40. Food hub

Civic food-access communities in various locales

Dockland Food Hub

a design-led food innovation for the community in Melbourne, Australia
Food category: Accessibility
Design category: Environment

Year of creation: 2015
Source: Ballantyne-Brodie et al. 2015

In August 2009, the community embarked on a "design-led innovation" project in Melbourne, Australia (Ballantyne-Brodie et al. 2015, 44). With the DO of a food hub in mind, they created "group think-tanks" comprised of experts from "design, law, community development, and economics" for incubation (48). After four months of giving intellectual form to the idea, they conducted a series of meetings with other members of their community to get "buy-in." In January 2010, the sixth month, they successfully developed a partnership with Open Channel, a media firm in Australia, that donated a design space for ease of access to the community. For four months starting in February 2010, they conducted co-design workshops with community stakeholders to develop the idea of a food hub further and apply for funding through proposal development and fundraising.

After successfully attaining funding, they were then able to secure a place in the community for the Food Hub through negotiations with a local developer, another stakeholder, and a "design champion" (48). The food hub was co-designed initially as a "garden" by community and business stakeholders starting in August 2010 (48). It officially opened in October 2010 with an appealing and persuasive story likely developed in concert with the media firm Open Channel, one of the early stakeholder partners. From November 2010 through November 2011, they sought and obtained additional funding to design a business model for the Food Hub to sustain both business and the community. These funded efforts generated a waste-auditing program and a shop to showcase products and run community events and educational workshops for the community (48). The design-led innovation process concluded with all-inclusive stakeholder discussions on how to sustain the food hub.

Healthy Food Hub

a food cooperative market in a Black community combating food deserts in
    Chicago, United States
Food category: Accessibility
Design category: Environment
Year of creation: 2009
Source: Figueroa 2017

Established in 2009 on the South Side of Chicago, the Healthy Food Hub is a community-based cooperative market, located in an area that was once a food desert, with the last Black-owned grocery store closing in 1995. Many of the Hub's older members are the children of sharecroppers from the Mississippi Delta, who fled to the area to escape the racial violence that prevailed following the murder of Emmett Till, a 14-year-old African-American teen, by white supremacists in 1955. The sharecroppers brought with them, and passed through the generations, a collective resilience and strategies for survival that resides in the Hub's community empowerment model (Figueroa 2017). The collective buying strengthens the community through solidarity. The overall economics of the Hub's operations are inspired by the African socialist concept of *ujamaa*, cooperative economics, which seeks to reinscribe the ideas of community, sustainability, and resilience through culture and material.

The Hub purchases healthy, fresh food for less as a collective, buying from Black farming communities to strengthen economic opportunities and cultural connections. It is a member-based organization, with nearly 500 families from the neighborhoods of south Chicago being served through a pre-order system. This system supports the co-op model and the participatory nature of building community. Being a member is an investment of money, time, skills, and knowledge, and in return community members retain control over their community wealth. While a traditional CSA has farmers selling memberships, this model has the members determining what they want to purchase. The distribution of the food takes place at a Market Day, and builds community as a social engagement space, with demos and education on subjects including cooking and farming. In addition, the Healthy Food Hub also maintains a 40-acre production center and eco-campus in the historic Black farming community in Pembroke Township, called the Black Oaks Center for Sustainable Renewable Living (Black Oaks). Black Oaks hosts events and educational seminars for students from the South Side of Chicago, as well as a Rotating Apprentice Farmers' Training Program with the Black farmers in the Pembroke area.

Meadow Well Food Hub

a civic food network for food democracy in Newcastle upon Tyne, Britain
Food category: Accessibility
Design category: Environment
Year of creation: 2019
Source: Prost 2019

The Meadow Well Food Hub (Meadow Well) in Newcastle upon Tyne in the United Kingdom, epitomizes this type of civic food network (CFN). According to Prost (2019):

> The Meadow Well estate is located in the suburban fringe of the Newcastle upon Tyne metropolitan area in North East England. It is inhabited predominantly by British white working-class and low-income families. Decades of neglect by local authorities resulted in a brief period of violent unrest in the mid-1990s. Despite political commitments, little has changed, and today the estate remains among the most deprived 10% neighbourhoods in England in terms of education, employment, income, health, and environmental quality.

(144)

For six months starting May 2017, a baker, a researcher, a community-based organization, and members of the Meadow Well estate community came together to develop the Meadow Well Food Hub using a participatory action research (PAR) approach. During iterative phases of PAR, these stakeholders engaged in "action and reflection" towards negotiating the final DO (145). The Meadow Well Food Hub effectuated from a collaborative design process of balanced decision-making powers between all stakeholders. On the one hand, it aims to "ethically source food" (149) within a marginalized community of Newcastle upon Tyne that is economically and environmentally sustainable for its local producers. On the other hand, Meadow Well Food Hub also aims to provide this locally sourced food to a community of consumers in a manner that is just and ethical through affordability and accessibility.

41. *International Potato Center*

A nutrition-sensitive agriculture intervention in Tigray and the Southern Nations,
*   Nationalities, and Peoples' regions, Ethiopia*
Food category: Accessibility
Design category: Experience
Year of creation: 2017
Source: Busse et al. 2017

In 2013, the International Potato Center introduced a three-year program to address food insecurity and malnutrition in two regions in Ethiopia: Tigray and Southern Nations, Nationalities, and Peoples' regions. To address vitamin A deficiencies and improve nutrition and food security, the intervention promoted an increase of production and consumption of orange-fleshed sweet potatoes, a proven method to reduce this deficiency in vulnerable populations (Busse et al. 2017). Working with a variety of stakeholders, the intervention was designed to increase smallholder farmers' production of the sweet potatoes, increasing consumption, strengthening value chains, and facilitating multi-sector nutrition policies (Busse et al. 2017). Regions or *woredas* (i.e., districts) were selected by the International Potato Center and regional Bureaus of Agriculture based on agroecology suitable for sweet potato production, food insecurity in the area based on the Government of Ethiopia's Productive Safety Net Programme, child malnutrition in the district, and the distance to a main road (Busse et al. 2017). Multiple stakeholders in the *woredas* were engaged to implement the interventions with the International Potato Center.

In Ethiopia's Southern Nations, Nationalities, and Peoples' regions, the International Potato Center's interventions promoted community gatherings over individual meetings, a focus on planting the sweet potato in small gardens due to hesitancy on the farmer's part to experiment with a new crop. Activities were led by trusted community organizations instead of outsiders. These efforts were important to improve nutrition and overall livelihoods (Busse et al. 2017).

In the Tigray region, the regional government plays a critical role in the community and has invested in increased food production (Busse et al. 2017). Understanding the need to respect culture and religious practices, the International Potato Center worked with existing government programs to make the orange-fleshed sweet potatoes a priority crop in the region. In addition, the International Potato Center worked to strengthen women's knowledge and empowerment on nutrition and feeding issues, enhancing their assets. This included strengthening women's development groups and cooperatives to make sure that women had access to the activities. Finally, the International Potato Center worked with educational institutions in a multi-sector approach to address systemic behavior through school programs (Busse et al. 2017).

Busse et al. (2017) worked to understand how to transform and strengthen community assets holistically in both the Tigray and Southern Nations, Nationalities, and Peoples' regions of Ethiopia. Understanding the multi-sector factors contributing to malnutrition in these regions, as well as the local assets, can help determine the impact, and support coordinated efforts across sectors to improve food security (Busse et al. 2017).

Consumption

Another sustainable approach to address global food security is insect-based food, rich in nutrients. Scientists are exploring how to prepare these foods in a way that consumers will eat them and how to raise the insects on an industrial scale (McClements 2020). While westerners may have a more challenging time with the idea of eating insects (Mancini et al. 2019), for many around the world insects are already part of their regular diet (Tao and Li 2018). In the European Union (EU), any new product for human consumption with insects requires assessment as a novel food,[8] which under EU regulation is food that was not significantly consumed prior to May 1997. Some feel that using insects instead of crops for animal feed might also be an option for sustainability (McClements 2020).

42. Edible insects

Alternative protein farming in various locales
Food category: Consumption
Design category: Object
Year of creation: Varied
Source: Kauppi et al. 2019; Feleke et al. 2021

Edible insects are a valuable source of sustainable protein for humans and for animals and have gained increased attention as a way to address global food insecurity. While many people across the globe already include insects as part of their diets, eating insects is still considered a novelty to some westerners. Eating insects is a way to address global food insecurity while also considering sustainability. Edible insects require less feed, water, and space, and emit fewer GHGs than other animal-based protein sources (Kauppi et al. 2019, 40). Regulations exist and vary for the distribution of insects for consumption. Design can serve as an important strategy to increase consumer acceptance of edible insects in the West.

in Finland

Year of creation: 2016
Source: Kauppi et al. 2019

Sirkkapurkki (Cricket Jar) was a glass jar with layers of different cricket-based granola ingredients visible through the glass. Originally sold in Finland in 2016, it was promoted as a kitchen decoration, since it was illegal to sell edible insects at the time. However, the company encouraged customers to share social media posts preparing and eating the cricket granola. Continued advocacy for legalization of edible insects was promoted in 2018 in Sweden, where whole roasted crickets in a translucent jar were introduced by Griidy. Both ento-preneurs, new insect food companies, sought to influence regulation by consumer demand, and eventually the local food authority in Finland amended regulations and accepted insects as food (Kauppi et al. 2019).

The Hive—Vienna, Austria, and Hong Kong

Year of creation: 2018
Source: Kauppi et al. 2019

The Hive by LivinFarms, operating out of Vienna, Austria, and Hong Kong, is an electronic home farming product designed to grow mealworms in a fast, controlled way using kitchen food waste as feed. By producing the mealworms at home, the owner avoids the high cost of purchasing insects and learns more about producing their own food. The goal is to increase awareness of the food system and shift food production from large industrial sources to the home and schools (EntoNation 2018).

This article is a result of the ENTOWASTE project "Design of Insect and Insect-based Food Products," funded by the Norwegian Research Council NFR under the ERA-NET LAC II scheme, a Network of the European Union (EU), Latin America and the Caribbean Countries (LAC) on Joint Innovation and Research Activities (Kauppi et al. 2019).

in Benin and the Democratic Republic of Congo

Year of creation: n.d.
Source: Feleke et al. 2021

One of the International Institute of Tropical Agriculture (IITA) circular bioeconomy bio-ecological interventions to address food insecurity and climate change

Figure 3.4 Example of edible insects. This image by Matthieu Lelievre is licensed under Creative Commons Attribution: ShareAlike 2.0 Generic (CC BY-SA 2.0): https://creativecommons.org/licenses/by-sa/2.0/

in Benin and the Democratic Republic of Congo is edible insects, developed in partnership with the University of Liverpool in the United Kingdom. To reduce or replace the consumption of farmed animals, thus reducing the carbon footprint by reducing GHG emissions, insects like termites are being developed for human consumption. Many parts of the world consume insects and caterpillars, termites, crickets, and palm weevils, and minimal land is needed to produce these edible insects. Socio-cultural factors need to be considered in changing the mindset about eating insects, which may be seen as unappealing or taboo compared to consuming other meats (Feleke et al. 2021).

43. Edible mushroom

A circular bioeconomy intervention in Benin and the Democratic Republic of Congo
Food Category: Consumption
Design Outcome: Object
Year of creation: n.d.
Source: Feleke et al. 2021

Edible mushrooms are another type of circular bioeconomy intervention to address food insecurity and climate change in Benin and the Democratic Republic of Congo. Edible mushrooms farming in the Democratic Republic of Congo has also led to job creation. IITA Youth Agripreneurs (IYA) run an edible mushroom farming business in Kinshasa, Democratic Republic of Congo. For more information about circular bioeconomy see DO #32 above.

Waste

As mentioned previously in Chapter 2, food waste deters environmental sustainability and undermines the United Nations (UN) 2030 Agenda for Sustainable Development. The DO called CEASE-DT (Massari et al. 2021) is a design thinking approach used to develop and analyze the impact of design innovation (e.g., Fleet Farming and the Food Flow[9] app) on sustainability by lessening food waste. Other interventions that address food insecurity by reducing food waste are animal feed development and food rescue services.

44. CEASE-DT

A design-thinking approach to food waste prevention in Rome, Italy, and the United States
Food category: Waste
Design category: Experience
Year of creation: 2021
Source: Massari et al. 2021

Food waste deters environmental sustainability and undermines the UN 2030 Agenda for Sustainable Development that was adopted by the organization in 2015. At that time, the UN adopted this agenda with 17 goals listed in Figure 1.5 of Chapter 1. The eleventh and twelfth goals, sustainable cities and communities and responsible consumption and production, respectively, are the aims of the DO titled CEASE-DT (Communities, Engagement, Actions, Shareability, Ecosystem Design Thinking Tool), proposed by Massari et al. (2021) "to support and maintain the sustainable food waste habits which emerged during the lockdown periods [of the COVID pandemic] and maintain a high level of consumer awareness" (2).

Massari et al. (2021) provide access to several DOs that show evidence of the positive impact on sustainability that making consumers aware of food waste can yield (3). The list includes a variety of innovative technologies from apps to platforms that optimize and catalyze the exchange and circulation of information and resources within local food systems towards greater multi-sustainability that is economical, equitable, and environmentally friendly. Massari et al.'s (2021) design thinking framework—CEASE-DT—builds on this success. CEASE-DT extends design thinking beyond an approach for business impact to an approach that measures sustainability through four parameters: desirability, feasibility, viability, and sustainability (4). As such, Massari et al. (2021) define CEASE-DT as an analytical tool that consists of the following four phases of inquiry:

1. Did the DT approach succeed in making the solution desirable for the community? Does the community (customer and users alike) want this solution? (4)
2. Is the new scenario designed by means of DT feasible for consumers? Did DT provide the right solution by means of a combination of build, partner, or acquire endeavors/activities? (4)
3. Did the DT model succeed in supporting emerging behavior styles based on values that are important to the community? How did DT build and provide the solution capable of creating value? (4)
4. Did the solutions provided by the application of DT provide scenarios that support more sustainable habits for the near future? Is the community able to manage their solutions proactively in order to account for their future development? (4)

CEASE-DT is a creative approach to making consumers aware of their environmentally unfriendly household habits around food management that lead to food waste and informs them on how to replace those habits with more sustainable ones. For instance, purchasing food using a shopping list, planning meals for the week, keeping track of food inventory, and learning how to cook can prevent food waste and contribute to environmental sustainability. CEASE-DT outcomes can be measured by the four criteria listed above.

CEASE-DT in process engages designers with consumers in participatory design thinking that progresses through five phases where together they empathize, define, ideate, prototype, and test. A question guides the activities of each phase of the participatory design thinking process of CEASE-DT. When empathizing, stakeholders address the question: How have communities approached food management practices during COVID-19? Then, during the definition phase, they address the question: How do we define the empowerment of emergent behaviors during COVID-19? Next, in the ideation phase, they respond to the question: What do we create to maintain food management practices? In the prototyping phase, they determine how they can create a shareable prototype and, finally, in the testing phase they determine how to test the long-term effect of their DOs on the ecosystem. Evaluation of DOs that take many qualitative and quantitative forms can include survey instruments that generate data relevant to consumers and businesses.

Fleet Farming

an urban agriculture program in Orlando, Florida, United States

In a qualitative study of Fleet Farming (FF), Massari's research team used CEASE-DT to analyze its impact on sustainability through lessening food waste. Fleet Farming is an urban agricultural program led by IDEAS for Us—a non-profit, non-governmental organization accredited by the United Nations (Massari et al. 2021, 5). The objective of Fleet Farming is to "transform lawns into sustainable farm plots while empowering all generations to grow food to increase local food accessibility" (5). According to Massari et al. (2021), lawns are one of the largest sources of U.S. pollution; the "40 million acres of grass that currently exists absorbs three million tons of chemical fertilisers and 30,000 tons of pesticides each year, while requiring over three and a half billion litres of petrol to mow them" (5).

Fleet Farming meets its objective through a system of actors and activities centered around consulting, training, and networking. FF volunteers consult with and assist community members in residential areas to transform their grass into edible gardens. FF also organizes community events that connect "different generations of people" with "tools for social change and food security" (5). While centered on transforming grasslands within residential communities, FF also serves "restaurants and markets" that may wish to contribute to their mission (5).

Food Flow

a food waste management app in San Francisco, California

Massari et al. (2021) used CEASE-DT to analyze Food Flow's impact on sustainability through lessening food waste. Food Flow is an app that was selected as one of the Top Ideas at the Food Waste Challenge launched by Open IDEO[10] in 2016 (5). Food Flow aims to contribute to sustainability by redirecting still-edible food from restaurants to homeless shelters. It also aims to engender agency and motivate behavioral change regarding food waste reduction among individual citizens.

45. *High-quality cassava peels (HQCP)*

Animal feed used in Benin and Rwanda
Year of creation: n.d.
Source: Feleke et al. 2021

When cassava is peeled it produces a significant amount of waste that can be turned into high-quality cassava peels (HQCP). To produce HQCP, the cassava peels are chopped and pressed using hydraulic machines which eliminates the toxic cyanide water and other toxins and forms a solid consumable ingredient for livestock and poultry feeds. IITA in collaboration with the International Livestock Research Institute (ILRI) worked to utilize the processing waste from cassava to produce animal feed in Nigeria and Rwanda. This bio-waste innovation creates jobs and reduces greenhouse gas emissions. This closed-loop agriculture recovers and recycles nutrients back into the soil. For more information about this DO in relation to circular bioeconomy see DO #32 above.

46. *SecondBite*

A food rescue service in Victoria, Tasmania, Queensland, and New South Wales, Australia
Food category: Waste
Design category: Context
Year of creation: 2005
Source: Lindberg et al. 2014

SecondBite is a non-profit food rescue organization in Australia organized in 2005 to address and support people dealing with food poverty in Victoria, Tasmania, Queensland, and New South Wales. Food rescue is an effort to reduce food waste, strengthen food networks, and to contribute to emergency food providers by collecting excess food from restaurants and other food businesses and redistributing to those in need (Lindberg et al. 2014).

In an analysis of SecondBite's data, three themes within the issue of food waste emerged for the organization including people in need, fresh food, and fresh food that was going to waste (Lindberg et al. 2014). While efforts exist to eliminate food waste throughout the world, SecondBite relies on the surplus food to help those in need of fresh food, creating a tension with the idea of eliminating all waste (Lindberg et al. 2014).

While food rescue is their major activity, SecondBite added educational nutritional and advocacy programs as part of their mission. Their food rescue program rescues food and delivers it to identified providers, and through Community Connect, provides facilitation of direct-donor-to-provider distribution of surplus

food. The food is used in pantries and meal programs in the community including schools and health organizations. SecondBite's nutrition education programs
were initiated in 2008 and in 2012, Fresh NED and FoodMate were established as
two nutrition programs supported by a full-time dietician (Lindberg et al. 2014).
While Fresh NED offers training to the volunteers at SecondBite, FoodMate is an
integrated approach to nutrition through case management with the goal to help
clients reach food independence (Lindberg et al. 2014). Focus groups indicated
that the advocacy program felt less defined and may be a symptom of being a
newer SecondBite program at the time (Lindberg et al. 2014).

Food is rescued for the SecondBite programs at markets, restaurants, and
major events, any food source that has an abundance of food that would alter-
natively go to waste. Recognizing the importance of healthy eating, SecondBite
was also working to develop a policy to rescue and redistribute 95% nutritious
food in line with the Australian Dietary Guidelines (Lindberg et al. 2014).
Additional resources of the organization include staff, both paid and unpaid, as
well as physical infrastructure including vans, cooling spaces, and warehouse storage (Lindberg et al. 2014).

While SecondBite provides healthy food to those in need, some critics suggest
that evidence is limited on whether those in need are receiving enough food, and
that the food is culturally and religiously appropriate (Lindberg et al. 2014). In
addition, Lindberg questions whether the process of food rescue and emergency
food is making food insecurity worse by lessening the government's responsibility to make sure a livable wage supports people to be food secure (Lindberg et al.
2014).

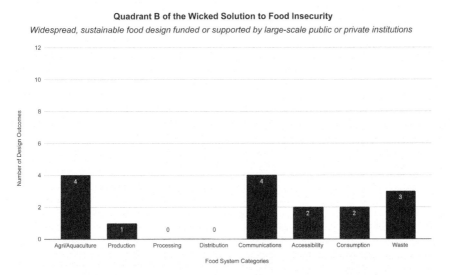

Figure 3.5 Quadrant B's DOs mapped according to the food system category to which they
contribute. Image courtesy of Audrey G. Bennett.

Places to intervene

The DOs in this quadrant show a high amount of top-down design activity to address food insecurity with sustainable food DOs that spread widely across regions, cities, states, and even countries. As Figure 3.5 shows, most of the sustainable food DOs that are top-down, widespread, and funded or supported by public or private institutions and have been peer-reviewed address aqua/agriculture, communications, and waste with minimal activity in the food supply phases of accessibility, consumption, and production. There are clear gaps in the food system of sustainable food DOs that address the processing and distribution phases. These gaps are the leverage points, that is, the places where designers can intervene and contribute to balancing the system towards food security that is equitable and just.

Notes

1 Note that the DOs in this quadrant come from peer-reviewed sources published after 2009—the founding of the International Food Design Society—though some of the DOs within the publications may have earlier creation or effectuation dates.
2 Based on peer-reviewed sources in English.
3 See: https://www.torontomu.ca/carrotcity/.
4 See: https://www.un.org/youthenvoy/2013/09/undesa-youth-focal-point/.
5 In German, Eidgenössische Technische Hochschule Zürich
6 See: https://www.nal.usda.gov/legacy/afsic/community-supported-agriculture.
7 See: https://parquedelapapa.org/.
8 For more information see https://www.efsa.europa.eu/en/topics/topic/novel-food.
9 While the Food Flow app was selected as one of the top ideas for Open IDEO's Food Waste Challenge, it does not appear to be still in use.
10 See: https://www.openideo.com/.

Bibliography

Ajzen, I. 1991. "The Theory of Planned Behavior." *Organizational Behavior and Human Decision Processes* 50, no. 2: 179–211.

Ashoka. 2022. "Laury Cullen." Accessed July 19, 2022. http://www.ashoka.org/fellow/laury-cullen.

Ballantyne-Brodie, Emily, Cara Wrigley, and Rebecca Ramsey. 2015. "Evolution of the Docklands Food Hub: A Design-led Innovation Approach to Food Sovereignty Through Local Food Systems." *Journal of Design, Business & Society* 1, no. 1: 43–55. https://doi.org/10.1386/dbs.1.1.43_1.

Barr, Jane, Angeline Gough, and Aimee Russillo. 2009. *Rapid Assessment Case Study: The Environmental Information Infrastructure of Pulse Production in Canada.* Winnipeg: International Institute for Sustainable Development. https://www.iisd.org/publications/report/rapid-assessment-case-study-environmental-information-infrastructure-pulse/.

The Bond Project. n.d. "Northern Fresian Woodlands Association (Noardlike Fryske Wâlden)." Accessed July 22, 2022. https://www.bondproject.eu/portfolio/northern-friesian-woodlands-association-nfw/.

Buehler, Devi, and Ranka Junge. 2016. "Global Trends and Current Status of Commercial Urban Rooftop Farming." *Sustainability* 8, no. 11: 1108. https://doi.org/10.3390/su8111108.

Busse, H. A., W. Jogo, M. Fofanah, H. Tesfay, M. Hadush, E. Kiflom, and S. Schulz. 2017. "Participatory Assessment of Factors Influencing Nutrition and Livelihoods in Rural Ethiopia: Implications for Measuring Impacts of Multisector Nutrition Programs." *Food and Nutrition Bulletin* 38, no. 4: 468–484. https://doi.org/10.1177/0379572117703265.

Caplow, Ted. 2009. "Building Integrated Agriculture: Philosophy and Practice." In *Urban Futures 2030: Urban Development and Urban Lifestyles of the Future*, edited by Heinrich Böll Foundation, 54–58. Berlin: Heinrich Böll Foundation.

Chapman, Benjamin, Tanya MacLaurin, and Douglas Powell. 2011. "Food Safety Infosheets: Design and Refinement of a Narrative-based Training Intervention." *British Food Journal* 113, no. 2: 160–186. https://doi.org/10.1108/00070701111105286.

Cullen, Jr., Laury, Keith Alger, and Denise M. Rambaldi. 2005. "Land Reform and Biodiversity Conservation in Brazil in the 1990s: Conflict and the Articulation of Mutual Interests." *Conservation Biology* 19, no. 3: 747–755. https://www.jstor.org/stable /3591064.

de la Salle, Janine. 2019. "Great Food Streets: Planning and Design for Urban Magnetism in Post-agricultural Cities." *Urban Design International* 24: 118–128. https://doi.org/10 .1057/s41289-019-00094-6.

Dignum, Frank, Barbara Dunin-Kęplicz, and Rineke Verbrugge. 2001. "Creating Collective Intention Through Dialogue." *Logic Journal of the IGPL* 9, no. 2: 289–304. https://doi .org/10.1093/jigpal/9.2.289.

EntoNation. 2018. "Podcast #50: 'With a Little Help from My Friends'." Accessed December 10, 2018. https://entonation.com/podcast-50-with-a-little-help-from-my -friends/.

Feleke, Shiferaw, Steven Michael Cole, Haruna Sekabira, Rousseau Djouaka, and Victor Manyong. 2021. "Circular Bioeconomy Research for Development in Sub-Saharan Africa: Innovations, Gaps, and Actions." *Sustainability* 13, no. 4: 1926. https://doi.org /10.3390/su13041926.

Figueroa, Meleiza. 2017. "Food Sovereignty in Everyday Life: Toward a People-centered Approach to Food Systems." In *The Politics of Food Sovereignty*, edited by Annie Shattuck, Christina Schiavoni, and Zoe VanGelder. London: Routledge. https://doi .org/10.4324/9781315226156-6.

Flood, Catherine, May Rosenthal Sloan, and Johanna Stephenson. 2019. *Food: Bigger Than the Plate*. London: V&A Publishing.

Fox, Thomas A., Thomas E. Barchyn, and Chris H. Hugenholtz. 2012. "Successes of Soil Conservation in the Canadian Prairies Highlighted by a Historical Decline in Blowing Dust." *Environmental Research Letters* 7, no. 1: 014008. https://doi.org/10.1088/1748 -9326/7/1/014008.

Geyrhalter, Nikolaus. 2006. "Our Daily Bread." Amazon Prime Video. https://www .amazon.com/Daily-Bread-Blu-ray-Nikolaus-Geyrhalter/dp/B07G24T847.

Gorgolewski, Mark, June Komisar, and Joe Nasr. 2011. *Carrot City: Designing for Urban Agriculture*. New York: Crown Publishing Group.

Government of Saskatchewan. 2014. "Growing Forward 2: Farm Stewardship Program." http://www.agriculture.gov.sk.ca/GF2-FarmStewardship.

Growing Home. n.d. "Our Model." Accessed July 19, 2022. https://www.growinghomeinc .org/our-model/.

Hart, Abigail K., Philip McMichael, Jeffrey C. Milder, and Sara J. Scherr. 2016. "Multi-Functional Landscapes from the Grassroots? The Role of Rural Producer Movements." *Agriculture and Human Values* 33, no. 2: 305–322. https://doi.org/10.1007/s10460-015 -9611-1.

Hartling, Xu (Cissy). 2019. "A Quick Guide to Building a Local Food System and Reducing Carbon Footprint." *E-Journal of Social & Behavioural Research in Business* 10, no. 2: 1–9.

Henderson, Elizabeth, and Robyn Van En. 2007. *Sharing the Harvest: A Citizen's Guide to Community Supported Agriculture.* White River Junction, VT: Chelsea Green Publishing.

Holt-Giménez, Eric. 2009. "From Food Crisis to Food Sovereignty: The Challenge of Social Movements." *Monthly Review* 61, no. 3. https://monthlyreview.org/2009/07/01/from-food-crisis-to-food-sovereignty-the-challenge-of-social-movements/.

Howard, George S. 1991. "Culture Tales: A Narrative Approach to Thinking, Cross-cultural Psychology, and Psychotherapy." *American Psychologist* 46, no. 3: 187–197. https://doi.org/10.1037/0003-066X.46.3.187.

"How Far Does Your Food Travel to Get to Your Plate?" CUESA, February 5, 2018. https://cuesa.org/learn/how-far-does-your-food-travel-get-your-plate.

Jacobs, Allan B. 1993. "Great Streets: Monument Avenue, Richmond, Virginia." *ACCESS Magazine* 1, no. 3: 23–27.

Kauppi, Saara-Maria, Ida Nilstad Pettersen, and Casper Boks. 2019. "Consumer Acceptance of Edible Insects and Design Interventions as Adoption Strategy." *International Journal of Food Design* 4, no. 1: 39–62. https://doi.org/10.1386/ijfd.4.1.39_1.

Lindberg, Rebecca, Mark Lawrence, Lisa Gold, and Sharon Friel. 2014. "Food rescue — An Australian Example." *British Food Journal* 116 no. 9: 1478–1489. https://doi.org/10.1108/BFJ-01-2014-0053.

Mancini, Simone, Roberta Moruzzo, Francesco Riccioli, and Gisella, Paci2019. "European consumers' readiness to adopt insects as food. A review." *Food Research International* 122, 661–678.

Massari, Sonia, Ludovica Principato, Marta Antonelli, and Carlo Alberto Pratesi. 2021. "Learning from and Designing after Pandemics. CEASE: A Design Thinking Approach to Maintaining Food Consumer Behaviour and Achieving Zero Waste." *Socio-Economic Planning Sciences* 82, no. part A: 101143. https://doi.org/10.1016/j.seps.2021.101143.

McClements, David Julian. 2020. "Future Foods: A Manifesto for Research Priorities in Structural Design of Foods." *Food & Function* 11, no. 3: 1933–1945. https://doi.org/10.1039/c9fo02076d.

McClinton, Blair, and Juanita Polegi. 2010. "Saskatchewan Soil Conservation Association." In *Landscapes Transformed: The History of Conservation Tillage and Direct Seeding,* edited by C. Wayne Lindwall, and Bernie Sonntag, 51–66. Saskatoon: Knowledge Impact in Society.

Prost, Sebastian. 2019. "Food Democracy for All? Developing a Food Hub in the Context of Socio-economic Deprivation." *Politics and Governance* 7, no. 4: 142–153. https://doi.org/10.17645/pag.v7i4.2057.

Schein, Edgar H. 1993. "On Dialogue, Culture, and Organizational Learning." *Organizational Dynamics* 22, no. 2: 40–51. https://doi.org/10.1016/0090-2616(93)90052-3.

Shannon, Claude E. 1948. "A Mathematical Theory of Communication." *The Bell System Technical Journal* 27, no. 3: 379–423. https://doi.org/10.1002/j.1538-7305.1948.tb01338.x.

Shiva, Vandana. 2000. *Stolen Harvest: The Hijacking of the Global Food Supply.* Cambridge, MA: South End Press.

Tao, Jaynie, and Yao Olive Li. 2018. "Edible Insects as a Means to Address Global Malnutrition and Food Insecurity Issues." *Food Quality and Safety* 2, no. 1: 17–26. https://doi.org/10.1093/fqsafe/fyy001.

Valladares-Padua, Claudio, Suzana M. Padua, and Laury Cullen, Jr. 2002. "Within and Surrounding the Morro do Diabo State Park: Biological Value, Conflicts, Mitigation and Sustainable Development Alternatives." *Environmental Science & Policy* 5, no. 1: 69–78. https://doi.org/10.1016/S1462-9011(02)00019-9.

Vodeb, Oliver. 2017. *Food Democracy: Critical Lessons in Food, Communication, Design and Art*. Bristol, UK: Intellect.

Wittman, Hannah. 2010. "Agrarian reform and the environment: Fostering ecological citizenship in Mato Grosso, Brazil." *Canadian Journal of Development Studies/Revue canadienne d'études du développement* 29, no. 3–4: 281–298. https://doi.org/10.1080/02255189.2010.9669259.

World Health Organization. 2022. "Food Safety." Accessed May 19, 2022. https://www.who.int/news-room/fact-sheets/detail/food-safety.

4 Quadrant C

Widespread, sustainable food design created by citizens

Sustainable food designs emerging since 2009 and created by citizens are few but far in reach. Quadrant C of the wicked solution to food insecurity shows peer-reviewed design outcomes[1] (DOs) created by citizens for a local context that propagates in multiple places, including countries, states, regions, cities, or communities. Quadrant C's citizen stakeholders include artists, innovators, local communities, and food activists. The DOs in this quadrant emerge from grassroots stakeholders who may initiate sustainable food design projects using their resources or collaborating, pooling, and soliciting resources. Some DOs will have a local place of origin before widespread propagation through commercial or cultural production. Quadrant C's DOs are alphabetically organized according to the part of the food system that they address, including agri/aquaculture, production, processing, communications, accessibility, and consumption. They are equally varied, including design objects, communications, environments, contexts, futures, and systems.

Figure 4.1 shows that the United States and Europe have the most sustainable food design activity.[2] The data from the integrative literature review suggests that the West is where citizens have effectuated the most sustainable food designs that have spread widely or have been propagated in other parts of the world. Citizen efforts to address food insecurity, inequity, and injustice for widespread propagation include:

47. **Aquaponics**: Government-funded fieldwork to engage with two communities of farming families in Bangladesh to modify a floating aquaponics cage system to include fishes and plants that are more suitable for a caged environment. Agricultural organizations in Milwaukee, Wisconsin, and Melbourne, Australia, identify challenges in local aquaponics by investigating how to sustain them best.
48. **Community gardening**: Community gardeners in the United States, France, and Britain grow food to address food insecurity in their local communities.
49. **Farm Hack**: To address an impending absence of farming knowledge, a coalition of young farmers in the United States came together to develop an open-source archive in which remotely located farmers can upload and share documentation of agricultural tools and resources.

DOI: 10.4324/9781003222026-5

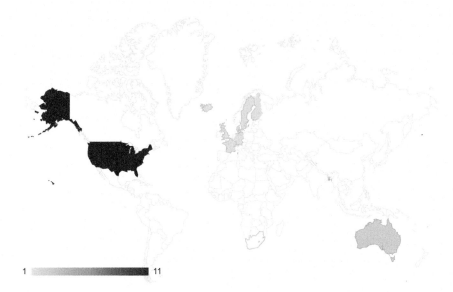

Figure 4.1 Quadrant C's DOs impact different parts of the world, including the continents of North America, Australia, Asia, and Europe. The shading indicates the density of sustainable food DOs we examined for that geographic region. Image courtesy of Audrey G. Bennett.

50. **Planetary Community Chicken**: A Belgian artist cross-breeds (or designs) cockerels in food-insecure locales worldwide as his creative practice.
51. **The Sausage of the Future**: A designer, chef, and butcher in Switzerland collaborate to design a more sustainable sausage with alternative types of proteins, vegetables, fruits, and other ingredients.
52. **Food Activist Handbook**: An American writer who is also a household food producer uses the form of a published book to advocate broadly and educate a mass audience about facilitating food security and sustainability in their households and communities.
53. **Banana Passport**: A group of design activists in Iceland collaborate to create a banana passport to communicate the long distances a banana traveled from Ecuador to Iceland.
54. **Food Futures Imagined**: Academic researchers convene a two-day workshop with designers, researchers, artists, and growers from Europe (Finland, Denmark, Sweden), Australia, and the United States to explore research methods and techniques in experimental future food design resulting in futures recipes and a published cookbook that is openly accessible on the World Wide Web.
55. **Sun Mad**: A US-based artist whose family of immigrants suffered adverse health consequences from exposure to pollution and pesticides on the farms of San Joaquin Valley in California creates artwork to spread the word widely about this injustice for immigrants.

56. **Supernatural**: A German artist uses the medium of art to paint a more sustainable natural landscape using food packaging.
57. **Fallen Fruit**: Residents in Los Angeles plant fruit trees on public lands and map their locations to provide free access to healthy food by local community members.
58. **Freeganism**: Activists tour the dumpsters in New York City and use the media and conversations with community members to call attention to the latter's unnecessary food waste habits and to persuade them to change their behaviors regarding food disposal and sustainability.
59. **Growing Food Justice for All Initiative**: A grassroots organization establishes a US-based food justice network to address racism in the food system by fostering collaborations through monthly meetings.
60. **SONO filter**: Two brothers team up to design a system to filter arsenic from the water in Bangladesh, Nepal, Pakistan, and India.

In the next section of this chapter, one can find quadrant C's DOs organized according to the phases of the food system that they address: aquaculture/agriculture, production, processing, distribution, communication, accessibility, consumption, and waste. Our integrative review of peer-reviewed literature shows sustainable food design activity in the food system for quadrant C, specifically in the phases of aquaculture and agriculture, processing, production, communication, accessibility, and consumption. Each food category begins with a summary of the challenges within the phase of the food system that existing DOs address, followed by descriptions of each DO. These descriptions provide more information about the actors and activities involved in their functionality, the type of design form they manifest, the year and geographical place where they were effectuated, and the literature source that provides the evidence that they are effective. Our aim in each food category is to give a summary overview gleaned from the respective peer-reviewed publication. This information includes: 1) the food insecurity, inequity, or injustice challenge the DO addresses and why it is a significant sustainability issue, 2) the global or local context/community the challenge impacts, 3) how the DO addresses the challenge, 4) how the DO works or functions and what qualities or components it comprises, 5) when and where the DO was effectuated, tested, or implemented, and found to be effective, and 6) who the stakeholders are and their activities. Sometimes, we rely on supplemental and credible gray literature sources to tell a more detailed story of the sustainable food DO. From this discussion, the chapter concludes with an analysis of the places the data suggests to intervene with further social innovation or appropriation by citizens towards sustainable food security, equity, and social justice for widespread impact.

Agriculture/Aquaculture

Generally, agricultural agency, that is, cognizance of one's power to grow and produce food and the resources to do so, is largely controlled by large and private organizations that are few in number, distant, and whose methods are closed.

Lack of access to the agricultural knowledge they hold hinders a sustainable future for farming and food security. As curator Cynthia Smith observes in the book titled *By the People: Designing a Better America*:

> American food production faces numerous challenges these days: floods and droughts; warmer winters and longer growing seasons due to climate change; an aging farming population (with an average age of fifty-eight); and young farmers having limited access to land. Modern agriculture comprises land consolidation, large-scale mechanization, synthetic fertilizers and pesticides, engineered seeds, and limited crop rotation and diversification.
>
> (2016, 232)

The evolving platform known as Farm Hack addresses these current and impending challenges by providing open access to farming tools and knowledge generated by its community members situated locally and globally.

Large-scale production has also been quite detrimental to farm animals. For instance, in the *New York Times* article titled "Commercial Production of Chickens Takes Toll on Genetic Diversity," science journalist Henry Fountain reported that with the loss of "fifty percent or more" of "diversity in ancestral chicken breeds," chicken production was becoming "more susceptible to disease outbreaks for which resistant genes have disappeared" (2008). Even more alarming is that the loss of diversity can be credited to "the advent of wide-scale commercial production in the 1950s" (2008). These findings are significant because "in 2019, the global poultry market increased by 6% to $231.5 billion, rising for the 3rd consecutive year," with China, the United States, and Brazil leading the world in their consumption of chicken—20 million, 19 million, and 12 million tonnes, respectively (Brockotter 2020). To address this food security challenge, Belgian citizen Koen Vanmechelen's creative practice includes designing planetary community chickens as sustainable food design.

Two other urban agriculture and aquaponics DOs in this quadrant rise to the wicked challenge of food insecurity caused by distant, large-scale food production. Urban agriculture refers to the public and private contexts in which food is grown and produced locally in front lawns, backyards, repurposed lots, rooftops, and various other indoor and outdoor gardens socially constructed in varying sizes. Urban agriculture is viewed as a way to address global food insecurity and food sovereignty, used as a tool to promote healthy living and healthy environments in communities and school settings within cities and food deserts, providing access to healthy foods and opportunities for supplemental income. However, government policy can create restrictions to urban agriculture due to climate change and other drivers like racism (Morales 2011, 201).

According to Vermeulen et al. (2012), agriculture and food production contribute significantly to the carbon footprint that has caused and is nurturing climate change. Kim (2017) calls this phenomenon the "carbon foodprint" (364). Specifically, Kim (2017) categorizes consumption patterns that contribute to the carbon foodprint as "food self-sufficiency, food shopping habits (e.g., shopping in supermarkets), dietary choices (e.g., eating meat), and food waste management" (380). As a result, food is an industry subject to emerging government regulations to reduce carbon emissions. For instance, in Britain, the Climate Change Act of 2008 mandated an 80% reduction in carbon emissions by 2050, which has recently been amended to 100% reduction (UK Government 2008). Its regulations are directed at a variety of industries including food (Kim 2017, 365). For instance, London has a target of 50% carbon reduction by 2025, making it necessary to shift London's carbon-intensive food consumption practices, including reliance on large grocery retailers, consumption of meat, and the abundance of food waste.

Community gardens, a form of urban agriculture, are viewed as a bottom-up movement for sustainable development in Britain and elsewhere worldwide, including the United States. While community gardens can serve as a source of healthy, accessible foods, they also promote socio-economic resiliency and environmental sustainability in their communities. Indeed, they have the potential to help reduce greenhouse gas emissions by increasing environmental awareness with consumers and promoting behavior changes in consumption habits. Kim (2017) argues that while many variables impact food consumption, community gardening offers one way to influence food environmental stewardship.

Community food security supports systems changes through environmentally sustainable approaches, including community gardening, which is often the most viable option in low-income neighborhoods. This movement seeks to democratize and restore local food movements over the long term to strengthen communities by giving access to fresh, healthy, culturally appropriate, and affordable food. Community gardening creates green spaces in urban areas and provides opportunities for mental and physical wellness; its success depends on the work of community residents. Community gardens benefit the most from a bottom-up approach, developed by the people for the people. Challenges include securing space and resources and assessing the soil.

While community gardening requires access to agricultural land, aquaponics, a form of aquaculture and hydroponics, is rising in popularity as a way to create localized and healthy food production systems that can address food shortages caused by reduced availability of suitable agricultural land due to population, environmental constraints, and complex weather systems that impact agriculture. Several sustainable food DOs provide examples of aquaponics applied in various geographic regions worldwide.

47. *Aquaponics*

Fish and vegetable farming in Bangladesh, Australia, and the United States
Food category: Aquaculture
Design category: Environment

in Bangladesh

Year of creation: 2014
Source: Sunny et al. 2019

The ponds in the Barisal area of Bangladesh are stocked with fish, and vegetables are cultivated on the pond dike. However, the fish often escape during heavy rains, and a lack of sunlight often inhibits plant growth due to the shade of large-area trees. While the practice of aquaponics, the integrated culture of both aqua-culture and hydroponics, has been practiced in Bangladesh for generations, this study examined how to further modify the integrated culture system to reduce costs of construction and increase productivity in the Barisal region (Sunny et al. 2019).

In conservative rural households in Bangladesh, women are restricted from working outside their homestead. Utilizing pond aquaponics provides an additional opportunity for women to harvest and collect vegetables. Thus, a design team of stakeholders modified an existing integrated floating cage system, and suitable fish and plants were identified that could prosper in the cage environment. The bottom of the three-square-meter bamboo-split cage frame has a nylon net, with the four corners weighted by a brick. Three sides are for plants, including leafy vegetables, and a horizontal trellis above the cage supports climbing plants. The fourth side is left open for the retrieval of fish and plants. The design team planted plants in inexpensive planters, including plastic bottles and bamboo baskets. They studied stocking density and fish species to optimize productivity, finding that lower-stocking densities are best for growth (Sunny et al. 2019).

The study was conducted in Bangladesh in 2014 from October to December, in the Bay of Bengal coastal zone, in two communities in the Char Kawa union under Sadar Upazila of Barisal district. The research was supported by the Aquaculture for Income and Nutrition (AIN) project, funded by the United States Agency for International Development (USAID). The stakeholders include the farmers and their families in the Barisal District of Bangladesh. While Sunny et al. (2019) argue that more research is needed, in its current state as a floating cage, this system could be implemented commercially and applied to other water bodies where communities could maintain an aquaponic system.

in the United States and Australia

Year of creation: 2008 (United States), 2010 (Australia)
Source: Laidlaw and Magee 2016

Comparative case studies were conducted in Milwaukee, Wisconsin, in the United States, and Melbourne, Australia, utilizing a cross-sectional approach to examine the stakeholders' impact on their struggling urban agriculture sustainable enterprises. Milwaukee's aquaponics organization was known as Sweet Water Organics (SWO). Melbourne's aquaponics was through the Centre for Education and Research Environmental Strategies (CERES), a project affiliated with an urban farm in Melbourne. SWO was established in 2008 and CERES aquaponics was built in 2010. Both organizations are similar in size and have less than ten stakeholder groups. Each case study was in an urban area and was community-focused and market-oriented. The studies happened from 2012 to 2013. They

included unstructured qualitative interviews with the key stakeholder organizations (five in Milwaukee and two in Melbourne) and site visits to review each
organization's history, current challenges, and plans. Additional stakeholders,
primarily volunteers, were given online surveys to complete. While the people
interviewed who were affiliated with SWO were enthusiastic, there had been
adverse reports in the news about unpaid wages. Neither city had personnel connected to urban agriculture or sustainable enterprise at the time, providing limited information on policy barriers. Both struggled with the challenges of the
intensive needs of aquaponic installations (Laidlaw and Magee 2016).

The researchers identified four distinct factors that contribute to the survival of urban aquaponics sustainable enterprises. These include an ongoing commitment of key stakeholders, supportive government environments,
availability of markets for the produce cultivated from urban aquaponics,
and diversification through training and education (Laidlaw and Magee
2016).

in Milwaukee, Wisconsin, United States

Year of creation: 2008
Source: Laidlaw and Magee 2016

Many individuals who are unemployed or underemployed lack access to fresh
foods. However, with affordable city real estate in Milwaukee, Wisconsin, at the
time of the research, the location served as a suitable trial for sustainable enterprise urban aquaponics (UA).

In 2008, Sweet Water Organics, an experimental urban aquaponics farm and
school, was set up in a large unused industrial building in the Bay View area of
Milwaukee to provide employment opportunities and affordable food to the local
community. In 2010, Sweet Water Foundation (SWF), a new organization, was
developed, and it split off from SWO with the goal of being a co-existing hybrid
supportive organization, together developing a for-profit urban farm and non-
profit aquaponics academy (Laidlaw and Magee 2016).

Many challenges arose when SWO realized the system they were using was
not scalable to commercial aquaponics in the large, dark warehouse. Costly adaptations had to be made, and continued support was provided by the Milwaukee
municipal government with ongoing scrutiny by local media. The two organizations also struggled to find their alignment, with each having a different operational structure with different visions and strategic plans. By 2013, the for-profit
side of SWO went into liquidation. That SWF emerged highlights the "robust
nature of entrepreneurial UA models which embed multiple business functions
and activities" (Laidlaw and Magee 2016, 581). When the for-profit business
operation failed, it did not shut down the whole operation; the non-profit component prevailed and continues providing community development and education,
run by volunteers and part-time employees (Laidlaw and Magee 2016), demonstrating the resiliency, commitment, and perseverance needed to make bottom-
up DOs endure.

Figure 4.2 Aquaponics system at Growing Power in Milwaukee. Growing Power was "an agricultural non profit that support[ed] people from diverse backgrounds by developing community-based food systems" (Smith 2016). This image by ryan griffis is licensed under the Creative Commons Attribution-Share Alike 2.0 Generic license: https://creativecommons.org/licenses/by-sa/2.0/deed.en.

in Melbourne, Australia

Year of creation: 2010
Source: Laidlaw and Magee 2016

With increased property prices in Melbourne, one can find Australia's food insecurity in pockets. However, at the time of the peer-reviewed publication, addressing food insecurity was not seen as a high priority in local or state government. CERES, the Centre for Education and Research in Environmental Strategies, is a not-for-profit organization that operates several for-profit businesses to support its not-for-profit work. It is a community environment park located in Melbourne, Australia. In 2010, a design team built the CERES experimental aquaponics system to address local food insecurity and diversify local food production (Laidlaw and Magee 2016).

Laidlaw and Magee write that the system used little energy and was easy to use (2016). The system for aquaponics was a floating deep-bed raft with two tanks for the fish tank, which were situated higher than the plant pool, situated in a shipping container. One side of the shipping container was a cut-out opening to the greenhouse, and water was pumped between the fish tank, plant bed, and back. Though still under refinement and not working at full capacity, the system itself was self-sufficient and provided enough produce to financially support the producer who maintained it. The farmers' wages were dependent on how much produce was produced. Initially, this produce was sold directly to the CERES Fair Food organic box delivery enterprise located nearby, with an income-sharing arrangement. However, as lessons were learned, the demands of the CERES project changed, and with the low volume of produce, the farmers then kept all of the income (Laidlaw and Magee 2016). Compared to horticulture urban agriculture, the daily care aquaponics requires is challenging. While CERES continues to be an environmental education organization with a community garden, urban farm, and a social enterprise hub in four locations across Melbourne, their current website does not mention the status of the aquaponics project.[3]

48. Community gardening

Urban agriculture in various locales
Food category: Agriculture
Design category: Environment

in London, Britain

Year of creation: 2014
Source: Kim 2017

Community gardens, a form of urban agriculture, are viewed as a bottom-up movement for sustainable development in Britain. While community gardens can serve as sources of healthy, accessible foods, they can also promote resiliency and sustainability in their communities. Kim (2017) discusses findings from a study that investigated community gardening in relation to consumption behavior among gardeners in Britain to identify food consumption patterns that reduce the "foodprint," the time commitment required to do community gardening, and the aspects of community gardening that contribute to behavior change in food consumption among community gardeners. The stakeholders conducted this research in 2014 for over a month and in two stages. First, they collected data through an online survey sent to gardeners connected to 95 community garden and food-growing organizations in London. Second, semi-structured interviews were conducted with community garden participants from the Drysdale Allotments in Chingford, London.

Kim (2017) found that community gardens indeed help reduce greenhouse gas emissions by increasing environmental awareness with consumers and promoting behavior changes in consumption habits, and that this change can be achieved through experiential and social teaching and learning. That is, through experiential learning, gardeners are exposed to the process of food production, become more aware of the seasons, and are introduced to a wide variety of produce. Connecting to other gardeners in the community also promotes social learning,

Figure 4.3 Example of community gardening across generations. This image by d-olwen-dee is licensed under the Creative Commons Attribution 2.0 Generic license: https://creativecommons.org/licenses/by/2.0/deed.en.

providing the space and opportunity to discuss food sustainability. While many variables might impact food consumption behavior, community gardening offers one way to influence food environmental behavior (Kim 2017).

in Marseille, France

Year of creation: 2012
Source: Martin et al. 2017

Five gardens managed by local social organizations located near social housing were identified, and the organizations introduced programs to assist gardeners weekly. Each volunteer gardener had a small plot for which they were responsible and shared tools. For the study, each had to be responsible for the food supply of their household, the 21 volunteers for the study were all women. Volunteers participated in a questionnaire and semi-structured interviews that explored their personal history with gardening, their links between gardening and food practices, and the social functions of gardening. Participants were in charge of a food log that recorded all food activity for a month, including purchases, harvests, gifts, and consumption. Based on this information, the design team built a nutri-economic database. The design team compared the food supplies of the gardeners with non-gardeners from the same neighborhoods, who logged their foods using the same procedure (Martin et al. 2017).

Results indicated that those with garden plots had more supplies of produce than those without, even though the study indicated this was not due to the access to produce in the garden. Instead, the study concluded that those house-holds purchased more produce, suggesting the possibility of the gardens' influence on dietary habits (Martin et al. 2017).

This study was conducted in the northern districts of the city of Marseille, France, with a culturally diverse population whose incomes were below the national average and who experienced high unemployment rates. Gardens in the study were created two to five years before the article's publication, beginning in 2012, and data collection took place over two months in 2014 (Martin et al. 2017).

in Baltimore, Maryland, United States

Year of creation: 2009
Source: Corrigan 2011

This study focuses on the Duncan Street Miracle Garden (DSMG), established in 1988 in the Broadway East neighborhood of historic East Baltimore in Maryland, and examines the challenges of community gardens and how community gardens can encourage connection and involvement with the local food system and help to address food insecurity (Corrigan 2011). The DSMG is supported by the Parks and People Foundation (PPF) and is located in a food desert in a historically Black neighborhood with high poverty rates. At the time of the peer-reviewed publication the garden had 17 plots, cared for by 11 gardeners, and surplus food from them was donated to those in need in the community.

Interviews were conducted with gardeners for two months in 2009 at the DSMG about food security and community gardens. The success of the DSMG includes the leadership of the community members in keeping the space tidy and having gardening knowledge and experience, as well as support from the city and other community organizations. The DSMG improves access to healthy foods in its neighborhoods but could benefit from further education, policy, and financial assistance to address food security (Corrigan 2011).

in New York City, United States

Year of creation: 2010
Source: Gregory et al. 2016

Community gardens provide access to healthy, nutritious food and community engagement and well-being opportunities. Challenges often exist related to sustainable food production, including soil issues, an excess of nutrients, and pest and insect problems. Understanding and building quality soil is critical to community garden success (Gregory et al. 2016).

Food-producing community gardens, administered by Green Thumb (a program of the New York City [NYC] Department of Parks and Recreation), growing vegetables and fruits in all five boroughs of NYC, were studied to develop ecological management practices for urban gardens. Other food-producing gardens may benefit from the findings. For two years, from 2010 to 2012, garden interviews and ecological measurements provided information on the gardens' spaces, challenges, shared-knowledge systems, and social and organizational structures. In addition, some plots were examined for land-use mapping, soil properties, plant species richness, and arthropod scouting (Gregory et al. 2016).

Community gardens are a valuable part of NYC neighborhoods. The produce grown in these gardens helps with food security, but challenges exist, including soil quality, pests, weeds, limited time, and access to water. Ecological knowledge and skills are needed to address issues through agroecological practices like cover crops, habitat management, and crop rotation. The researchers' findings suggest educational programs on ecological concepts and follow-up support as gardeners integrate new techniques and provide better gardening education access (Gregory et al. 2016).

in Rockford, Illinois, United States

Year of creation: 2014
Source: Furness and Gallaher 2018

Impacted by the loss of manufacturing jobs, Rockford, Illinois, is a midwestern city in the United States with high unemployment, crime, and poverty rates.

Figure 4.4 U.S. Agriculture Secretary Tom Vilsack participates in community gardening at Frederick Douglass High School in Baltimore, Maryland, in 2016.

Most parts of the town are segregated, with Black people living on the west and southwest sides and white people living on the east. Food deserts exist primarily in the non-white population areas, and barriers to healthy food access exist, including lack of transportation. While community gardens have been known to benefit communities, the actual impact on food security is arguably not known (Furness and Gallaher 2018).

Community gardens can improve access to healthy, fresh foods. Rockford's community gardens include allotment gardens and growing communal spaces. Many donate their produce to local pantries, primarily the Rock River Valley Pantry (RRVP), or allow participants to get their produce directly from the garden. In addition, some gardens grow food for others, although many donate some of their produce and promote youth-oriented gardening. While a few gardens have been around for a long time, most of the spaces have been in place since the 2010s. The most significant

Figure 4.5 Q Gardens community garden in Brooklyn, New York City, in 2022. This image by Wil540 art is licensed under the Creative Commons Attribution-ShareAlike 4.0 International: https://creativecommons.org/licenses/by-sa/4.0/deed.en.

barrier to access seems to be a lack of awareness, seemingly a direct result of the donation-model gardens, that create a disconnect between the local garden and the local produce distributed in the pantries. Some participants chose store produce over local produce in the pantries because it looked more uniform. The donation model has had mixed results in Rockford; while pantry clients do consume locally grown produce, there is limited variety and the pantry allows only one visit per month. Gardeners contribute to the food resources in Rockford, though the overall impact on the food system remains small. Food pantry clients remain disconnected from the source of the produce, and the donation-model garden may perpetuate the structural inequalities in the food system (Furness and Gallaher 2018).

49. Farm Hack

An open-source farm tools information database for online/offline use across the United States
Food category: Agriculture
Design category: System
Year of creation: 2010
Source: Smith 2016

To address the barrier to agricultural knowledge and resources imposed by closed systems run by large-scale, industrial, and agricultural entities, in 2010 a group of citizens came together to launch an organization known as National Young Farmers Coalition to sustain and share agricultural knowledge and tools. They developed an open platform called Farm Hack[4] with a network of over 400,000 people who have contributed over 150 open-source agrarian tools (Smith 2016, 232). Farm Hack functions multimodally. Online, it facilitates the sharing of agricultural resources. It also brings technologists, agrarians, and designers belonging to Farm Hack together for face-to-face activities centering on agricultural knowledge development (232).

50. *Planetary Community Chicken (PCC)*

Performing art installation to cross-breed chicken in Belgium; Zimbabwe; Detroit, Michigan, United States; and Ethiopia
Food category: Agriculture
Design category: Environment
Year of creation: 2016
Source: Flood and Sloan 2019, 52, 56–57

To address the food security threat of chicken production becoming more susceptible to disease outbreaks moving forward, Belgian citizen Koen Vanmechelen cross-breeds (or designs) cockerels known as "cosmopolitan chickens" with

Figure 4.6 Farm Hack's open-source tilling solution. "Farm Hack's tilling solution." by Engineering for Change is licensed under CC BY-SA 2.0. To view a copy of this license, visit https://creativecommons.org/licenses/by-sa/2.0/?ref=openverse.

"small-scale commercially farmed hens" in economically challenged and food-insecure locations across the globe as an art practice (Flood and Sloan 2019, 52). As Vanmechelen notes on his website[5]:

> The project starts with the idea that every year, a rooster of the newest [PCC] cross-breed will be paired with a local commercial hen somewhere in the world. This chicken will absorb the genetic pool of the [PCC] and the local commercial hen and produce a vital community chicken that can provide its host community with eggs and meat.
>
> (Vanmechelen)

Integrating the cosmopolitan with the local yields a new kind of localized chicken with the genes to resist disease. This integration is done through an art exhibition venue as an art installation. "The new cross-bred chicks hatch in the galleries and museums—with exhibition materials often constructed and recycled

Figure 4.7 Planetary Community Chicken (DO #50). (Top) The Cosmopolitan Chicken Project – Mechelse Bresse, 2000Photo by Patrick Despiegelaere Storm Centers, Poeziezomer van Watou (BE) Curated by Jan Hoet and Gwy Mandelinck; (Bottom left) Mechelse Koekoek – C.C.P., 2000; (Bottom right) Poulet De Bresse – C.C.P., 2000. Images courtesy of Koen Vanmechelen.

by local communities—before being transferred to selected free-range flocks" (Vanmechelen).

Since the first chick was born in Sint-Truiden, Belgium, more have propagated in other parts of the world in Zimbabwe, Detroit, and Ethiopia.

Production

The food system has evolved from an arguably simplified past of hunting and gathering where the individual is the producer and consumer. In the complex present, however, the individual is the consumer and the producer of their food is likely someone else who leads a private organization located far away in a distant locale from the individual consumer. The impact of this shift has been and is continuing to be detrimental to the health and welfare of the individual consumer, members of their household, local and global communities, and the environment. Ali Berlow's 2015 book, *The Food Activist Handbook: Big and Small Things You Can Do to Help Provide Fresh, Healthy Food for Your Community* provides learned lessons and resources for other households to address these issues.

51. The Sausage of the Future

Sustainable protein in Switzerland
Food category: Processing
Design category: Object
Year of creation: 2014
Source: Flood and Sloan 2019, 126

Designer Carolien Niebling, a self-identifying food futurist, addresses the impact of meat consumption on sustainability through the redesign of sausage for greater sustainability. Niebling's sausage of the future, a design object featured in Britain's V&A Museum's exhibition titled "Food: Bigger than the Plate Exhibit" and also in the book by Niebling titled "The Sausage of the Future." The latter book project was funded by a Kickstarter campaign.[7] The Sausage of the Future is the manifestation of a collaborative and creative exploration of sustainable protein development. Niebling teamed up with a molecular gastronomy chef and a butcher to create an alternative to sausages made of meat. In their future sausage, one can find combinations of insects, nuts, legumes, and other ingredients (e.g., see the fruit salami recipe in Appendix VI); the sausage is particularly significant as a design form as it is "one of mankind's first-ever designed foods" to address potential meat scarcity (Niebling 2018).

Processing

Animal-based and highly processed foods continue to undermine present-day society. According to the World Counts, humanity consumes around 350 tons of meat annually.[6] To top off this alarming statistic, meat consumption is rising globally as the human population and its affluence increase, and while meat does provide essential nutrients, it also has significant negative consequences on the environment and human health, contributing to global warming and chronic, life-threatening diseases in humans (Godfray et al. 2018). So too do highly processed foods that have been manipulated through science and technology. "In the past, the food industry has focused on creating cheap, convenient and tasty foods, but have often ignored their health and environmental impacts" (McClements 2019, 342). Like animal-based food, food processing negatively impacts the environment with pollution, land and water use, and greenhouse gas emissions (Poore and Nemecek 2018; Willett et al. 2019). While studies debate what defines ultra-processed food, there is a consensus that processed food consists of high levels of salt, sugar, and fat, which contribute to poor health outcomes, including obesity, diabetes, and heart issues (Gibney et al. 2017).

While there is an increasing demand for food that is less processed, more authentic, and sustainable, most foods today continue to be manipulated by science and technology, with fruits and vegetables in the supermarket, for instance, having been through years of selective genetic traits breeding and controlled harvesting (McClements 2019). Varying levels of processing impact most of the food on the grocery store shelf.

New and existing companies are trying to create healthier and more sustainable foods. Using animals in food production can impact the environment significantly, and international organizations have recommended reducing the consumption of meat and animal products in diets (Poore and Nemecek 2018; Willett et al. 2019). Challenges to this include that meat is a significant part of many cultures' diets, people enjoy it and don't want to change how they eat, and some nutritional aspects can be vital. "There is, therefore, a need to produce foods that consumers can easily incorporate into their diets without making large lifestyle or cultural changes, but which are not higher in calories, saturated fat, salt, and sugar than the foods they are replacing, still make a significant contribution to essential micronutrients, and have enhanced sustainability credentials" (McClements 2019, 342).

To address these issues in the food system and the sustainability of the environment, technological approaches are being used to create alternatives to meat, fish, milk, cheese, and eggs. Non-animal-based foods are being designed and developed by academic researchers and industrial scientists based on principles in chemistry, physics, biology, and engineering (Specht 2018). Even artists and designers are contributing alternatives to animal-based foods like the Sausage of the Future, designed by self-identified food futurist and designer Carolien Niebling.

Additionally, plant-based foods are being created to mimic traditional animal products like milk, meat, and fish. Alternative kinds of milk come from almonds, coconut, flaxseed, oat, and soybean. As a result of food chemistry, these often have less of an impact on the environment, though not always (Poore and Nemecek 2018). While the calories of plant-based milks are usually less, some contain high sugar levels and less protein than bovine milk—many need to be fortified with micronutrients. Meat and fish plant-based alternatives include products by companies such as Impossible Foods and Beyond Meat. These may have a lower environmental impact than animal-based products but often have less protein, vitamins, and minerals and include more calories, total fat, and salt (McClements 2019). "The more widespread adoption of these products may be held back by semantics. In many countries, legislation or debates about introducing legislation will limit the use of words such as 'meat,' 'milk,' and 'eggs' to animal products only" (McClements 2019, 343).

Another approach to alternative food is called cellular agriculture (Mattick 2018) and uses biotechnology to grow "clean meat" from animal cells in a bioreactor, without having to kill any animals. This approach tends to have less impact on the environment. The meat-like products include burgers and sausages. While these products have many of the nutritional qualities of real meat, they are highly processed. Bacteria, fungi, and algae can be food too, grown in fermentation tanks. A micro-fungus, fusarium venenatum, is used to produce meat-free products on the grocery shelf, including Quorn (McClements 2019). Many companies seek to develop these new foods to improve healthy eating habits through scientific and technological advances. And through science and technology healthy and more sustainable processed foods can be developed (McClements 2019).

52. *Food Activist Handbook*

A handbook on food activism made in the United States
Food category: Production
Design category: Communication
Year of creation: 2015
Source: Berlow 2015

In the foreword to Ali Berlow's book titled *The Food Activist Handbook: Big and Small Things You Can Do to Help Provide Fresh, Healthy Food for Your Community*, Alice Randall notes the following about the book's author:

> Ali Berlow eats in a territory located between feast and famine. She lives with her husband and three sons in a kind of elaborate treehouse above plots for vegetables and pens for livestock on an island off the coast of Massachusetts. Her kitchen is at the end of a rough country road. When I walked into her home for the first time, I recognized our common cause: a desire to use our pots and pans to connect our families to the land, justice, pleasure, and health. Ali has watched obesity threaten to rob her of her father, and food illiteracy and immersion in processed foods threaten the long-term health of her adopted son, a gifted athlete. She fought back with her fork, farm, and cell phone.
>
> (Randall, in Berlow 2015, 6)

How many, like Ali Berlow, are challenged by maintaining food-secure households? How many experience low food security and the adverse health and environmental ramifications of such on a personal level and desire to improve their situation? How many observe others in their household and local communities experiencing low food security and the adverse health and environmental ramifications and want to help them but may not know how?

Ali Berlow's book addresses these questions with a comprehensive set of resources on educating, building, growing, connecting, speaking, harvesting, feeding, cooking, and engaging for sustainable food security, equity, and justice. From getting to know one's food community to planning one's meals, Berlow provides sage food advice in a globally accessible book format at prices ranging from $2 to $20. Storey Publishing in North Adams, Massachusetts, published this resourceful book.

Communications

Flood and Sloan (2019) note that "[d]esigners have long been engaged with the visual elements of the food industry through packaging and marketing" (74). However, ever since Garland's "First Things First" manifesto's publication in 1964, the design discipline has grappled more with the ethics of their professional practice. Do they continue to focus solely on putting food on the table, so to speak, by designing whatever the client requests despite its impact on the world, or do they allow ethics to inform their creative choices?

In 2002 renowned designer Milton Glaser (2002) created a set of ethical questions for designers to consider, including the following two that pertain to food: 1) Would you design a package for a cereal aimed at children with low nutritional value and high sugar content? 2) Would you design a promotion for a diet product that you know doesn't work? Subsequently, in 2009, designer David Berman issued a clarion call to the design discipline with a critical publication, reminding professional designers to "Do Good Design" by embracing sustainability. Artist Ester Hernandez's "Sun Mad" artwork responds indirectly to this call by challenging the impact of Sun-Maid's agribusiness on communities, whereas German artist Uli Westphal creates landscape collages from food packaging. These artists exemplify how graphic art design resources can play an activist role in the food system through communication art as a vehicle for sustainable food visual rhetoric.

Another example of graphic design resources being used to galvanize social change can be seen in the work of artist Carolien Niebling, designer of the sausage of the future, who unassumingly uses the power of a typeset recipe published in the book form of an exhibition catalog to share her fruit salami food design with the world (Flood and Sloan 2019). Meat will arguably soon be a scarce commodity, and suppliers will be unable to meet the high demand for it due to the population increase and our human love for consuming it. Also, due to the negative impact of meat production on the environment and our health after consumption, we must produce and consume alternatives to this protein. Fighting global warming requires a collaborative effort, with each person contributing to the solution by eating an alternative protein rather than contributing to the problem by eating meat. Niebling's work inspires others globally to adopt this alternative meat in their diets.

We've all arguably seen the small typeset text on food packages in supermarkets communicating the origin of the food we consume. According to the 2013 *New Yorker* article titled "What Does the 'Made-In' Label Mean Anymore?," the need to know where food comes from originated in 1887, when the British, intent on "stigmatizing imitation goods from Germany," passed a law forcing foreign companies to make the origins of their products clear on the packaging. While journalist Renuka Rayasam notes that this requirement has become optional for certain goods, many countries, including the United States, still enforce and require their use on food packaging. Designers Björn Steinar Blumenstein and Johanna Seelemann integrate the food origin phenomenon through a banana passport they designed that document's one banana's travel from Ecuador to Iceland (Flood and Sloan 2019).

"While design contributes to social and ecological un-sustainability, it can also play a pivotal role in bringing us towards more positive, inclusive ways of living and being within the planetary ecosystem" (Wilde et al. 2021, 115). The ways of designers have contributed to transformative thinking and action (Maldonado 1972) in the world. Wilde et al. (2021) advocate that experimentation with theories, methods, and practices is needed, in the locally situated spaces, to address the global challenges related to food.

53. *Banana Passport*

An artwork in Iceland
Food category: Communication
Design category: Object
Year of creation: 2017
Source: Flood and Sloan 2019

There is controversy over what origin labels mean, as most food goods do not travel directly from their origin. Take the banana, for instance. In 2017, designers Björn Steinar Blumenstein and Johanna Seelemann "found that the average banana travels 8,800 kilometers on its 14-day journey to Iceland and is touched by 33 people per day" (Yalcinkaya 2018). The banana passport they designed documents one banana's travel from Ecuador to Iceland. As a creative design, Flood and Sloan (2019) describe it as functioning "poetically... leveraging the [power] of art [and design] to make the "hidden visible," and hold this particular aspect of the food system accountable (17).

54. *Food Futures Imagined*

a food futures participatory workshop in Denmark, Finland, Australia, Sweden, and the United States
Food category: Communications
Design category: Experience
Year of creation: 2020
Source: Wilde et al. 2021

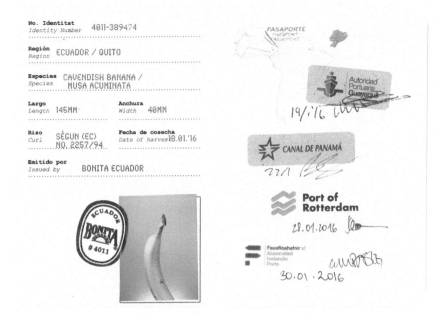

No. Identitat
Identity Number   4011-389474

Región
Region   ECUADOR / QUITO

Especies   CAVENDISH BANANA /
Species   MUSA ACUMINATA

Largo
Length   145MM

Anchura
Width   40MM

Rizo
Curl   SEGUN (EC)
NO. 2257/94

Fecha de cosecha
*Date of harvest*18.01.'16

Emitido por
Issued by   BONITA ECUADOR

PASAPORTE

CANAL DE PANAMÁ

Port of Rotterdam

Figure 4.8 Banana passport designed by Björn Steinar Blumenstein and Johanna Seelemann (DO #51). Image courtesy of Björn Steinar Blumenstein and Johanna Seelemann.

Food Futures Imagined was a two-day online conference workshop that used experimental food design research methods to explore food futures and climate resilience through the lens of values, concerns, and imaginaries. "The objective was to explore possibilities of transitioning human food and technology practices towards resilient regenerative and justice-oriented (more-than-human) system, both fantastical and plausible" (Wilde et al. 2021, 116).

A diverse group of 33 participants from around the world met online for two days to explore two themes using tools including Zoom and Miro. They included designers, researchers, artists, and growers. The first-day theme was "Fantastic(e) ating Food Futures: Reimagining Human Food Interactions," which explored food, technology, and social practice interdependencies. Day 2 was "Designing with More-than-Human Food Practices for Climate Resilience," which looked at ideas for regenerative, climate-resilient food futures. As a component of the activities, existing food sustainability projects were observed to identify how often they do not include a multi-species plurality (Dolejšová et al. 2020). In thinking about "more-than-human" perspectives, participants were encouraged to shift their food future thinking from fantastical to plausible. Wilde et al. (2021) note that "unlike other design materials, food is edible, perishable and compostable, and as such supports research through ecologically accountable design" (117).

To prototype, participants were each given a deck of Food Tarot cards[8] and directed to select an item in their home that reflected the card and focused on food-tech practices. The identified items served as an impetus for the workshop activity. The cards include 22 imagined food tribes, like the Davatores and Turing Foodies, each impacted by technology.

The workshop resulted in a co-authored, open-access book titled *More-than-Human Food Futures Cookbook*[9] which includes the food futures recipes co-developed in the workshop. The researchers received funding from the European Union's Horizon 2020 research.

55. Sun Mad

An artwork by Ester Hernandez from the collection of the Smithsonian American Art Museum in the United States
Food category: Communications
Design category: Object
Year of creation: 1982
Source: Flood and Sloan 2019, 73

The food system in its complex state tends to generate unevenly distributed profits. Large food producer companies, like Sun-Maid, typically retain most of the profits at the expense of the environment, public health, and its workers. Artist Ester Hernandez's family was exposed to polluted water and pesticides in the San Joaquin Valley in California due to Sun-Maid's agribusiness (Hernandez 1982). So, she created the artwork titled "Sun Mad Raisins" to shed light on this atrocity. It is a screenprint that "subverts the Sun Maid brand to highlight the very harsh working conditions of the immigrant farm workers" (Flood and Stone 2019, 73).

56. Supernatural

An artwork by Uli Westphal of Berlin, Germany
Food category: Communications
Design category: Object
Year of creation: 2010
Source: Flood and Sloan 2019

Artists, too, have used their graphic design resources at the intersection of climate change and food insecurity. For instance, in 2010, German artist Uli Westphal created "a series of landscape collages fabricated from imagery found on food packaging" (Flood and Sloan 2019, 75). These pieces "subtly comment on the discord between the stories we are told about our food and the unseen realities of how it is produced and sold" (74)

Accessibility

Historically, the food movement has critiqued industrial agriculture as overly harmful to the environment, health, and social ecosystem. It advocates for society to pivot from industrially produced and processed foods to fresh, local, and organic options (Alkon and Agyeman, eds. 2011, 14). To date, suburban regions have been empowered to make this shift easily. However, marginalized communities like those in food deserts populated predominantly by people of color and immigrants face challenges when pivoting due to systemic racism caused by government policy that hinders access to intellectual, organizational, and financial resources for sustained food access, equity, and security (Morales 2011, 201). For instance, consider the Christian Doctrine of Discovery, a federal law "legalizing the removal of Indigenous people from their homelands" (215).

Access to healthy food is a life-threatening challenge in Los Angeles (LA), which harbors many food deserts. According to a 2021 report by the University of Southern California's Dornsife College of Letter, Arts, and Sciences, LA's population that experiences low food security comprises predominantly low-income women, and Latinos between the ages of 18 and 40 (Miller 2021). Artists in LA are working diligently to address this challenge. Food as a medium of art and design activism affords unconventional spaces. It can extend off of the blank canvas in the artist's private studio to collaborative and public spaces on street corners and sidewalks. Its tools are equally eclectic, spanning a spectrum ranging from manufactured like a photograph or performance to natural like a community tree and its fallen fruit. Appropriately, Fallen Fruit is the name of a residency art project in Los Angeles that engages community members in LA in planting fruit trees in and over public spaces and then mapping them (Flood and Sloan 2019, 19) to provide free access to their fallen fruit, thus facilitating the performative "creative" and collective action of community members gathering the fruit for nourishment. The Growing Food Justice for All Initiative (GFJI), founded in 2006, is a network of food justice organizations collaborating to dismantle racism and enable a more sustainable food system for people of color in marginalized communities and food deserts. GFJI grew out of the organization and food movement known as Growing Power with a focus on promoting "individual and organizational empowerment through training, networking, and creating a supportive community" (207).

Then, the anti-consumerist movement, also known as freeganism, includes activities like dumpster diving, guerilla gardening in empty urban lots, and voluntary unemployment. Freegans, a combination of the words "free" and "vegan," are often radical community activists who embrace community and, through minimal consumption, limit their participation in consumerism. Most active freegans retrieve food by dumpster diving, supplementing what they don't find through purchasing food. Freegan[10] meetings often include time for sharing out of recent dives and findings. Others downplay the role of dumpster diving in freeganism, are mindful of the stigma of eating food from the trash, and highlight other components, including bike and sewing workshops and wild food foraging events. Some freegans dumpster dive in groups of about twenty people, referred to as trash tours, to orient prospective freegans to the practice, a large percentage of whom will not return. These tours are designed with scouts determining the best sites to visit (i.e., which give away the best food), optimizing the experience, and highlighting to newcomers both the food waste problem and the opportunity for edible waste (Barnard 2011).

57. *Fallen Fruit*

A residency art project originating in Los Angeles, United States
Food category: Accessibility

Design category: Experience
Year of creation: 2004
Source: Flood and Sloan 2019, 19

"Fallen Fruit," a 2004 residency art project featured in Britain's V&A Museum's exhibit titled "Food: Bigger than the Plate," engages community members in Los Angeles (LA) and other cities around the world in planting fruit trees in and over public spaces and then mapping them to provide free access to fruit and perform "creative" and collective action to address food insecurity caused by lack of access (Flood and Sloan 2019, 19). Another part of Fallen Fruit's community action is its Public Fruit Jam (pun intended) which brings together community volunteers in a public indoor or outdoor space to socialize and make jam from the fallen fruits collected (see Appendix V). Fallen Fruit takes a bite out of the problem of low food security in LA through public performance art.

58. Freeganism

Dumpster diving in New York City, United States
Food category: Accessibility
Design category: Context
Year of creation: n.d.
Source: Barnard 2011

With garbage pick-up every night on a schedule, waste is typically placed on the public sidewalk curb in New York City. This practice provides a consistent resource for dives. Fieldwork conducted in 2008 and 2009 in New York City examined trash tours. These trash tours have established protocols, with the homeless having first rights to diving, the findings being first utilized for group gatherings, and anything left over can be distributed to individuals. In addition, trash bags need to be opened from the top, and the area should be free of disarray after the dive to keep the practice above scrutiny from shop owners. Freegans on these trash tours approach unsuspecting community members with food found on the dumpster dive and are willing to talk to the media to highlight their movement. In one instance, highlighting a store's waste on the news resulted in the business changing its practices and reducing waste. This accomplishment eliminated it as a dumpster dive for food but also resulted in social change that freeganism ultimately desires (Barnard 2011).

59. Growing Food Justice for All Initiative (GFJI)

Network to dismantle racism in Wisconsin, Oklahoma, and Minnesota, United States
Food category: Accessibility
Design category: System
Year of creation: 2006
Source: Morales 2011

GFJI conducts monthly conference calls with its member organizations to dis-cuss topics and share ideas around "antiracist tools of sustainable agriculture"

(Morales 2011, 211). Some of its member organizations include the Fondy Food Center in Milwaukee, Wisconsin, which works to create family-sustaining jobs in the Hmong-American community and get locally grown produce into the inner city from their farms (212). Another GFJI member organization, the Mvskoke Food Sovereignty Initiative & Earth-keepers Voices for Native America, works with Native American communities in Oklahoma to "reintroduce farming and

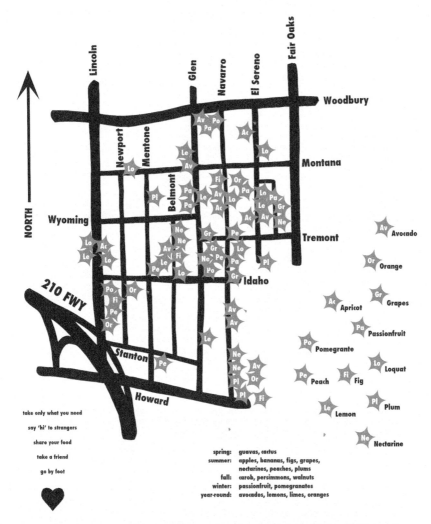

Figure 4.9 Fallen Fruit map of Pasadena (DO #56). Fallen Fruit (David Allen Burns, Matias Viegener, Austin Young), Public Fruit Map, City of Pasadena, dimensions variable, 2009.

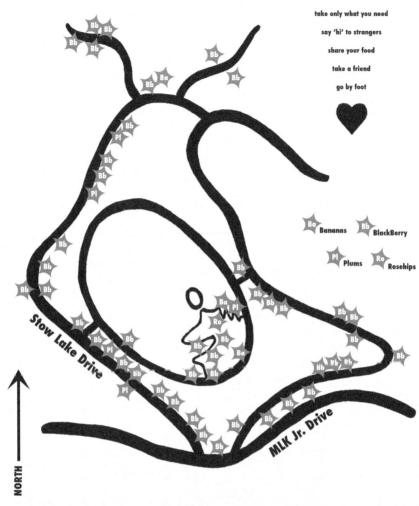

Figure 4.10 Fallen Fruit map of San Francisco (DO #56). Fallen Fruit (David Allen Burns, Matias Viegener, Austin Young), Public Fruit Map, City of San Francisco, Golden Gate Park, dimensions variable, 2008.

Figure 4.11 A freegan foraging for food in the East Village, New York City. This image by
Carlos A. Martinez is licensed under the Creative Commons Attribution 2.0
Generic license: https://creativecommons.org/licenses/by/2.0/deed.en.

food preparation methods that are more culturally and ecologically appropriate and contribute to building a sense of community and healthier lifestyle" (215). Then, there is the Rural Enterprise Center (REC), formerly known as the Latino Enterprise Center, in Northfield, Minnesota that nurtures an immigrant community of new farmers of color in 1) constructing an identity as an entrepreneur (rather than laborer) and establishing networks with other local immigrants, 2) learning how to farm collaboratively and in context to gain valuable insight, 3) training formally by applying new knowledge in a REC-developed, incubation farming process, and 4) implementation of a new farm or processing unit.

Consumption

Bangladesh faces a public health crisis because the naturally occurring inorganic arsenic contaminates its drinking water. Arsenic-related illnesses can develop between 2 and 20 years, depending on exposure and accumulation in the body. The shallow wells built in the 1970s and 1980s are contaminated with arsenic from the ground soil, and the resulting poisoning kills over 40,000 people in Bangladesh every year.

Large organizations like WHO, UNICEF, and other NGOs continue to address this issue, and according to Ahmed et al. (2017) the government has three primary strategies:

1. Labeling arsenic tube wells green for safe arsenic levels and red for dangerous levels.
2. Providing deep tube wells in areas contaminated with arsenic.
3. Providing treated, safe water through pipes, and increasing awareness.

While the Arsenic Mitigation Water Supply Project, supported by GoB World Bank, is working on this, the technology is still not economical, sustainable, or technically possible. Thus, two brothers instead created a SONO filtration system to address this issue in Bangladesh that is now propagated worldwide through commercialization.

60. SONO *filter*

A water filtration system in Bangladesh, Nepal, Pakistan, and India
Food category: Consumption
Design category: Object
Year of creation: 1999
Source: Ahmed et al. 2017

The development of the SONO arsenic water filter was begun in 1997 by Abul Hussam and his brother Abul K.M. Munir to address the arsenic crisis in Bangladesh. Iteration and adaption refined the product for commercialization

(Ahmed et al. 2017). The SONO Filter on the market[11] lasts for five years and comprises:

> two buckets. [The u]pper bucket contains [a] 4–5 cm thick layer of composite iron (mixture of metal iron and iron hydroxides) covered by sand layers, where arsenic is adsorbed and co-precipitated. The lower bucket contains sand and a charcoal layer to remove the iron hydroxides, and organic matter is released from the upper bucket.

It is affordable at around $40 per filter, easy to use and maintain, and does not impact the water quality or create an issue with toxic waste. NGOs have distributed them throughout Bangladesh, Nepal, Pakistan, and India, providing training on usage.

Places to intervene

The DOs in this quadrant show that citizen designers are innovatively using their creative agency to innovate sustainable food DOs that are replicated widely and address food insecurity, inequity, and injustice starting in their communities and spreading further. Figure 4.12 shows that most of the sustainable food DOs that are widespread and created by citizen designers and have been peer-reviewed address aqua/agriculture, communications, and accessibility with minimal production, processing, and consumption activity. Apparent gaps in the food system

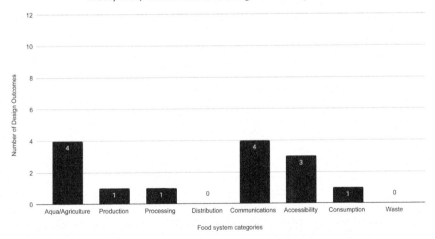

Figure 4.12 Quadrant C's DOs mapped according to the food system category to which they contribute. Image courtesy of Audrey G. Bennett.

of bottom-up and widespread sustainable food DOs exist in the distribution and waste phases. These gaps are the leverage points or places where citizen food designers can intervene and contribute to balancing the system towards food security, equity, and justice.

Notes

1 Note that the DOs in this quadrant come from peer-reviewed sources published after 2009—the founding of the International Food Design Society—though some of the DOs within the publications may have earlier creation or effectuation dates.
2 Based on peer-reviewed sources in English.
3 See: https://ceres.org.au.
4 See: https://farmhack.org/tools.
5 See: https://www.koenvanmechelen.be/planetary-community-chicken-pcc.
6 See: https://www.theworldcounts.com/challenges/consumption/foods-and-beverages/world-consumption-of-meat.
7 See: https://www.kickstarter.com/projects/1036543319/the-future-sausage.
8 See: https://foodtarot.tech/.
9 See: https://foodfutures.group/2021/01/21/more-than-human-food-futures-cook-book/.
10 See: https://freegan.info/.
11 See: https://www.hwts.info/products-technologies/e154da31/sono-filter/technical-information.

Bibliography

Alkon, Alison Hope, Yuki Kato, and Joshua Sbicca. 2020. *A Recipe for Gentrification: Food, Power, and Resistance in the City*. New York: NYU Press. https://play.google.com/store/books/details?id=TWnnDwAAQBAJ.

Alkon, A. H. and Agyeman J. eds., 2011. *Cultivating food justice: Race, class, and sustainability*. Cambridge: MIT Press.

Ahmed, Jashim Uddin, Wahida Shahan Tinne, Md. Al-Amin, and Maliha Rahanaz. 2017. "Social Innovation and SONO Filter for Drinking Water." *Business and Society Review* 13, no. 1: 15–26. https://doi.org/10.1108/SBR-08-2017-0060.

Barnard, Alex V. 2011. "'Waving the Banana' at Capitalism: Political Theater and Social Movement Strategy among New York's 'Freegan' Dumpster Divers." *Ethnography* 12, no. 4: 419–444. https://doi.org/10.1177/1466138110392453.

Berlow, Ali. 2015. *The Food Activist Handbook: Big & Small Things You Can Do to Help Provide Fresh, Healthy Food for Your Community*. North Adams, MA: Storey Publishing. https://play.google.com/store/books/details?id=kX3VCQAAQBAJ.

Berman, David B. 2008. *Do Good Design: How Design Can Change Our World*. Hoboken, NJ: Peachpit Press.

Brockotter, Fabian. "Popularity of Poultry Continues Globally." *Poultry World*, July 20, 2020. https://www.poultryworld.net/poultry/popularity-of-poultry-continues-globally/.

Cawst. "Technical Information." SONO Filter. Accessed August 17, 2022. https://www.hwts.info/products-technologies/e154da31/sono-filter/technical-information.

"Climate Change Act 2008." Legislation.gov.uk. Statute Law Database, 2019. https://www.legislation.gov.uk/ukpga/2008/27/section/1.

Corrigan, Michelle P. 2011. "Growing What You Eat: Developing Community Gardens in Baltimore, Maryland." *Applied Geography* 31, no. 4: 1232–1241. https://doi.org/10.1016/j.apgeog.2011.01.017.

Dolejšová, Markéta, Sjef van Gaalen, Danielle Wilde, Paul Graham Raven, Sara Heitlinger, and Ann Light. 2020. "Designing with More-than-Human Food Practices for Climate-Resilience." In *Companion Publication of the 2020 ACM Designing Interactive Systems Conference*, edited by Ron Wakkary, Kristina Andersen, Will Odom, Audrey Desjardins, and Marianne Graves Petersen. New York: Association for Computing Machinery. https://doi.org/10.1145/3393914.3395909.

Flood, Catherine, and May Rosenthal Sloan. 2019. *Food: Bigger Than the Plate*. London: V&A Publishing.

Fountain, Henry. 2008. "Commercial Production of Chicken Takes Toll on Genetic Diversity." *The New York Times*, November 3, 2008. https://www.nytimes.com/2008/11/04/science/04obchicken.html.

Furness, Walter W., and Courtney M. Gallaher. 2018. "Food Access, Food Security and Community Gardens in Rockford, IL." *Local Environment* 23, no. 4: 414–430. https://doi.org/10.1080/13549839.2018.1426561.

Garland, Ken. 1964. "First Things First Manifesto." *The Guardian* 24.

Gibney, Michael J., Ciarán G. Forde, Deirdre Mullally, and Eileen R. Gibney. 2017. "Ultra-Processed Foods in Human Health: A Critical Appraisal." *The American Journal of Clinical Nutrition* 106, no. 3: 717–724. https://doi.org/10.3945/ajcn.117.160440.

Glaser, M. 2002. "This is What I Have Learned." In AIGA *National Design Conference 2002 More Than Ever: Proceedings of the Washington DC Conference March 21–23*. https://www.macacos.com.uy/material/pdf/glaser_aiga_2002.pdf.

Godfray, H. Charles J., Paul Aveyard, Tara Garnett, Jim W. Hall, Timothy J. Key, Jamie Lorimer, Ray T. Pierrehumbert, Peter Scarborough, Marco Springmann, and Susan A. Jebb. 2018. "Meat Consumption, Health, and the Environment." *Science* 361, no. 6399: eaam5324. https://doi.org/10.1126/science.aam5324.

Gregory, Megan M., Timothy W. Leslie, and Laurie E. Drinkwater. 2016. "Agroecological and Social Characteristics of New York City Community Gardens: Contributions to Urban Food Security, Ecosystem Services, and Environmental Education." *Urban Ecosystems* 19, no. 2: 763–794. https://doi.org/10.1007/s11252-015-0505-1.

Hernandez, E. 1982. *Sun Mad*. Smithsonian American Art Museum. Accessed July 18, 2022. https://americanart.si.edu/artwork/sun-mad-34712.

Kim, Ju Eun. 2017. "Fostering Behaviour Change to Encourage Low-Carbon Food Consumption through Community Gardens." *International Journal of Urban Sciences* 21, no. 3: 364–384. https://doi.org/10.1080/12265934.2017.1314191.

Laidlaw, Julia, and Liam Magee. 2016. "Towards Urban Food Sovereignty: The Trials and Tribulations of Community-based Aquaponics Enterprises in Milwaukee and Melbourne." *Local Environment* 21, no. 5: 573–590. https://doi.org/10.1080/13549839.2014.986716.

Maldonado, Tomás. 1972. *Design, Nature, and Revolution: Toward a Critical Ecology*. New York: Harper & Row.

Martin, Pauline, Jean-Noël Consalès, Pascale Scheromm, Paul Marchand, Florence Ghestem, and Nicole Darmon. 2017. "Community Gardening in Poor Neighborhoods in France: A Way to Re-Think Food Practices?" *Appetite* 116: 589–598. https://doi.org/10.1016/j.appet.2017.05.023.

Mattick, Carolyn, S., 2018. "Cellular agriculture: the coming revolution in food production." *Bulletin of the Atomic Scientists* 74, no. 1: 32–35.

McClements, David Julian. 2019. *Future Foods: How Modern Science Is Transforming the Way We Eat*. Cham: Springer Nature Switzerland AG. https://play.google.com/store/books/details?id=SrPlwAEACAAJ.

———. 2020. "Future Foods: A Manifesto for Research Priorities in Structural Design of Foods." *Food & Function* 11: 1933–1945. https://doi.org/10.1039/c9fo02076d.

Morales, Alfonso. 2011. "Growing Food and Justice: Dismantling Racism Through Sustainable Food Systems." In *Cultivating Food Justice: Race, Class, and Sustainability*, edited by Alison Hope Alkon, and Julian Aygeman, 198–233. Cambridge, MA: MIT Press. Kindle.

Niebling, Carolien. 2018. *The Sausage of the Future*. Zurich: Lars Muller Publishers.

Poore, J., and T. Nemecek. 2018. "Reducing Food's Environmental Impacts Through Producers and Consumers." *Science* 360, no. 6392: 987–992. https://doi.org/10.1126/science.aaq0216.

Rayasam, Renuka. 2013. "What Does the 'Made In' Label Mean Anymore?" *The New Yorker*, August 30, 2013. https://www.newyorker.com/business/currency/what-does-the-made-in-label-mean-anymore.

Schwab, Katharine. 2017. "The Sausage Gets a Radical Redesign." *Fast Company*, April 17, 2017. https://www.fastcompany.com/90109023/the-sausage-gets-a-radical-redesign.

Smith, Cynthia E. 2016. *By the People: Designing a Better America*. New York: Cooper Hewitt, Smithsonian Design Museum.

Specht, Liz. 2018. "Is the Future of Meat Animal-Free?" *Food Technology* 72, no. 1. https://www.ift.org/news-and-publications/food-technology-magazine/issues/2018/january/features/cultured-clean-meat.

Sunny, Atiqur Rahman, Mohammad Mahmudul Islam, Mizanur Rahman, Mohammad Yusuf Miah, Mohammad Mostafiz, Naimul Islam, Mohammad Zakir Hossain, Mohammed Anas Chowdhury, Mohammed Ariful Islam, and Hendrik Jan Keus. 2019. "Cost-Effective Aquaponics for Food Security and Income of Farming Households in Coastal Bangladesh." *Egyptian Journal of Aquatic Research* 45, no. 1: 89–97. https://doi.org/10.1016/j.ejar.2019.01.003.

The UK Government. 2008. *Climate Change Act 2008*. London. https://www.legislation.gov.uk/ukpga/2008/27/section/1.

The World Counts. n.d. "Globally, We Consume Around 350 Million Tons of Meat a Year." Accessed July 18, 2022. https://www.theworldcounts.com/challenges/consumption/foods-and-beverages/world-consumption-of-meat.

Vanmechelen, K. n.d. "Planetary Community Chicken (PCC)." koenvanmechelen. Accessed July 18, 2022. https://www.koenvanmechelen.be/planetary-community-chicken-pcc.

Vermeulen, S. J., P. K. Aggarwal, A. Ainslie, C. Angelone, B. M. Campbell, A. J. Challinor, J. W. Hansen, J. S. I. Ingram, A. Jarvis, P. Kristjanson, C. Lau, G. C. Nelson, P. K. Thornton, and E. Wollenberg. 2012. "Options for Support to Agriculture and Food Security Under Climate Change." *Environmental Science & Policy* 15, no. 1: 136–144. https://doi.org/10.1016/j.envsci.2011.09.003.

Wilde, Danielle, Markéta Dolejsova, Sjef van Gaalen, Ferran Altarriba Bertran, Hilary Davis, and Paul Graham Raven. 2021. "Troubling the Impact of Food Future Imaginaries." In *Nordes 2021: Matters of Scale*, edited by E. Brandt, T. Markussen, E. Berglund, G. Julier, and P. Linde, 15–18. https://doi.org/10.21606/nordes.2021.10.

Willett, Walter, Johan Rockström, Brent Loken, Marco Springmann, Tim Lang, Sonja Vermeulen, Tara Garnett, David Tillman, Fabrice DeClerck, Amanda Wood, Malin Jonell, Michael Clark, Line J. Gordon, Jessica Fanzo, Corinna Hawkes, Rami Zurayk,

Juan A. Rivera, Wim De Vries, Lindiwe Majila Sibanda, Ashkan Afshin, Abhishek Chaudhary, Mario Herrero, Rina Augustina, Francesca Branca, Anna Lartey, Shenggen Fan, Beatrice Crona, Elizabeth Fox, Victoria Bignet, Max Trolle, Therese Lindal, Sudvir Singh, Sarah E. Cornell, K. Srinath Reddy, Sunita Narain, Sanya Nishtar, and Christopher J. L. Murray. 2019. "Food in the Anthropocene: The EAT-Lancet Commission on Healthy Diets from Sustainable Food Systems." *The Lancet* 393, no. 10170: 447–492. https://doi.org/10.1016/S0140-6736(18)31788-4.

Yalcinkaya, Gunseli. 2018. "Banana Passport Explores Issues Surrounding Food Exportation." *Dezeen*, April 7, 2018. https://www.dezeen.com/2018/04/07/graduates -create-passport-banana-explore-issues-surrounding-food-exportation-graphics -design/.

5 Quadrant D

Local, sustainable food design created by citizens

Quadrant D of the wicked solution to food insecurity includes design outcomes[1] (DOs) created by citizens for a limited geographic region that may be a single country, state, region, city, local community, or household. Quadrant D's citizen stakeholders include artists, innovators, food activists, and even local communities working with other professional stakeholders. The DOs emerge bottom-up and localized from individual and pooled grassroots resources and collaborations. This chapter's DOs are alphabetically organized according to the part of the food system that they address, including agriculture, processing, communications, accessibility, and waste, and the design forms used, including objects, environments, contexts, systems, and experiences.

As Figure 5.1 shows, a small but significant amount of peer reviewed, sustainable food design activity has emerged since 2009 by citizens worldwide to address local food insecurity, inequity, and injustice. Our integrative literature review shows that the United States leads North America and the rest of the world in citizen-driven sustainable food design activity with five DOs.[2] Citizen-driven DOs contributing to the global effort to eradicate food insecurity, inequity, and injustice include:

61. **Food planning**: Community-based stakeholders practice historically informed food planning through various types of food agricultural, distribution, and accessibility strategies to address food insecurity in the local food system of Detroit, Michigan.
62. **Home gardening**: University stakeholders, low-income community members with outdoor garden space, and a community service organization in San José, California, design sustainable home vegetable gardens.
63. **Hoop house gardening**: Native community members in Wapekeka, Canada, design a hoop house garden in their community in a participatory manner with local academic researchers.
64. **Non-flower for the Hoverfly**: An architect in Reykjavik, Iceland, using advanced imaging and simulation technologies, studies how hoverflies recognize their food and model their ideal environment to help them flourish amid climate change.

DOI: 10.4324/9781003222026-6

Figure 5.1 Quadrant D's DOs impact different parts of the world, including the continents of North America, Africa, Australia, Asia, and Europe. The shading indicates the density of sustainable food DOs we examined for that geographic region. Image courtesy of Audrey G. Bennett.

65. **Pā to Plate**: A community-based, participatory food supply chain loop intended to increase New Zealand's Indigenous community's connections to ancestral food traditions and landscapes and return the economic value generated.
66. **Sack gardening**: Residents in poor communities in Kenya use vertical gardening with sacks to address the lack of access to farmland and rampant food insecurity.
67. **Indigiearth**: An Australian entrepreneur creates food products that use heritage ingredients from the local Indigenous cultural tradition and land to yield food security and economic sustenance.
68. **Mark Olive**: An Australian entrepreneur creates food products that promote Indigenous materials and ingredients from native Australian plants returning economic value generated to local Indigenous communities.
69. **Fresh Moves Mobile Market**: A community-based initiative in which professionals work with a graffiti artist to convert Illinois transit buses into storefronts to provide low-income communities access to fruits, vegetables, and herbs.
70. **Humane Borders Water Station and Warning Posters**: Local citizens team up to create a network of emergency water stations and accompanying posters in the Sonoran Desert in Arizona to prevent migrants crossing the border by foot from dying from lack of water.

71. **Community cooker**: In Kenya, a community creates a public oven where residents exchange trash they've collected from the streets of their communities for time to cook.
72. **Daily Dump**: An artist in India aestheticizes composting pots to make the practice of composting in households resonate more.
73. **Food rescue**: Citizens of Göteborg, Sweden, municipal officials, community organizations, and businesses create a waste prevention initiative.

In the next section of this chapter, DOs are organized according to the food system's categories: aquaculture/agriculture, production, processing, distribution, communication, accessibility, consumption, and waste. Our integrative review of peer-reviewed literature shows sustainable food design activity in the food system specifically in the phases of agriculture, processing, communication, accessibility, and waste only. Each food category begins with a summary of the challenges within the phase of the food system that existing DOs address, followed by descriptions of each DO that provide more information about the actors and activities involved in their functionality, the type of design form they manifest, the year and geographical place where designers effectuated them, and the literature source that provides the evidence that they are effective. Our aim in each food category is to provide a brief summary overview gleaned from the respective peer-reviewed publication. This information includes: 1) the food insecurity, inequity, or injustice challenge the DO addresses and why it is a significant sustainability issue, 2) the global or local context/community the challenge impacts, 3) how the DO addresses the challenge, 4) how the DO works or functions and what qualities or components it comprises, 5) when and where the DO was effectuated, tested, or implemented, and found to be effective, and 6) who the stakeholders are and their activities. Sometimes, we rely on supplemental sources to tell a more detailed story of the sustainable food DO. From this discussion, the chapter concludes with an analysis of the places the data suggests to intervene with further design innovation or appropriation by citizens towards sustainable food security, equity, and justice in local contexts.

Agriculture

Our analysis of sustainable food design driven by citizens pursuing food security, equity, and justice in their local communities begins with agricultural challenges in specific BIPOC (Black, Indigenous, People of Color) communities in the United States and Canada. The residual negative impact of colonization, systemic racism, climate change, and environmental contaminants on present-day food supply chains continues to ravage these marginalized communities. For instance, in Canada's northern region, Indigenous populations face challenges of food insecurity and increasing rates of health issues, including obesity and diabetes. Many of these issues in Indigenous communities are caused by restrictions imposed by the government that have infringed upon the Indigenous people's right to manage their land, and to hunt, fish, and gather.

For example, many Indigenous societies utilized a hunter-gatherer economy where ecosystem relations required great mobility. Forced assimilation attempted to destroy these ways of life by introducing Western farming, in many cases through the residential school system with children separated from their parents and being taught that their culture and ways were uncivilized. Gardening in this context was a disciplinary tactic in the Foucauldian sense of subject formation. And yet today, in the Native community of Wapekeka, Canada, hoop houses and community gardening have proven effective at sustaining Indigenous land-use practices. This reversal—from farming as assault to farming as means of cultural survival—is emblematic of the transformations made possible by bottom-up, citizen-driven agency in food justice practices.

A similar transformation took place in the city of Detroit, Michigan, which has experienced rapid racialized depopulation in its history that has contributed to the economic decline and food deserts, in its predominantly Black communities, it is known for in its present day. Food planning is an evolving design system that is working to address these issues. Food planning is a system of strategies that provide or strengthen links between food supply chain actors and activities to achieve food and economic sustenance for all community members. These strategies include "urban agriculture, neighborhood farm markets, and retail grocery, and community-based food entrepreneurship" (Pothukuchi 2015, 419). For instance, community gardens, a form of urban agriculture, effectively address food insecurity in Detroit. However, economic crises and other environmental factors can exacerbate food insecurity in cities like Detroit and curb their impact. While sustaining these urban agriculture programs after crises has been challenging, still many endure due to the dynamic relationships in community gardens.

Yet, in other cities worldwide, urban gardens are ending due to urban development or because they can be challenging for many to access and require an ongoing commitment from volunteers. As a result, home gardens are proving even more effective at providing easier access to nutritious foods. However, while a home garden may work to alleviate food insecurity in some urban contexts, some households lack growing spaces for gardening and farming. For these households without land rights of their own, growing healthy, accessible food is often not an option. Hence, the use of sacks by low-income households in Kenya, for instance, for vegetable gardening.

Marginalized BIPOC communities also grapple with climate change which can damage the agricultural ecosystem, including human and non-human actors. For instance, worldwide, one finds insects (e.g., bees, butterflies), birds, and bats playing a crucial role in agriculture and food security. They fertilize food crops that depend on pollinators. These crops include cowpea, coffee, avocado, tomato, soybean, mango, beans, oilseed, shea, and vegetables (e.g., cabbage, cauliflower, okra, pumpkin, squash, lettuce, and carrot) (USAID Office of Forestry and Biodiversity 2020). However, one of the adverse effects of climate change is the generally known steady decline of these pollinators' populations, particularly bees. With over 75% of leading food crops that contribute to sustainable food security relying on pollinators (USAID Office of Forestry and Biodiversity 2020), it is clear that the decline of pollinator populations contributes to food insecurity globally. By shifting to biodiverse Indigenous cropping systems, many communities have seen a corresponding rise in the ecological health surrounding these farms, including pollinator populations (Figueroa-Helland et al. 2018; Henríquez-Piskulich et al. 2021). The compensation for climate change need not be limited to decolonization. For example, Thomas Pausz, a concerned citizen and architect in Reykjavik, Iceland, uses the creative technologies of 3D printing and virtual reality to study how hoverflies recognize their food to create the ideal "material and sensory conditions for them to flourish" (Flood and Sloan 2019, 53). Putting these two approaches, decolonization and computational affordances together, Eglash et al. (forthcoming 2023) have called for new "phyto-human alliances" in which computing plays the role of restorative prosthetic.

The sustainable DOs gleaned from our integrative literature review that address these agricultural challenges include food planning, home gardening, hoop house gardening, Non-flower for the Hoverfly, Pā to Plate, and sack gardening.

61. *Food planning*

Urban agriculture and food entrepreneurship in Detroit, Michigan, United States
Food category: Agriculture
Design category: Systems
Year of creation: n.d.
Source: Pothukuchi 2015

As noted previously, the city of Detroit has faced racialized depopulation and subsequent economic decline. Food planning can help sustain the city and address the devastating socio-economic ramifications of poverty, including food insecurity, inequity, and injustice. Food planning is a comprehensive approach to strengthening the links between food systems and the community to achieve food and economic sustenance, and food planning has been rising in Detroit, Michigan, over the last decade and a half, taking the aesthetic forms of "urban agriculture, neighborhood farm markets, and retail grocery, and community-based food entrepreneurship" (Pothukuchi 2015, 419). Pothukuchi (2015) further notes historical precedence for food planning in Detroit that can provide lessons for more sustainable food planning moving forward. Food planning entails conducting historical research on what has worked and not worked in a locale to determine how to move forward by innovating new forms of sustainable agricultural design practices, appropriating old methods for present contexts, or repairing those that are working. It is an evolving system of agricultural design practices that impacts the present towards a more sustainable food future that is more secure, equitable, and just.

62. *Home gardening*

Urban agriculture in San José, California, United States
Food category: Agriculture

Design category: Environment
Year of creation: 2010
Source: Gray et al. 2014

This DO, a home gardening environment, expands research from public community gardening to the less-studied domestic agricultural spaces. Gray et al. (2014) examine its use in the context of a primarily low-income Latinx community in the San José, California, region of the United States near Silicon Valley. In this area, access to affordable, healthy, and fresh food in the local neighborhoods of Alma, Gardner, and Washington can be a life-threatening challenge. These areas are low-income communities with high poverty and gang violence, which contribute to food insecurity. Home gardens provide culturally appropriate food for the households in these communities through La Mesa Verde (LMV), a network of urban gardeners who build access to healthy food in San José. LMV generally aims to empower those in need, particularly low-income families, by providing training on how to grow organic vegetables in their homes. LMV creates home gardens for people to make their food, like the ingredients for salsa, including cilantro, chiles, tomatoes, tomatillos, and onions. Participants in the program must have garden space and, if renting their home, permission for a garden bed to be built with access to sunlight. They attend a series of nutrition and gardening classes organized by LMV. Once completed, the participants receive the materials and assistance to develop their garden bed and seedlings. With feedback, the program has evolved from a needs-based service delivery model to one more asset-based, utilizing participatory design (Gray et al. 2014).

Gray et al. (2014) started the LMV project in 2010 after the 2008 financial crisis in the United States. The stakeholders include organizers of La Mesa Verde, a project of the Sacred Heart Community Service, who facilitated the project; University of California Cooperative Gardeners of Santa Clara County, who assisted with community education; and community members in the communities of Alma, Gardner, and Washington, who participated in the project.

63. Hoop house gardening

Indigenous agriculture in Wapekeka, Canada
Food category: Agriculture
Design category: Environment
Year of creation: 2017
Source: Thompson et al. 2018

The hoop house gardening DO was effectuated in Canada's northern Indigenous population, specifically in the Oji-Cree First Nation community of the Wapekeka. There, researchers engaged in community-based participatory design to implement a hoop house and community garden to contribute to local food production, develop the community's skills and knowledge, engage the community, including the youth, and align with traditional Indigenous land-based practices. Community members were hired as staff to oversee the gardens, and a hoop house was constructed after deliberation on its location. It was erected with and by the community near a school to connect it to local youth. This design activity fostered connection and empowerment within the community as well as a sense of their ownership of the hoop house (Thompson et al. 2018).

Key stakeholders are the Oji-Cree First Nation in the community of Wapekeka. The researchers partnered with the Indigenous Health Research Group (IHRG) at the University of Ottawa. Funding was secured in 2017, with corresponding research being conducted then. The project was supported by the Michaëlle Jean Center for Global and Community Engagement and by IHRG. The team also secured funding from the Students for Canada's North scholarship and the Alex Trebek Challenge and Innovation Fund (Michaëlle Jean Center funding programs).

64. Non-flower for the Hoverfly

A pollen container in Reykjavik, Iceland
Food category: Agriculture
Design category: Object
Year of creation: 2017
Source: Flood and Sloan 2019, 53–4

One of the adverse effects of climate change is the steady decline of pollinator populations. Hoverflies, second to bees, are among the most prolific pollinators globally (Flood and Sloan 2019, 54). Thus, Thomas Pausz, an architect in Reykjavik, Iceland, has used 3D printing and virtual reality to study how hoverflies recognize their food and to "create the material and sensory conditions for them to flourish" (53). The resulting non-flower is Pausz's ecological intervention featured in the 2019 "Food: Bigger than the Plate" exhibition at the V&A museum in Britain. Non-flowers integrated within a field of food crops can assist in attracting hoverflies to pollinate the crops. "In contrast to the animal-human relations based on control and exploitation" that exists within traditional animal farming, Pausz's approach offers "a model of cooperation and coexistence for reconfiguring the interactions between human and non-human systems" (53) within the scope of food.

65. Pā to Plate

A food value chain loop in the Bay of Islands, New Zealand
Food category: Agriculture
Design category: Context
Year of creation: 2016
Source: Kawharu 2019

For Indigenous communities interested in socio-economic growth and enterprise development in food, interpreting values may help develop a new approach to food supply chains, as exemplified by the design innovation occurring in the New Zealand Māori kin.

This DO, called Pā to Plate, emerged from a community-based participatory design project focused on the marae. Marae communities of the Bay of Islands, New Zealand, serve as an economic center and the cultural center of communities; but they also refer to people who attend events in those spaces. Pā to Plate aims to increase communities' connections to the traditions and landscapes of ancestral food. It is about food sovereignty and reclaiming economic connection to ancestral land. Pā to Plate is a socio-economic enterprise concept that is a marae-value chain model, providing access to foods and resources from the landscapes of their ancestors.

Kawharu (2019) conducted the research from 2016 through 2018 with and in the Māori communities in the Bay of Islands with additional community conversations over a more extended period. The researchers and organizations providing support include Ngā Pae o Te Maramatanga and the Our Land and Water National Science Challenge. Community stakeholders are the New Zealand Māori kin.

66. Sack gardening

Urban agriculture in Nairobi, Kenya
Food category: Agriculture
Design category: Environment
Year of creation: 2008
Source: Gallaher et al. 2015

In the poverty-stricken Kibera region of Nairobi, Kenya, it is impossible to farm due to the lack of access to land for farming. Thus, sack gardening has emerged as a more viable option for densely populated living spaces and potentially other similar regions across the globe. While this research specifically focuses on the areas of Kibera, Gallaher et al. (2015) note that sack gardening is also being done in other cities around the world, but limit their research to Kenya.

Sack gardening, also referred to as vertical gardening, is a form of urban agriculture that allows for planting directly on the sides and tops of sacks of soil. The process of sack gardening consists of 20 to 40 plants being planted by farmers on the top and side of sacks of soil, fully utilizing the vertical space of the sack (2). Sack gardening was introduced in Kibera by Solidarites, a French nongovernmental organization, which in 2008 provided free seedlings and advice to help address food insecurity after a period of post-election violence. This program ended in 2012, but Kibera still uses sack gardens.

The key stakeholders in this study were the residents of Kibera, East Africa's largest slum area. There are ten villages, including Makina, Mashimoni, Laini Saba, Kianda, Kisumu Ndogo, Soweto East, Soweto West, Gatwekera, and Silanga. In addition, researchers worked in collaboration with the University of Nairobi. The researchers used a sustainable livelihood approach to look at the ability of farming in high-poverty regions. Gallaher et al. (2015) conducted this research on the impact of sack gardening from 2010 to 2011.

Processing

In the past, Indigenous communities relied on local food, culture, and traditions rooted in their connection to the land to support trade activities. However,

Figure 5.2 Sack gardening (DO #66). "Albert demonstrating watering the sack garden" by Colleen_Taugher is licensed under CC BY 2.0.

more Indigenous people live in cities, making them less connected to the land. Entrepreneurship can promote tradition and culture, and support economic development within Indigenous communities, though legal and administrative barriers can make it hard for these business ventures to succeed. The DO in this food category titled Indigiearth highlights a food-processing venture that provides economic, social, environmental, and ecological sustainability to Indigenous communities in Australia. Indigiearth is a significant example of how to connect food to cultural tradition and land through Indigenous entrepreneurship in Central West New South Wales in Australia.

67. Indigiearth

Indigenous entrepreneurship in Central West New South Wales, Australia
Food category: Processing
Design category: Context
Year of creation: 2012
Source: Ratten and Dana 2015

A Ngemba Weilwan woman, Sharon Winsor, founded Indigiearth in 2012, a business that highlights Indigenous culture by producing and selling products connected to Indigenous land and cultural traditions in Central West New South Wales in Australia.

While Indigiearth products include biscuits and cookies, bush secret plum puddings, and chocolate macadamias, they are most known for their native range of products, including herbal teas, jams, and sauces. In addition, Indigiearth sells natural soaps and skincare products, which can also be found in hotels across Australia. In addition, BP also sells Indigiearth's products in its stores and donates 50 cents of each product sold to Indigenous children's literacy and numeracy foundation early language programs. The stakeholders are the Indigenous people of Australia as well as distributors and consumers of various products.

Communications

The Indigenous people of Australia are linked to nature and the land, connecting their culture and traditions to native herbs, spices, and foods. With an increased global interest in locally grown food, Indigenous people have an opportunity to improve their socio-economic development through food entrepreneurship (Ratten and Dana 2015). The DO in this food category is the brand Mark Olive, which represents a celebrity chef and food entrepreneur in Australia. Olive has brought significant attention to the Indigenous food movement in Australia by using communication conventions like a television show and a corresponding cookbook to market the Indigenous-sourced ingredients of his catering business and restaurant.

68. Mark Olive

Indigenous entrepreneurship enterprise in Melbourne, Australia
Food category: Communication
Design category: Context
Year of creation: 2008
Source: Ratten and Dana 2015

Descended from the north coast of New South Wales Bundjulung people, Mark Olive, known as "The Black Olive," is an Australian indigenous food entrepreneur who utilizes native herbs and spices in his cooking and food products.

Mark Olive has brought attention to the food cultures and traditions of the Indigenous people of Australia by appearing as a celebrity chef on "The Outback Café" and by publishing a corresponding cookbook. In addition, he had a catering business named Black Olive and a restaurant called Tjanabi. Mark uses Indigenous materials from native Australian plants for cooking, and his popularity has corresponded with market demand for Indigenous meats like kangaroo, emu, and crocodile.

Accessibility

The city of Chicago is a hotbed for food insecurity and injustice, with an abundance of food deserts in low-income communities. Those predominantly affected by low food security in Chicago are African-Americans and Latinx communities (Smith 2016, 132). As a result, a group of socio-economically diverse stakeholders have designed mobile farmers' markets facilitated by transit buses transformed into vegetable storefronts to transport food to communities living in these food deserts.

Along the border between the United States and Mexico, migrants more than occasionally die from dehydration. Journalist Alyssa Marksz of Cronkite News reports in the article titled "Migrant Deaths in the Desert at Record Levels as Heat Wave Pounds West" that near the beginning of the summer of 2021, the remains were found of a record number of migrants who had attempted unsuccessfully to cross the Arizona desert during a record-breaking heatwave. Thus, concerned citizens designed a system of emergency water stations and posters in the Sonoran Desert in Arizona to provide water to these migrants, communicate the dangers of attempting to cross the desert, and dissuade them from doing so. For those who still venture forward and take on the risk, the posters also show a map of all the locations of the emergency water stations.

69. Fresh Moves Mobile Market

A mobile farmers' market in Illinois, United States
Food category: Accessibility

Design category: Object
Year of creation: 2009–present
Source: Smith 2016

Before the 2011 rise of static farmers' markets in Chicago to facilitate access to healthy food, the idea of a mobile market emerged in 2009 as the way to transport healthy food to these food desert communities (Smith 2016, 132). Transit buses with the Illinois Link system already integrated were appropriated to take the form of mobile markets for use in low-income communities. Their interior spaces were redesigned to function like storefronts with "shelves filled with fresh fruit, vegetables, and herbs" (132). Professionally branded as "Fresh Moves Mobile Markets," the project reached fruition through the collaborative efforts of an agricultural non-profit organization, an architecture firm, and a local graffiti artist. "These markets make over forty weekly stops in ten underserved neighborhoods" thus contributing to the 40% decline of people living in food deserts in Chicago (132).

70. Humane Borders Water Stations and Warning Posters

A system of emergency water stations and posters in the Sonoran Desert in Arizona,
   United States
Food category: Accessibility
Design category: System
Year of creation: 2000
Source: Smith 2016

To address the food challenge of migrants succumbing to dehydration while attempting to cross the desert, a group of citizens in Tucson, Arizona, came together to design a system of water stations situated strategically at different locations throughout the Sonoran Desert (Smith 2016, 134). According to curator Cynthia Smith in her book titled *By the People: Designing a Better America*, the water stations evolved from a large trash can filled with water with a 30-foot high pole and flag mounted on it to make it visible to a small tank painted a vibrant blue and branded "Humane Borders (Fronteras Compasivas)" and the Spanish word *AGUA* that means water (134).

Formalizing into a non-profit organization known as Humane Borders, these humanitarians map the specific locations of places in the Sonoran Desert where migrant remains have been found. They use this map and its alarming data to populate warning posters that they design with Spanish headlines, "Don't go! There is not enough water! It isn't worth it!" These posters alert prospective migrants and deter migration. At the same time, the water tanks quench the thirst of those who persist onward and prevent dehydration and fatality.

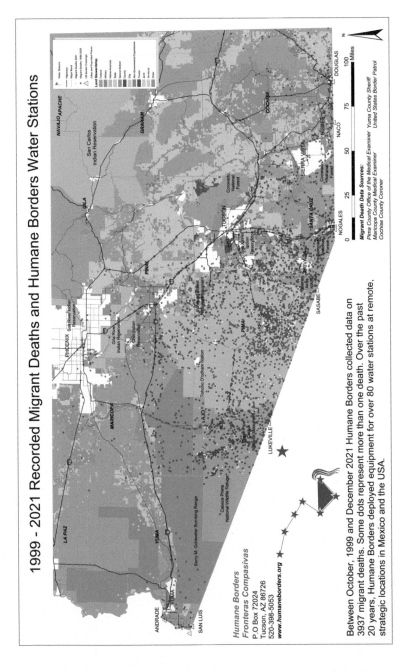

Figure 5.3   Migrants Deaths, Rescue Beacons, Water Stations 2000–2021 that can be downloaded and printed in letter and poster sizes free of charge at https://humaneborders.org/printable-maps-and-posters/. (DO #70). Image courtesy of Human Borders.

Waste

Many factors contribute to climate change, including agriculture, which emits the greenhouse gases methane and nitrous oxide (Gregory et al. 2005). On the other end of the food supply chain, waste discarded in household trash also creates greenhouse gases when disposed of in landfills. When these factors and others coexist excessively and increasingly, they cause climate change, and, if left unmanaged and unaddressed, climate change, in turn, negatively impacts the food supply system in varying ways, depending on the region, "ranging from crop production (e.g., changes in rainfall leading to drought or flooding, or warmer or cooler temperatures leading to changes in the length of the growing season), to changes in markets, food prices, and supply chain infrastructure" (2139).

Accordingly, the United Nations Environmental Program, in their 2021 Food Waste Index report, estimates that "around 931 million tonnes of food waste was generated in 2019," of which "61 percent came from households" (UNEP 2021, 8). In India, household food waste is estimated at about 68.7 million tonnes annually (NDTV 2021). Reducing household food waste helps to mitigate climate change worldwide while moving us towards greater food security. For instance, in India, handcrafted terracotta composting pots sold under the brand Daily Dump are used to improve households' daily waste management.

In the 2017 *Washington Post* article titled "Drowning in Garbage," photographer Kadir van Lohuizen reports that the world "produces more than 3.5 million tons of garbage a day" and that that figure will "grow to 11 million tons by the end of the century." Using multiple modes—text, photos, and videos—van Lohuizen relays a compelling story of his journeys to the cities of Jakarta, Tokyo, Lagos, New York City, São Paulo, and Amsterdam to investigate their waste management. In the article, van Lohuizen asks: "Is this just garbage, or is it a resource?" Transforming waste from garbage to resource is critical to curbing its impending growth worldwide as the population grows. Addressing van Lohuizen's question is crucial in impoverished informal settlements worldwide as mounds of mismanaged rubbish grow in the middle of cities near rivers and schools, and domestic spaces creating health hazards (Community Cooker, n.d.). A DO that addresses waste mismanagement is the *jiko ya jamii* (Swahili for "community cooker") in Nairobi. The *jiko ya jamii* serves as a quintessential example of how we can transform rubbish into an asset for greater sustainability through better waste management.

As the increase in waste significantly impacts sustainability in the world, one result is that some European cities have moved from waste management to waste prevention, viewed as the most desirable action. Cities are responsible for navigating this change within their communities through regulation and policy, as well as introducing and educating residents on the importance of this shift. Previous plans emphasizing waste reduction have been criticized for expressing

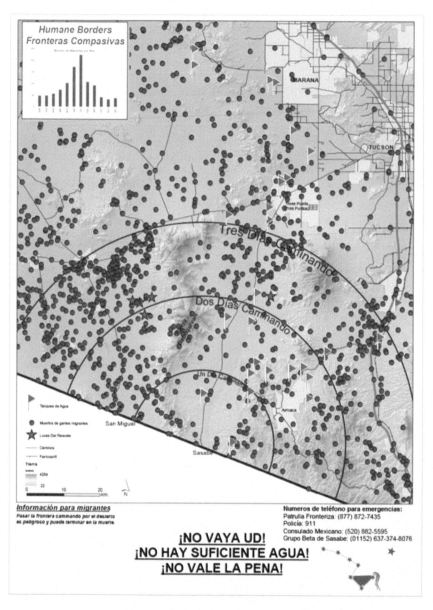

Figure 5.4 This warning poster is one of four downloadable at https://humaneborders.org/
printable-maps-and-posters/ that is used to deter migration across the Sonoran
Desert. It reads in Spanish "Don't go! There is not enough water! It isn't worth
it!" (DO #70). Image courtesy of Human Borders.

intent but lacking results (Zapata and Zapata Campos 2018). As the idea of waste prevention moves to the forefront of waste management, the city of Göteborg was an early adopter of waste prevention and has become one of Sweden's leaders in the emerging field (Zapata and Zapata Campos 2018).

71. *Community cooker* (jiko ya jamii)

A community oven in Nairobi, Kenya
Food category: Waste
Design category: Object
Year of creation: 1993
Source: Smith 2011

The community cooker in Nairobi, *jiko ya jamii*, the Swahili expression for community cooker, serves as a quintessential example of how we can transform rubbish into an asset for greater sustainability through better waste management. The community cooker is featured in the Smithsonian Institute's Cooper Hewitt Museum collection.[3] It was designed in 1993 by James Howard Archer, Momu Musuva, and Planning Systems Services. It functions as a community-based and publicly situated oven where local residents exchange collected trash for cooking time on the community cooker. The community cooker is managed by a "community-based organization" known as *Ushirika Wa Usafa* ("corporation of cleanliness" in Swahili) that sorts the trash as it feeds a burning box.

72. *Daily Dump*

Aesthetic pottery for home composting in Bangalore, India
Food category: Waste
Design category: Object
Year of creation: 2006
Source: Flood and Sloan 2019, 37

Daily Dump's aesthetically pleasing handcrafted terracotta pots that featured in the "Food: Bigger than the Plate" exhibition in Britain at the V&A Museum address the challenge and stigma of household food waste in India and are used pervasively in households there. Daily Dump challenges the stigma of handling waste by changing our perceptions of it from something that is gross and shameful to something that can generate visual beauty in the household. ("Food Bigger than the Plate," 2019)

Figure 5.5a Community cooker (5.5DO #71.)

Figure 5.5b Community cooker (5.5DO #71.)

Figure 5.5c Community cooker (5.5DO #71.)

Figure 5.6 Daily Dump's compost pots of varying sizes aim to change the stigma of household composting (DO #72).

73. Food rescue

Citizen-driven waste reduction initiative in Göteborg, Sweden
Food category: Waste
Design category: Experience
Year of creation: 2013
Source: Zapata and Zapata Campos 2018

This DO, an experience design, comes from waste prevention research on existing successful waste prevention projects and workshops with practitioners to highlight opportunities for how cities can become institutional entrepreneurs in the waste prevention space. To comply with European regulations, the Swedish Waste-Prevention Programme was launched in December 2013, focusing on Göteborg, Sweden and four of its waste prevention initiatives, including Alelyckan Reuse Park, Living the Life, GreenHackGBG, and Preventing Waste in Göteborg.

By examining the four existing waste prevention projects from 2014 to 2017, Zapata and Zapata Campos (2018) identified innovative practices that mobilized people and resources, rationales, and relations. Data collected included observations, reviews of documents, websites, social media, and interviews examining how waste prevention was conducted in the four identified initiatives.

Due to size and resources, the researchers acknowledge challenges in replicating and scaling this work of environmental policies and projects in other cities. Stakeholders are the citizens of Göteborg, Sweden, along with municipal officials, community organizations, and businesses.

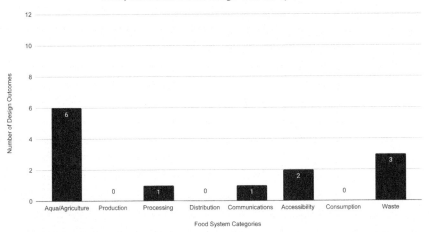

Quadrant D of the Wicked Solution to Food Insecurity
Local, sustainable food design created by citizens

Figure 5.7 Quadrant D's DOs are categorized according to the food system category to which they contribute. Image courtesy of Audrey G. Bennett.

Places to intervene

The DOs discussed in this quadrant emerge bottom-up and localized from individual and pooled grassroots resources and collaborations. They provide evidence that citizens without formal training in design are utilizing their design agency to fight food insecurity. The bar chart in Figure 5.7 shows most of the sustainable food DOs that are local and created by citizen designers and have been peer-reviewed to address agriculture, accessibility, and waste with minimal activity in processing, and communications. Clear gaps in the food system of sustainable food design occur in the production, distribution, and consumption phases. These gaps are the leverage points or places where designers can intervene and contribute to balancing the system towards greater food security, equity, and justice.

Notes

1 Note that the DOs in this quadrant come from peer-reviewed sources published after 2009—the founding of the International Food Design Society—though some of the DOs within the publications may have earlier creation or effectuation dates.
2 Based on peer-reviewed sources in English.
3 See: https://collection.cooperhewitt.org/objects/420778907/.

Bibliography

"Community Cooker: Jiko Ya Jamii: Planning Systems Services Ltd." Archello. Accessed August 16, 2022. https://archello.com/project/community-cooker-jiko-ya-jamii.
Eglash, Ron, Audrey Bennett, Lionel Robert, Kwame Robinson, Matthew Garvin, and Mark Guzdial. 2023, forthcoming. "Decolonization, Computation, Propagation:

Phyto-human Alliances in the Pathways towards Generative Justice." In *Plant by Numbers*, edited by Jane Prophet, and Helen Pritchard. London: Bloomsbury Publishing PLC.

Figueroa-Helland, L., C. Thomas, and A. P. Aguilera. 2018. "Decolonizing Food Systems: Food Sovereignty, Indigenous Revitalization, and Agroecology as Counter-Hegemonic Movements." *Perspectives on Global Development and Technology* 17, no. 1–2: 173–201.

"Food: Bigger than the Plate." *ITSLIQUID*, April 13, 2019. https://www.itsliquid.com/food-bigger-than-the-plate.html.

Flood, Catherine, and May Rosenthal Sloan. 2019. *Food: Bigger Than the Plate*. London: V&A Publishing.

Gallaher, Courtney M., Antoinette M. G. A. WinklerPrins, Mary Njenga, and Nancy Karanja. 2015. "Creating Space: Sack Gardening as a Livelihood Strategy in the Kibera Slums of Nairobi, Kenya." *Journal of Agriculture, Food Systems, and Community Development* 5, no. 2: 1–19. https://doi.org/10.5304/jafscd.2015.052.006.

Gray, Leslie, Patricia Guzman, Kathryn Michelle Glowa, and Ann G. Drevno. 2014. "Can Home Gardens Scale-up into Movements for Social Change? The Role of Home Gardens in Providing Food Security and Community Change in San Jose, California." *Local Environment* 19, no. 2: 187–203. https://doi.org/10.1080/13549839.2013.792048.

Gregory, P. J., J. S. I. Ingram, and M. Brklacich. 2005. "Climate Change and Food Security." *Philosophical Transactions of the Royal Society of London B, Biological Sciences* 360 no. 1463: 2139–2148. https://doi.org/10.1098/rstb.2005.1745.

Henríquez-Piskulich, Patricia A., Constanza Schapheer, Nicolas J. Vereecken, and Cristian Villagra. 2021. "Agroecological Strategies to Safeguard Insect Pollinators in Biodiversity Hotspots: Chile as a Case Study." *Sustainability* 13, no. 12: 6728. https://doi.org/10.3390/su13126728.

Kawharu, Merata. 2019. "Reinterpreting the Value Chain in an Indigenous Community Enterprise Context." *Journal of Enterprising Communities: People and Places in the Global Economy* 13, no. 3: 242–262. https://doi.org/10.1108/jec-11-2018-0079.

Marksz, Alyssa. "Migrant Deaths in the Desert at Record Levels as Heat Wave Pounds West." Cronkite News. Arizona PBS, July 13, 2021. https://cronkitenews.azpbs.org/2021/07/13/migrant-deaths-in-the-desert-at-record-levels-as-heat-wave-pounds-west/.

Miller, Jenesse. 2021. "Food Insecurity Returns to Pre-Pandemic Levels, but More than 1 in 10 Angelenos Are Still Struggling." UCS News. University of Southern California, October 13, 2021. https://news.usc.edu/193049/food-insecurity-los-angeles-county-usc-research/#:~:text=Nearly%201%20million%20Los%20Angeles,by%20USC%20Dornsife%27s%20Public%20Exchange.&text=One%20in%203%20Los%20Angeles,during%20April%20to%20December%202020.

NDTV. 2021. "India Wasted Over 68 Million Tons Of Food In 2019: UN Report." March 15, 2021. https://www.ndtv.com/india-news/india-wasted-over-68-million-tons-of-food-in-2019-globally-931-million-tons-food-wasted-un-report-2384225.

Pothukuchi, Kameshwari. 2015. "Five Decades of Community Food Planning in Detroit: City and Grassroots, Growth, and Equity." *Journal of Planning Education and Research* 35, no. 4: 419–434. https://doi.org/10.1177/0739456X15586630.

Ratten, Vanessa, and Léo-Paul Dana. 2015. "Indigenous Food Entrepreneurship in Australia: Mark Olive 'Australia's Jamie Oliver' and Indigiearth." *International Journal of Entrepreneurship and Small Business* 26, no. 3: 265–279. https://doi.org/10.1504/ijesb.2015.072391.

Smith, Cynthia E. 2011. *Design with the Other 90%: Cities*. New York: Cooper-Hewitt, National Design Museum.

Smith, Cynthia E. 2016. *By the People: Designing a Better America*. New York: Cooper Hewitt, Smithsonian Design Museum.

Thompson, Heather A., Courtney W. Mason, and Michael A. Robidoux. 2018. "Hoop House Gardening in the Wapekeka First Nation as an Extension of Land-Based Food Practices." *ARCTIC* 71, no. 4: 407–421. https://doi.org/10.14430/arctic4746.

United Nations Environment Programme. 2021 *Food Waste Index Report 2021*. Nairobi.

USAID Office of Forestry and Biodiversity. "The Importance of Wild Pollinators for Food Security and Nutrition." USAID, July 2020.

van Lohuizen, K. 2017. "Drowning in Garbage." *The Washington Post*. https://www.washingtonpost.com/graphics/2017/world/global-waste/.

Zapata, Patrik, and María José Zapata Campos. 2018. "Cities, Institutional Entrepreneurship and the Emergence of New Environmental Policies: The Organizing of Waste Prevention in the City of Gothenburg, Sweden." *Environment and Planning C: Politics and Space* 37, no. 2: 339–359. https://doi.org/10.1177/2399654418783205.

6 Concluding remarks and future research

Our investigation began with the question of where *should* designers intervene in the current food system, such that they can contribute to shifting it towards a future of sustainable food security that is equitable and just. In this book, we introduced critical mapping, a problematizing, reflective approach to design inquiry that investigates how existing design outcomes (DOs) can be coupled to address a wicked problem. We used critical mapping to develop a "wicked solution" to the wicked problem of food insecurity, in order to see the current state of the system—in terms of what is effective (i.e., according to peer review) and to identify "leverage points" (Meadows 1999) or gaps for further innovation or appropriation of an existing sustainable food design outcome. First, we conducted an integrative literature review of peer-reviewed scholarship since 2009, the year that marks the founding of the International Food Design Society. We found 49 peer-reviewed publications from which we gleaned 73 DOs that epitomize sustainable food design. Next, to determine the places to intervene in the system to attain a more sustainable food future, we categorized the 73 DOs into four different quadrants in a wicked solution visualization. Out of the total 73 DOs, we grouped:

- 30 DOs in Quadrant A that have been funded or supported by public or private institutions for implementation within local geographic contexts. These DOs are top-down and localized emerging from a variety of professionals and have been implemented through cultural or commercial production limited to a geographic region.
- 16 DOs in Quadrant B that have been funded or supported by public or private institutions for implementation on a more widespread scale. These DOs are top-down and memetic emerging from a few professionals for widespread propagation across local or global, spatial boundaries, from households to nations.
- 14 DOs in Quadrant C that have been designed by citizens for implementation on a more widespread scale. These DOs are bottom-up and memetic emerging from citizens or grassroots organizations and have been implemented through cultural or commercial production in ways that permeate local or global, spatial boundaries, from communities to global networks.

DOI: 10.4324/9781003222026-7

- 13 DOs in Quadrant D that have been designed by citizens for implementation on a local scale. These DOs are bottom-up and memetic emerging from a citizen or grassroots community and have been implemented through cultural or commercial production in ways that are limited to a local context.

Collectively, these 73 sustainable food DOs provide a proof of concept for the wicked solution to food insecurity that enables us to see more clearly the state of the food system and where leverage points exist to intervene. The question becomes: what kinds of design interventions should be developed to move the food system towards a greater balance that is sustainable, secure, equitable, and just? What we see includes:

- Leverage points in sustainable food design activity in quadrant A's food system include the phases of production and processing and minimal activity in consumption, waste, and distribution. Most top-down activity seems to be occurring in the agricultural/aquacultural, communications, and accessibility phases of the food system.
- Leverage points in sustainable food design activity in quadrant B's food system include the phases of processing and distribution and relatively minimal activity in the rest of the phases.
- Leverage points in sustainable food design activity in quadrant C's food system include the phases of distribution and waste. The agri/aquaculture and communications phases had the most sustainable food design activity while the rest of the phases had relatively minimal activity.
- Leverage points in sustainable food design activity in quadrant D's food system include the phases of production, distribution, and consumption. The agricultural/aquacultural phase had the most sustainable food design activity while the rest of the phases had relatively minimal activity.

This critical mapping of sustainable food design is a process that can facilitate understanding of the design solutions in one's community, country, and around the world, and supports the important principle in Constanza-Chock's "design justice principles" (2020), that before implementing any new design solution, it is important to understand what is already being done in the community and also to recognize and honor traditional, Indigenous, and local knowledge and practices in this work.

The principles of "design justice" (Costanza-Chock 2020) listed in Chapter 1 provide a map to guide designers seeking to work to address food insecurity. This work benefits from a transdisciplinary team inclusive of designers and those working in food and most importantly community members most impacted by any design outcome, recognizing that everyone has lived experiences that add value to the collaborative design process. As Costanza-Chock (2020) indicates, the design's impact should take priority over any intention of the designers, who should serve as facilitators and share their knowledge, process, and tools with the communities they are working with. In this important work of social design, innovation, and appropriation, the goal is to work towards sustainable, community-led and -controlled outcomes, solutions that are non-exploitative and work towards reconnecting us with the earth and each other.

Limitations

The layered complexity of the food system, the ubiquitous nature of design, and the wide scope of sustainability inherently create limitations in this work. Within each community across the world, there are innovative design solutions to address food insecurity, equity, and justice that are not published in peer-reviewed journals. Multiple barriers exist in publishing peer-reviewed materials, including time, resources, access, and limited journals, that often prevent impactful, innovative efforts from being assessed and shared more widely. And, for many designers traditionally trained in creating artifacts, design research and publishing peer-reviewed papers about their DOs may be outside of their scope of experience or even interest. Oftentimes the work necessary to create, implement, and sustain these design solutions with limited resources prevents effectuation through research or further amplification of the work through published peer-reviewed journals, though some may be found written about in gray literature (i.e., magazines or newspapers, and other news outlets and social media). The selected DOs in this book were limited to peer-reviewed articles to share a selection of what currently exists in a scholarly realm, and to encourage designers of all breeds to publish peer-reviewed research on the subject in the future to expand the critical mapping of sustainable food design, which can be done in local, regional, national, and global spaces, and to bring more designers' diverse voices into scholarly conversations where important decisions are being made that will impact the future of society and our environment.

Indeed, these selected DOs do not represent all peer-reviewed DOs addressing food insecurity. The field of sustainable food design is still emergent, and this research limited its scope to reviewing peer-reviewed articles beginning in 2009, the year of the founding of the International Food Design Society, through an integrative literature review outlined in Chapter 1. Other DOs certainly exist that were published prior to 2009. With the field of sustainable food design still emerging, the operationalization of it is still evolving, requiring the narrowing of DOs to be further curated based on our 8E's of sustainability criteria, with a focus on sustainable food design for food security and specifically through the authors' lenses of experience as visual communication designers who are scholars. The DOs were organized in each quadrant by phases of the food system, but as noted in Chapter 1, not all phases of the food system are represented in each quadrant as a result of our not identifying any peer-reviewed DOs for that phase from the integrative literature review we conducted. Based on the information we found about each DO, we placed it in one category of the food system in a particular quadrant, recognizing that some could be placed in multiple categories of the same quadrant and possibly multiple quadrants.

This collection of sustainable food DOs recognizes that design is a broad term. It was applied to peer-reviewed articles and research conducted with a transdisciplinary lens, identifying DOs outside of what might be considered traditional design fields, conducted by researchers not necessarily considered designers or not self-identifying as such. DOs were primarily derived from qualitative research with DOs that may be relevant for a transdisciplinary team, including designers conducting critical mapping of sustainable food DOs. Based on the information extracted from the peer-reviewed sources, some DOs may provide more context than others, and readers are encouraged to seek the source to find out more. DOs were only considered from articles in English, though additional peer-reviewed content exists in other languages.[1] It is acknowledged that this limits the broad cross-cultural critical mapping we intended. Finally, as the field of sustainable food design emerges and as society continues to be impacted by world events, some of the relevant DOs included may not endure or may be altered in some way. On the one hand, this may be an indication that more effort is needed to address sustainability. On the other hand, sustainable food DOs that have not endured lie dormant in refereed publications like the seeds of wild plants before emerging and propagating.

While some of these DOs exist globally in different contexts and have universal qualities that can be appropriated to communities across the world, not all of these DOs are relevant or applicable to all spaces. Sustainable design innovation begins by identifying what assets already exist and work within a specific community or space. Who is already doing what work in the community affected, and how can designers work together across cultures to spark the energy of collective creativity and address these issues? As indicated by the wicked solutions four-quadrant grid, limitations can occur for designers dependent on the quadrant where their work or employment aligns, but as described in this book, the goal is to move designers and others beyond solution-focused superficial DOs that become unsustainable without the investment and engagement of the community affected, perpetuating social problems.

Manzini (2014) describes designers leading bottom-up social innovation as having the flexible ability to design with and for communities. In designing with communities, designers can serve as facilitators, collectively engaging community stakeholders to co-design (62). The designer's skill set in this scenario is the ability to connect social actors and lead participatory engagement in building out shared visions while also identifying existing resources in the community to activate and combine. Manzini describes designing for communities as observing typologies of collaborative service, identifying strengths and weaknesses, and intervening and developing solutions where gaps and challenges exist (62). Designers develop solutions for collaboration and other artifacts that may increase access and effectiveness (62). Included in the designer's skill set is the ability to simply "make things happen" (Manzini 2014, 66) by starting new conversations through "discursive design" (Tharp and Tharp 2019) or by "shaping dynamic social conversations about what to do and how" (Manzini 2014, 66), like developing visual thinking approaches for building interpersonal relationships across geographic and cultural distances (Murdoch-Kitt and Emans 2020).

We intend our critical mapping of sustainable food DOs to spark a new conversation in design that centers equity and justice in the pursuit of design solutions to perennial societal problems. We intend critical mapping for sustainable design framework to be used by a variety of community and professional stakeholders including those who may or may not identify as designers to 1) understand and apply critical mapping of sustainable DOs to developing their own wicked solutions to other wicked problems, to determine how and where to intervene, 2) explore sustainable DOs that have been effectuated that can be appropriated or adapted to new geographic, community, and domestic spaces, and 3) identify the areas where more peer-reviewed design research may be needed on how to make local food systems more efficient and resilient to external factors.

Conducting a transdisciplinary design inquiry

An important question emerges from our pilot study: how can a designer participate in sustainable food design moving forward?

The question of how to participate in sustainable food design can be addressed through the development of a research agenda for collaborative and transdisciplinary design inquiry that engages the community. In Table 6.1[2], we attempt to "operationalize the components of a research agenda with questions, tools, and sources in which to engage when developing a viable research plan of action" (Bennett 2019) that can facilitate one's participation in sustainable food design.

Bennett (2019) proposed this process to define and execute a research agenda based on an autoethnographic look at her 21-year experience as a design scholar at a research university. Other research inquiry experiences and algorithms may exist, and more opportunities are needed in the discipline to compile those perspectives to delineate a clear path to transdisciplinary research for *all* designers that is fruitful for the sake of humanity (including the environment). In the meantime, we propose later in this chapter the development of an open platform that facilitates multimodal access to the wicked solutions to wicked problems including food insecurity.

The question of what kinds of design interventions should be developed can be deduced by analyzing the charts in Figures 6.1, 6.2, 6.3, and 6.4 that categorize the 73 sustainable DOs in terms of their design form and the quadrant of the wicked solution to food security that they fit.

Figure 6.1 maps the different categories of design represented by the 30 sustainable food DOs (out of 73) grouped in Quadrant A. It shows more activity in the design categories of experience and communications, respectively, and minimal activity in the categories of object, environment, context, systems, and futures. In the design categories of identity, service, and interaction, we found no activity.

Figure 6.2 maps the different categories of design represented by the 16 sustainable food DOs (out of 73) grouped in Quadrant B. It shows the same relatively high amount of activity in the design categories of object and experience, and minimal activity in the categories of environment, communications, context,

Table 6.1 Developing a Research Agenda: Components, Questions, Tools, and Sources

Components	Questions	Tools	Sources
Topic	Which issues in society interest you and why? Is there a challenge that you or your community experiences that you might want to address through research?	Literature review: What do we know about this topic? Which questions about this topic have been investigated previously? Informal observation of context	Broad array of materials including popular media, texts, journals, interdisciplinary peer-review articles/ journals, etc. Private and public contexts of life experiences
Research Question	What specific question do you aim to address? Will answering it make an original contribution to knowledge? If your question aims to test a theory, can the question be answered with either "yes" or "no"? If so, then it is falsifiable.	Literature review: What research has already been conducted in this area that can inform the development of your own research question?	Interdisciplinary peer-review articles/ journals, books, and gray literature. The latter can be sourced for evidence that confirms the dire need to address the question.
Hypothesis/ Objective	What do you propose as a solution or suitable outcome? Which design resources can address the question? Who are the stakeholders affected by the question and what role can/will they play in answering the question?	Literature review: Creativity and informal/formal observation (through ethnography and fieldwork) and other qualitative, quantitative, or mixed methods approaches	Interdisciplinary peer-review articles/ journals. A local or remote field site
Rationale	Why is the question important? Why is answering it essential? Which community benefits from the answer and how?	Literature review: What existing facts or statistics show the significance of this line of inquiry or the anticipated outcomes?	Credible sources for statistics, and facts (e.g., Pew Research Center; governmental or organizational research reports)

(*Continued*)

Table 6.1 (Continued)

Components	Questions	Tools	Sources
Theory	Which existing theory contributes to helping you understand the challenge or your hypothesis and scholarly objectives or directs you to an appropriate existing methodology or method for carrying out the research project?	Literature review: Which art, design, literary, marketing, social, or humanities theories can inform this study?	Interdisciplinary literature on contemporary or classic theories that relate to your topic or can inform your question or your approach to answering the question
Methodology	Which methodology and methods are most appropriate for answering the question? What kind of data do you need to gather, generate, or review to address your question?	Literature review: Which past studies related to your study have been conducted? Which method(s) were used?	Refereed journal articles and informational reading on methods that are unfamiliar to you
Budget	Where might/will you apply for funding to support or enable your research?	Funding databases at your institution or within professional organizations; governmental funding databases	Government Private companies Crowdfunding Professional organizations internal and external to your discipline (e.g., Design Incubation)
Dissemination	What are the flagship, refereed journals, publishers, conferences for the publication and presentation of scholarly work in your discipline and related disciplines? Which cohort of readers are you targeting?	Academia, Researchgate, Google Scholar, Editing: Grammarly Writing: Scrivener, writing groups and retreats	Peer-review journals and conferences in professional organizations within one's discipline and external to one's discipline

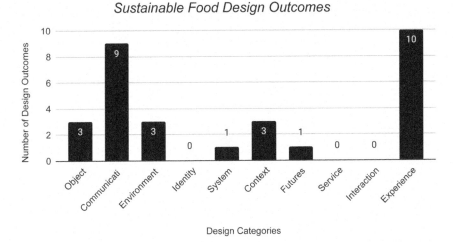

Figure 6.1 Quadrant A's sustainable food DOs grouped by the type of design form that they represent. Image courtesy of Audrey G. Bennett.

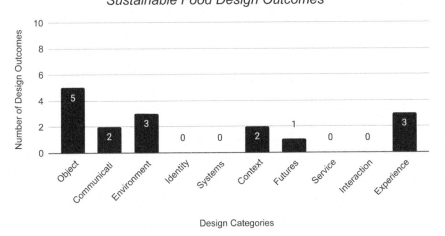

Figure 6.2 Quadrant B's sustainable food DOs grouped by the type of design form that they represent. Image courtesy of Audrey G. Bennett.

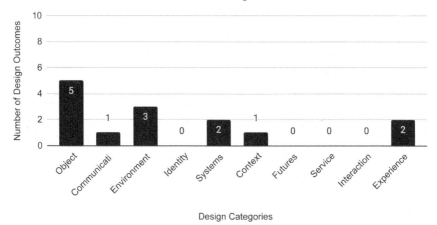

Figure 6.3 Quadrant C's sustainable food DOs grouped by the type of design form that they represent. Image courtesy of Audrey G. Bennett.

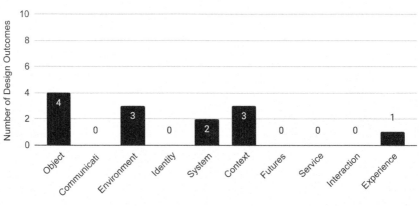

Figure 6.4 Quadrant D's sustainable food DOs grouped by the type of design form that they represent. Image courtesy of Audrey G. Bennett.

and futures. In the design categories of identity, systems, service, and interaction, we found no activity.

Figure 6.3 maps the different categories of design represented by the 14 sustainable food DOs (out of 73) grouped in Quadrant C. It shows that while sustainable food design activity is relatively abundant around the development or creation of objects and environments, there is minimal activity regarding sustainable food design communications, systems, contexts, and experiences. Furthermore, our integrative literature review revealed no DOs taking design form as identities, futures, services, and interactions.

Figure 6.4 maps the different categories of design represented by the 13 sustainable food DOs (out of 73) grouped in Quadrant D. It shows that while sustainable food design activity is relatively high in the categories of objects, environments, and contexts, there is minimal activity in the categories of sustainable food design systems and experiences. Furthermore, our integrative literature review revealed no design communications, identities, futures, services, and interactions emerging from peer-reviewed research findings.

Figures 6.1–6.4 suggest that there is a more top-down sustainable food design activity that may be due to the availability of more resources and power to deploy them. These figures suggest that some sub-disciplines of design are participating more or less than others in the fight for food security, equity, and justice. Finally, the figures imply that the question of what kinds of design interventions should be developed in the fight for food security that is equitable and just may be adequately addressed by the inclusion of more design perspectives in the evolving conversation on sustainable food design and its future, particularly the voices of designers who contribute to multiple realms of the design categories. Those who seem to be contributing the least, if anything, to sustainable food design activity across the four quadrants are designers of identities, interactions, and services.

However, why these designers are missing from the quadrants may have many reasons already discussed earlier in this chapter. Some designers are not engaging in transdisciplinary research on sustainable food design, or they are engaging in research but not disseminating findings in peer-reviewed journals. Yet another reason could be that they are engaging in creative practice as research outside of academia where they develop design interventions that are deployed publicly often without peer review.

When diving into an emerging field that straddles the wide berth of food, design, and sustainability, it is necessary to start somewhere, as limiting as it may be. We started by intentionally choosing DOs from peer-reviewed work to emphasize the importance of evidence-based design, but also to recognize how this process contradicts our underlying aim to be inclusive. Thus, our future research described below seeks to address this issue by providing a venue for access to scholarly and academic resources and networking. For now, by building a small repertoire of existing peer-reviewed DOs, we begin to establish a baseline, to indicate this is what exists, this is what we found, these are the patterns we are seeing in regard to sustainable food design. And as designers we know that by inviting others in, we can collectively see more, and iterate forward together to strengthen the work and build a resource archive of networks within networks. This book serves as an invitation to designers, food researchers, community partners, and others to collaborate on sustainable food design research moving forward. We invite them to share their resulting innovative work through peer-reviewed scholarship. It is our hope that this book serves as an impetus—so that in the near future, an entire new set of sustainable food design peer-reviewed DOs would be available to populate a possible future edition of this book, and in doing so, begin to solve the wicked problem of food insecurity.

Future research

As poverty-induced environmental and socio-economic inequities continue to challenge the health of marginalized communities, we recognize the need for research findings that can make positive and broad impacts on impoverished communities desperate for collective action and resources. The potential impact of our research on developing a wicked solution to food insecurity visualization includes 1) an analysis of the current state of the food system by socio-economically diverse stakeholders to identify gaps for "tuning" the system through further innovation or appropriation, and 2) networking among socio-economically diverse stakeholders that enables health equity for underserved and economically challenged communities and "generative justice" or the bottom-up generation and circulation of value through unalienated forms (Eglash 2016).

However, existing socio-economic and environmental disparities may hinder ease of access to knowledge in scholarly forms, like this book, and the lack of access to these sustainable food design exemplars contributes to perpetuating food insecurity. Thus, we posit that what is missing is multimodal interaction with our wicked solution to food insecurity. Multimodality describes the combination of communication modes, including human and non-human technologies, to relay information and meaning cross-culturally and broadly or expansively (Van Leeuwen 2011). In addition, interactive aesthetics (Bennett 2002a; Bennett 2002b; Bennett 2021) was introduced to explain the phenomenon of cross-cultural, remote, and local interaction in the graphic design process towards social justice. Our future work aims to integrate these concepts with critical mapping and operationalize them in the context of local communities struggling with food insecurity. We posit that critically mapping a wicked solution for multimodal access through interactive aesthetics can facilitate access to sustainable food DOs more inclusively, pervasively, and fluidly.

The future wicked solution to food insecurity visualization we imagine is one that would employ interactive aesthetics to implement a web-based platform that facilitates cross-disciplinary and lay-design experts plotting their own assets or seeking design solutions to local contexts. This embedded information would be systemically linked and retrieved using communication technologies (e.g., smartphones) to deploy resources that might be inserted into marginalized communities. This type of deployment would parallel the addition of emergency phones strategically placed along the footpaths of a college campus for enhanced security. To this end, the first author in collaboration with undergraduate and graduate researchers at the University of Michigan has started to develop an interactive visualization system called "wsdom.io" (pronounced "wisdom dot eye oh") that represents the fluidity of the interventional process, permitting one to see the ebb and flow of the wicked solution to food insecurity through sustainable food design in-process and over time.

However, we acknowledge the inherent limitations with digital platforms, even those that are open. Personal and public communication technologies (e.g., computers, smartphones, and even mapping resources within an open-source, web-based platform) do not guarantee access to the underserved communities most in need of them. Therefore, our future work on the wicked solution to food insecurity will entail evaluating the wsdom.io platform's ability to enable all stakeholders—marginalized local communities, designers, and other professional stakeholders—to locate and share food assets broadly with each other. Primary research needs to be conducted through local community workshops that engage community members in identifying, analyzing, and plotting existing local food design assets not already included in the evolving wicked solution to food insecurity, and adapting existing design assets that may be relevant to and appropriate for a local community context.

⁂

Four years after the founding of the International Food Design Society, design historian Victor Margolin encouraged consideration of both food and design as embedded in differing social, economic, and academic systems, and advocated for initiating a mapping process to define the scope of each system and identify points of connection between the two. In this way, he notes we can expand the conceptual space of each field and consequently discover themes and issues that may result in new methodological, narrative, and activist approaches by scholars in both of them (2013). The conceptual space of creative problem solving by designers is indeed expanding to include complex societal problems, including food insecurity, that require a new methodological framework. Manzini (2014; 2015) argues that while "social innovation design" has always existed, there is a particular need to focus on it today as global society transitions to sustainability and scurries to deal with its current economic crisis among other wicked problems—complex challenges for which there is no singular solution. Wicked problems tend to be transdisciplinary in nature, and require a more robust design inquiry process than traditional creative problem solving provides.

By "robust design" we do not mean the hunt for the perfect solution. Indeed, the very meaning of "wicked" is the fact that solving the problem will require many experiments in multiple domains. But one must also be wary of the ways that reward systems work for designers; too often creating variation simply for the sake of novelty or a fresh look is promoted over long-term iteration. The distinction really comes down to iteration. Real design research turns innovation into a feedback loop, one that many times may be humbling; but that is how wicked solutions have to progress, in a kind of Darwinian process of many mutations and much weeding out. And as in Darwin, the key is the relationship between those adaptations and their context: success is only meaningful if we understand which quadrant it is located in and how that particular confluence of resources (vertical axis) and dissemination structures (horizontal axis) gave rise to the design's sustainability. That is what makes peer-reviewed scholarship a crucial component. It asks for help from our critics in finding areas of improvement and for confirmation that what we see as progress is indeed that. This book advocates for harvesting the wisdom of peer-reviewed scholarship to set the stage for an evidence-driven design future that can facilitate more transformative social impact through sustainable design.

Notes

1 Juri et al. (2022) note that "Revista Latinoamericana de Food Design (Urdinola-Serna 2020), was founded in 2020 and features peer-reviewed articles mainly in Spanish and Portuguese."
2 Reprinted from *Decipher, Volume 1*, part of the Dialogue Proceedings Series, with permission from the AIGA Design Educators Community (DEC).

Bibliography

Bennett, Audrey. 2002a. "Dynamic Interactive Aesthetics." *The Journal of Design Research* 2 no. 2: 91–104. https://doi.org/10.1504/JDR.2002.009820.

———. 2002b. "Interactive Aesthetics." *Design Issues* 18, no. 3: 62–69. https://doi.org/10.1162/074793602320223307.

———. 2012. "Good Design is Good Social Change: Envisioning an Age of Accountability in Communication Design Education." *Visible Language* 46 no. 1/2: 66–79.

———. 2019. "Defining and Executing a Graphic Design Research Agenda (If Only for the Sake of Justice)." *Iridescent: Icograda Journal of Design* 2, no. 3: 2–10. https://doi.org/10.1080/19235003.2012.11428510.

———. 2021. "Agentic Design: An Emergent Approach to Generative Justice." *New Design Ideas* 5, no. 1: 5–20. http://jomardpublishing.com/UploadFiles/Files/journals/NDI/V5N1/BennettA.pdf.

Bougette, Patrice, Oliver Budzinsky, and Frédéric Marty. 2019. "Exploitative Abuse and Abuse of Economic dependence: What Can We Learn from an Industrial Organization Approach?" *Revue d'economie politique* 129 no. 2: 261–286. https://doi.org/10.3917/redp.292.0261.

Buchanan, Richard. 1992. "Wicked Problems in Design Thinking." *Design Issues* 8, no. 2: 5–21. https://doi.org/10.2307/1511637.

Chase, Lisa, and Vern Grubinger. 2014. *Food, Farms, and Community: Exploring Food Systems*. Durham, NH: University of New Hampshire Press.

Churchman, C. West. 1967. "Guest Editorial: Wicked Problems." *Management Science* 14, no. 4: B141–B142. https://www.jstor.org/stable/2628678.

Costanza-Chock, Sasha. 2020. *Design Justice: Community-led Practices to Build the Worlds We Need*. Cambridge, MA: MIT Press.

Eglash, Ron. 2016. "An Introduction to Generative Justice." *Revista Teknokultura* 13, no. 2: 369–404. http://doi.org/10.5209/rev_TEKN.2016.v13.n2.52847.

Juri, Silvana, Sonia Massari, and Pedro Reissig. 2022. "Editorial: Food+ Design-Transformations via Transversal and Transdisciplinary Approaches." In*DRS2022: Bilbao* edited by D. Lockton, S. Lenzi, P. Hekkert, A. Oak, J. Sádaba, and P. Lloyd, 25. https://doi.org/10.21606/drs.2022.1060.

Manzini, Ezio. 2014. "Making Things Happen: Social Innovation and Design." *Design Issues* 30, no. 1: 57–66. http://doi.org/10.1162/DESI_a_00248.

Manzini, Ezio. 2015. *Design, When Everybody Designs: An Introduction to Design for Social Innovation.* Translated by Rachel Coad. Cambridge, MA: MIT Press.

Meadows, Donella H. 1999. *Leverage Points: Places to Intervene in a System.* Hartland, VT: The Sustainability Institute. https://donellameadows.org/wp-content/userfiles/Leverage_Points.pdf.

Murdoch-Kitt, Kelly M., and Denielle J. Emans. 2020. *Intercultural Collaboration by Design: Drawing from Differences, Distances, and Disciplines Through Visual Thinking.* London: Routledge.

Margolin, Victor. 2013. "Design Studies and Food Studies: Parallels and Intersections." *Design and Culture* 5, no. 3: 375–392. https://doi.org/10.2752/175470813X13705953612327.

Serna, Diana Urdinola. 2020. "N°1 Revista latinoamericana de food design comes lo que eres." *Revista Latinoamericana de Food Design (ReLaFD)* 1: 1–265.

Tharp, Bruce M., and Stephanie M. Tharp. 2019. *Discursive Design: Critical, Speculative, and Alternative things.* Cambridge, MA: MIT Press.

Van Leeuwen, Theo. 2011. "Multimodality." In *The Routledge Handbook of Applied Linguistics*, edited by James Simpson. London: Routledge. https://doi.org/10.4324/9780203835654.ch47.

Afterword

by Francesca Zampollo

Designers hold the power to bring into the world what the world has never seen before. Designers hold the power to change what needs improving, revise what needs defining, develop what needs clarity, and amend what needs cleaning. Designers hold this power because designers have the tools, skills, and knowledge to *design*.

As Spider-Man's uncle reminds us all, "with great power comes great responsibility." Wisdom can come from anywhere and this remark to me has always spoken about design. In holding these "powers," these tools, skills, and knowledge, designers also hold the biggest responsibility. We are the people proposing and often actualizing change, therefore we have the responsibility about the type of change we want to propose and actualize.

The past hundred years or so has seen quite a bit of mindless design. We have witnessed thoughtless, ridiculous, and sometimes shameful outcomes from architecture, product manufacturing, marketing, etc. Fortunately we see it less and less, because more and more *design* is being pursued, taught, used. Today the damage done to planet Earth and the incongruence between the society in which we want to live and the society in which we actually live are more and more clear. For this reason, today the design discipline is filled with people who feel this impending need to follow that inner flame that calls us to change lives, to bring smiles, to better society, to bring our light into the world, and to make this world a little better than we found it. Today the design discipline is filled with people who understand the responsibility that comes from *doing design* and that are ready to take action.

The book you hold in your hands is the result of the work of such people, who have understood the responsibility designers hold and who are following their own call to make this world a little better than they found it. Firstly, this book identifies the path worth walking for designers, the path of localized design innovation, security, equity, and justice. These are the goals that emerge when we zoom out from any company brief, for example, apply a systemic approach, and understand the full spectrum of implications of any design choice we make. Secondly, this book uses and gives a tool to make sense of complexity and to use such complexity—inherent to any project to which we apply a zoomed-out systemic view—to make informed decisions. Critical mapping in fact helps make sense of complex information and aids the process of outlining the trajectory for our projects. I believe this method could very well be incorporated into what I call food design thinking, the food-specific design thinking process I have been working on for the past ten years. Thirdly, the book is itself a repository of information and inspiration: a map of current design work, applications, and innovation, as well as critical analysis for all of us to use and refer to.

Finally, this book does all of this in the specific design discipline of food design, to which I have dedicated my entire career. To see work like that presented in this book applied to the Food Design discipline fills me with joy, humility, respect, and hope.

I consider food the most inspiring material to design with because it is meant to be consumed, and therefore because it disappears. Most designers designing with tangible materials design stuff that lasts years or centuries. Food designers designing with edible materials don't. They have to design for memories, because those are the only elements that may last years or decades.

I consider food design the most exciting design discipline because of the variety of outcomes one could design, the result of the different food design sub-disciplines one could design for: *Food Product Design* where we design food for manufacturing: *design for food* where we design products to prepare, cook, serve, contain, and transport food; and *design with food* where we design the edible material itself, its texture, look, flavors, colors, etc. (for example what comes from gastronomy and food science); *Food Space Design* where we design the space where eating or cooking happens; *Eating Design* where we design the entire eating situation (with the term "eating situation," I broadly mean any situation in which there is someone eating something, which incorporates designing eating events and beyond); *Food Service Design* where we design food services (e.g., restaurants, cafes, supermarkets, food trucks, hot dog cards, etc.); *Critical Food Design* (or speculative food design) where we design with the goal of "making people think" about issues that are for us relevant or pressing; *Food System Design* where we design our intervention in the food system at hand; and finally, of course, *Sustainable Food Design*. The risk of creating a sub-discipline is that it then takes the pressure off the mainstream: surely we want every food design project to include consideration of sustainability, systemic effects, critical thinking, and so on. But that tension between expanding through sub-disciplines and integrating into the main is part of the reason why Food Design has such a powerful array of possibilities.

I consider Food Design the most exciting design discipline because it is where we could apply positive change in the most immediate and fast-spreading way, because food is in everybody's life, every day. If we all ate food that is truly economically, socially, and environmentally sustainable, we would change the world tomorrow. If we designed food products, services, systems that are truly economically, socially, and environmentally sustainable, we would change the world tomorrow.

I consider Food Design the most exciting design discipline because it seems to me to be the space with the most potential to bring light into issues that are rooted into the core of being a human being. Food is one of our most basic needs like water, air, and shelter. Food is one of our most basic human rights, but unfortunately and incredibly still is not available to each human being on this planet. We all need it, we don't all have it. We all should have access to growing our own food, but we don't all have that either. Food dependency seems to have been spread more than food independency, both for individuals as well as for communities. Today we see and recognize the geographical vastness, and the physiological, psychological, and social depth of this issue and are willing to implement change. Today we see more and more *design* for food sovereignty, and this book helps us in this movement.

This book brings a tool and framework for sustainable food design, to *do* food design through the lens of sustainability in its threefold composition: economic, social, and environmental sustainability. Moreover this book is interested in walking a specific path of design that leads towards localized design innovation, food security, equity, and justice. The content of this book is therefore written by, and for, people who know what type of impact they want to have in the world. This is what excites me the most: not only the type of impact pursued here, but also awareness of this interest and drive.

What has become most obvious to me throughout the years is that design has a twofold effect. From the perspective of those who *do* design, design moves from within to without, and from without to within. When designers design, they—these people, these conscious human beings with a personality, a life, a past, preferences, and stories—produce something from their knowledge and skills that goes out into the world and has an impact on the planet and on people: from within to without. At the same time the act of *designing* itself, the act of creating something, as well as the outcome itself of what we design has an impact on designers themselves: from without to within, where the "without" is the design project, the design process, and the outcome, and the "within" is the designer's personal life journey. *Designing* changes the world as well as designers themselves. This without-to-within effect happens because—and this is something not many designers really think about and incorporate—design is a conscious process.

Designing is the process of making a series of choices. Most specifically, designing is the process of consciously making a series of choices, which means that designers know why they're choosing what they're choosing, and that they are aware—or should be aware—of the impact of these choices on the outcome itself, on their business, on individuals and societies, and on the planet. When awareness is brought to the without-to-within effect, designers become aware of the impact that the project and each design choice they make has on themselves, on the person that they are. When we realize that each choice we make defines who we are because it influences who we are, we also realize that each choice we make can define the person that we want to become and the impact we want to have in the world. With each choice we make in life, from the smallest to the biggest, and whether part of a design project or not, we can ask ourselves: "does this align with who I want to be and what I want to bring to the world?" When we bring this awareness to the creative process, with each answer we define who we want to be and what we want to bring to the world. As a consequence, the outcome of the design process speaks of who we are, the project has an impact on us (without-to-within), and we have a conscious impact on the world (within-to-without) that is aligned with who we want to be and what we want to bring to this world.

Defining who we want to be and what we want to bring to this world is the essence of our spiritual journey as human beings, whether the choices that we make are about what to have for breakfast or part of our design project, whatever the outcome. We all walk our spiritual journey, whether we are aware of it or not, whether we think about it or not. Whether we pay attention to our choices or not, they define who we are and who we want to be. Since design—once again—is a conscious act, we get to be aware of our choices, and we can choose who we want to be through design itself. When we are aware of the full impact of our design choices we can fully embrace that responsibility we know comes with our "powers" and use them consciously and conscientiously.

Awareness of our spiritual journey through design can be cultivated, but spirituality is already embedded into design. Therefore, to what was the well-known sustainability triangle, where the three corners are economic sustainability, environmental sustainability, and social sustainability, I've added a fourth corner and lifted it up to make it connect to all three other corners, transforming this 2D sustainability triangle into a 3D sustainability pyramid. The fourth vertex I added is spiritual sustainability, acknowledging not only how design can explicitly

Sustainability Pyramid ©Francesca Zampollo

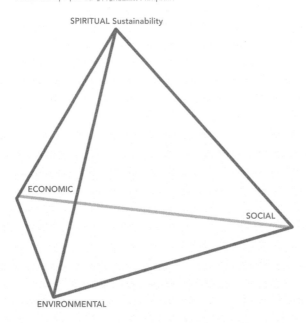

Figure A.1 Sustainability pyramid. ©Francesca Zampollo.

accompany people on their own journey of self-discovery, but also the spiritual journey of designers themselves and how what they design impacts their own lives too. Design can be an act of self-actualization (Maslow's highest human need).

The content provided in this book provides the type of information and tools that someone interested in pursuing spiritual sustainability will need. When interested in being aware of the impact of our choices on ourselves as the person we're creating (or designing!) and the world we want to create, inevitably the path towards equity and justice lays itself in front of us, and for those of us who walk this path in the food design discipline, this path leads to food security and food sovereignty.

I therefore commend Jennifer and Audrey for writing this book, for their time, effort, accuracy, and perspicacity in conducting the research that brought us to these findings, and finally for their kindness and generosity in sharing them with the community.

Francesca Zampollo

Author of *Food Design Thinking for Product and Services*, *Think like a Food Designer*, and *Food Design Voices 2022*. Design and food design consultant, facilitator, and teacher. Author of the Food Design Thinking methodology. Founder of the Online School of Food Design.

Appendix I
Publications from integrative literature review

A total of 49 publications—including peer-reviewed journal articles, conference proceedings' articles, edited books, and monographs—from which sustainable food design outcomes were gleaned that fit the 8E's criteria. The far right column shows the part of the food system that the peer-reviewed publication and its design outcome(s) address.

Key

WS# = Wicked Solution Number

	Peer-reviewed Publication	Type of Publication	Source	Quadrant(s)	WS#	Food Category
1	*Agriculture and Human Values*	journal	Hart et al. 2016	B	34	agriculture
			Healy and Dawson 2019	A	6	agriculture
			Zepeda and Reznickova 2017	A	24	accessibility
2	*American Journal of Public Health*	journal	Rose and O'Malley 2020	A	4	agriculture
3	*Applied Geography*	journal	Corrigan 2011	C	48	agriculture
4	*Appetite*	journal	Martin et al. 2017	C	48	agriculture
5	*Arctic*	journal	Thompson et al. 2018	D	63	agriculture
6	*BMC Public Health*	journal	Su 2015	A	23	accessibility
7	*British Food Journal*	journal	Chapman et al. 2011	B	36	communications
			Lindberg et al. 2014	B	46	waste
8	*Business and Society Review*	journal	Ahmed et al. 2017	C	60	consumption
9	*By the People: Designing a Better America*	book	Smith 2016	D	69	accessibility
				D	70	accessibility
				C	49	agriculture
10	Carrotcity.org	online database	Gorgolewski et al. 2011	B	31	agriculture
11	*Cultivating Food Justice: Race, Class, and Sustainability*	book	Morales 2011	C	59	accessibility
12	*Design for the other 90%: Cities*	book	Smith 2011	D	71	waste
13	*Design Issues*	journal	Manzini 2014	A	3	agriculture
14	*e-Journal of Social and Behavioral Research in Business*	journal	Hartling 2019	B	33	agriculture
15	*Egyptian Journal of Aquatic Research*	journal	Sunny et al. 2019	C	47	agriculture
16	*Environment and Planning C: Politics and Space*	journal	Zapata and Zapata Campos 2018	D	73	waste
17	*Ethnography*	journal	Barnard 2011	C	58	accessibility
18	*Food Activist Handbook*	book	Berlow 2015	C	52	production
19	*Food and Nutrition Bulletin*	journal	Busse et al. 2017	B	41	accessibility

(Continued)

	Peer-reviewed Publication	Type of Publication	Source	Quadrant(s)	WS#	Food Category
20	Food Bigger than the Plate (exhibition catalog)	book	Flood and Sloan 2019	B	38	communications
				C	50	agriculture
				C	51	processing
				C	53	communications
				C	55	communications
				C	56	communications
				C	57	accessibility
				D	64	agriculture
				D	72	waste
21	Food Democracy: Critical Lessons in Food, Communication, Desgn and Art	book	Vodeb 2017	B	39	communications
22	Food Security	journal	Leakey 2018	A	1	agriculture
23	Globalizations	journal	Figueroa 2015	B	40	accessibility
24	International Journal of Behavioral Nutrition and Physical Activity	journal	Brennan et al. 2021	A	17	communications
25	International Journal of Design	journal	Lee et al. 2020	A	12	communications
26	International Journal of Entrepreneurship and Small Business	journal	Ratten and Dana 2015	D	67	processing
					68	communications
27	International Journal of Environmental Research and Public Health	journal	Mikkelsen et al. 2018	A	18	communications
			Toft et al. 2018	A	18	communications
28	International Journal of Food Design	journal	Campagnaro and Ceraolo 2017	A	29	waste
			Reynolds 2017	A	11	communications
			Bordewijk and Shifferstein 2020	A	5	agriculture
			Leer 2020	A	30	waste
			Mouritsen and Styrbæk 2020	A	21	communications
				A	28	consumption
29	International Journal of Urban Sciences	journal	Kauppi et al. 2019	B	42	consumption
30	Iridescent	journal	Kim 2017	C	48	agriculture
			Carlson and Peake 2013	A	9	communications

No.	Source	Type	Citation	Code	No.	Category
31	*JMIR mHealth and uHealth*	journal	O'Malley et al. 2014	A	19	communications
			Gallaher et al. 2015	D	66	agriculture
			Santino 2021	A	10	communications
32	*Journal of Design, Business & Society*	journal	Ballantyne-Brodie et al. 2015	B	40	accessibility
33	*Journal of Enterprising Communities*	journal	Kawharu 2019	D	65	agriculture
34	*Journal of Hunger and Environmental Nutrition*	journal	Frank et al. 2021	A	26	accessibility
			Shukaitis and Elnakib 2021	A	20	communications
			Reyes and Ohri-Vachaspati 2021	A	27	consumption
35	*Journal of Planning Education and Research*	journal	Pothukuchi 2015	D	61	agriculture
36	*Journal of Public Affairs*	journal	Fernhaber et al. 2018	A	22	accessibility
37	*Local Environment*	journal	Furness and Gallaher 2018	C	48	agriculture
38	*New Design Ideas*	journal	Gray et al. 2014	D	62	agriculture
39	*Nordic Design Research*	conference proceedings	Laidlaw and Magee 2016	C	47	agriculture
			Johnson and Eglash 2021	A	25	accessibility
			Wilde et al. 2021	C	54	communications
40	*Politics and Governance*	journal	Prost 2019	B	40	accessibility
41	Proceedings of the 95th International Conference on Communities & Technologies—Transforming Communities	conference proceedings	Heitlinger et al. 2019	A	7	agriculture
42	Proceedings of the XXVI ISPIM Conference—Shaping the Frontiers of Innovation Management	conference proceedings	Nobre and Biscaia 2015	A	2	agriculture
43	*Progress in Community Health Partnerships: Research, Education, and Action*	journal	Nu and Bersamin 2017	A	16	communications
44	*Renewable Agriculture and Food Systems*	journal	Weissman and Potteiger 2020	A	14	communications

(*Continued*)

	Peer-reviewed Publication	Type of Publication	Source	Quadrant(s)	WS#	Food Category
45	Socio-Economic Planning Sciences	journal	Massari et al. 2021	A	15	communications
				B	44	waste
46	Sustainability	journal	Buehler and Junge 2016	B	35	production
			Feleke et al. 2021	B	32	agriculture
					42	consumption
					43	consumption
					45	waste
47	Urban Design International	journal	Nemat et al. 2020	A	13	communications
48	Urban Ecosystems	journal	de la Salle 2019	B	37	communications
49	USEP: Journal of Research Information in Civil Engineering	journal	Gregory et al. 2016	C	48	agriculture
			Yahaya and Akande 2018	A	8	distribution

Appendix II
Design outcomes grouped by quadrant

Quadrant A

Local, sustainable food design funded or supported by public and private institutions

WS#	Design Outcome	Food Category	Design Category	Country	Year of Creation	Source
1	3-step solution	subsistence farming strategy	agriculture	experience	Cameroon	n.d.	Leakey 2018
2	Brazilian Mandala System	family farming system	agriculture	system	Brazil	2000	Nobre and Biscaia 2015
3	Feeding Milan	participatory design with the largest agricultural park	agriculture	experience	Italy	2010	Manzini 2014
4	Food Access 3.0	food access intervention	agriculture	context	United States	1993	Rose and O'Malley 2020
5	Rainforest preservation	social enterprise to preserve rainforests	agriculture	environment	Indonesia	2020	Bordewijk and Shifferstein 2020
6	Seed to Kitchen Collaborative	participatory plant-breeding method	agriculture	experience	United States	2013	Healy and Dawson 2019
7	Speculative and participatory design approach for facilitating bottom-up, smart urban food-growing futures	co-designing with urban food growers	agriculture	futures	Britain	2018	Heitlinger et al. 2019
8	Pot-in-pot cooler	energy efficient food and drug cooling device	distribution	object	Nigeria	2018	Yahaya and Akande 2018
9	Communicating food recall information to consumers	strategies for communicating food recall information to millennials	communications	communications	United States	2012	Carlson and Peake 2013

No.	Name	Description			Country	Year	Citation
10	EMERGE CT	Restorative food justice program	communications	communications	United States	2020	Santino 2021
11	Farm School NYC	urban-situated, educational program	communications	environment	United States	2010	Reynolds 2017
12	Food design cards	Food design process tool	communications	communications	Netherlands	n.d.	Lee et al. 2020
13	Food packaging	a visualization strategy to enable material recovery	communications	communications	Sweden	2019	Nemat et al. 2020
14	FoodPlanCNY	participatory food system planning	communications	experience	United States	2012	Weissman and Potteiger 2020
15	Instock	a restaurant rescuing food to address food waste	communications	communications	Netherlands	2014	Massari et al. 2021
16	Neqa Elicarvigmun (Fish-to-School)	curriculum and community activities to encourage consumption of salmon	communications	communications	United States	n.d.	Nu and Bersamin 2017
17	Project Daire	school-aged curriculum intervention on the food system	communications	communications	Ireland	2018	Brennan et al. 2021
18	Project SoL	community intervention to improve health	communications	communications	Denmark	2012–2015	Mikkelsen et al. 2018; Toft et al. 2018
19	Reactivate Mobile App	intervention for adolescent obesity management	communications	communications	Ireland	2014	O'Malley et al. 2014

(*Continued*)

WS#	Design Outcome	Food Category	Design Category	Country	Year of Creation	Source
20	Yumbox	healthy eating tool	communications	object	United States	n.d.	Shukaitis and Elnakib 2021
21	Sustainable food tourism	academic field trip to the Faroe Islands	communications	experience	Denmark	2019	Leer 2020
22	Co-creating solutions in food deserts	design thinking approach to food access	accessibility	experience	United States	2018	Fernhaber et al. 2018
23	Obesity Prevention Tailored for Health II	online obesity intervention tool	accessibility	experience	United States	n.d.	Su 2015
24	Slow Food University of Wisconsin	social innovation for food democracy	accessibility	environment	United States	2013	Zepeda and Reznickova 2017
25	Urban farms GUI	generative production network facilitated by an online marketing and purchasing GUI	accessibility	context	United States	2021	Johnson and Eglash 2021
26	Free Food on Campus!	utilization of existing instructional technology to address food insecurity and food waste	accessibility	experience	United States	n.d.	Frank, Finkbinder, and Powell 2021

27	Implementation of school gardens through the Healthy Hunger-Free Kids Act	school garden in New Jersey	consumption	context	United States	2010	Reyes and Ohri-Vachaspati 2021
28	Umamification of vegetable dishes for sustainable eating	taste rack of ingredients for vegetable umamification	consumption	experience	Denmark	2020	Mouritsen and Styrbæk 2020
29	Egg of Columbus	participatory design workshop on food transformations and storage process	waste	experience	Italy	2015	Campagnaro and Porcellana 2015
30	Fresh boxes	food design to limit food waste	waste	object	Netherlands	2016	Bordewijk & Shifferestein 2020

Quadrant B

Widespread, sustainable food design funded or supported by public or private institutions

WS#	Design Outcome	Food Category	Design Category	Country	Year of Creation	Source
31	Carrot City	Urban agriculture archive with accompanying book	agriculture	environment	Canada	2011	Gorgolewski et al. 2011
31	Edible Estates Regional Prototype Garden	a food art installation by Fritz Haeg	agriculture	environment	United States		Gorgolewski et al. 2011
31	The Edible Schoolyard	urban agriculture program for school children	agriculture	environment	United States	1995	Gorgolewski et al. 2017
31	Wood Street Urban Farm	a certified organic farm	agriculture	environment	United States	2008	Gorgolewski et al. 2017
32	Circular bioeconomy intervention	Aflasafe (bio-control of aflatoxin)	agriculture	object	Nigeria	2021	Feleke et al. 2021
32	Circular bioeconomy intervention	Biochar	agriculture	object	Ghana	2014	Feleke et al. 2021
32	Circular bioeconomy intervention	Biochar	agriculture	object	Kenya		Feleke et al. 2021
32	Circular bioeconomy intervention	Biodiesel	agriculture	object	Benin	2021	Feleke et al. 2021
32	Circular bioeconomy intervention	Biodiesel	agriculture	object	Mali		Feleke et al. 2021
32	Circular bioeconomy intervention	Edible insects	agriculture	object	Benin		Feleke et al. 2021
32	Circular bioeconomy intervention	Edible insects	agriculture	object	Democratic Republic of Congo		Feleke et al. 2021
32	Circular bioeconomy intervention	Edible mushrooms	agriculture	object	Benin		Feleke et al. 2021

32	Circular bioeconomy intervention	Edible mushrooms	agriculture	object	Democratic Republic of Congo		Feleke et al. 2021
32	Circular bioeconomy intervention	Genetically modified cassava	agriculture	object	Nigeria	2021	Feleke et al. 2021
32	Circular bioeconomy intervention	HQCP (Animal Feed)	agriculture	object	Benin		Feleke et al. 2021
32	Circular bioeconomy intervention	Insect-based feed	agriculture	object	Rwanda		Feleke et al. 2021
32	Circular bioeconomy intervention	HQCP (Animal Feed)	agriculture	object	Benin		Feleke et al. 2021
32	Circular bioeconomy intervention	Insect-based feed	agriculture	object	Rwanda		Feleke et al. 2021
32	Circular bioeconomy intervention	NoduMax, bio-fertilizer	agriculture	object	Nigeria	2021	Feleke et al. 2021
33	Community-supported agriculture farm	food production and distribution localization	agriculture	experience	Japan	1960	Hartling 2019
33	Community-supported agriculture farm	food production and distribution localization	agriculture	experience	United States	1985	Hartling 2019
34	Grassroots rural producer movement	ANAPQUI	agriculture	futures	Bolivia	1983	Hart et al. 2016
34	Grassroots rural producer movement	Northern Friesian Woodlands	agriculture	futures	Netherlands	1992	Hart et al. 2016
34	Grassroots rural producer movement	Potato Park	agriculture	futures	Peru	2000	Hart et al. 2016
34	Grassroots rural producer movement	Rural Landless Workers' Movement	agriculture	futures	Brazil	1984	Hart et al. 2016

(Continued)

WS#	Design Outcome		Food Category	Design Category	Country	Year of Creation	Source
34	Grassroots rural producer movement	Saskatchewan Soil Conservation Association and crop diversification	agriculture	futures	Canada	2016	Hart et al. 2016
35	Urban rooftop farm	zero-acre agriculture	production	context	United States	1995–2015	Buehler and Junge 2016
35	Urban rooftop farm	zero-acre agriculture	production	context	Egypt	1995–2015	Buehler and Junge 2016
35	Urban rooftop farm	zero-acre agriculture	production	context	China	1995–2015	Buehler and Junge 2016
35	Urban rooftop farm	zero-acre agriculture	production	context	Canada	1995–2015	Buehler and Junge 2016
35	Urban rooftop farm	zero-acre agriculture	production	context	Spain	1995–2015	Buehler and Junge 2016
35	Urban rooftop farm	zero-acre agriculture	production	context	Germany	1995–2015	Buehler and Junge 2016
35	Urban rooftop farm	zero-acre agriculture	production	context	Singapore	1995–2015	Buehler and Junge 2016
35	Urban rooftop farm	zero-acre agriculture	production	context	Netherlands	1995–2015	Buehler and Junge 2016
35	Urban rooftop farm	zero-acre agriculture	production	context	France	1995–2015	Buehler and Junge 2016
35	Urban rooftop farm	zero-acre agriculture	production	context	Britain	1995–2015	Buehler and Junge 2016
35	Urban rooftop farm	zero-acre agriculture	production	context	Egypt	1995–2015	Buehler and Junge 2016
35	Urban rooftop farm	zero-acre agriculture	production	context	India	1995–2015	Buehler and Junge 2016
36	Food safety info sheets	a communication design tool for food safety training	communications	communications	United States	2011	Chapman et al. 2011

No.	Case	Description			Country	Year	Reference
36	Food safety info sheets	a communication design tool for food safety training	communications	communications	Canada	2011	Chapman et al. 2011
37	Great food street	Commercial Drive	communications	environment	Canada	n.d.	de la Salle 2019
37	Great food street	Eastern Market	communications	environment	United States	n.d.	de la Salle 2019
37	Great food street	Gore Street	communications	environment	Canada	n.d.	de la Salle 2019
37	Great food street	Trackside Cantina	communications	environment	Canada	n.d.	de la Salle 2019
37	Great food street	Wilder Snail	communications	environment	Canada	n.d.	de la Salle 2019
37	Great food street	Rue Mouffetard	communications	environment	France	n.d.	de la Salle 2019
37	Great food street	Campo de' Fiori	communications	environment	Italy	n.d.	de la Salle 2019
38	Why Cheap Art?	poster	communications	object	United States	1984	Flood and Sloan 2019
39	Memefest	festival of socially responsive communication, design, and art	communications	communications	Australia	2013	Vodeb 2017
40	Food hub	a civic food access community	accessibility	environment	Australia	2015	Ballantyne-Brodie et al. 2015
40	Dockland Food Hub	design-led food innovation for the community	accessibility	environment	Australia	2015	Ballantyne-Brodie et al. 2015
40	Healthy Food Hub	a food cooperative market in a Black community combating food deserts	accessibility	environment	United States	2009	Figueroa 2015
40	Meadow Well Food Hub	civic food network for food democracy	accessibility	environment	Britain	2019	Prost 2019
41	International Potato Center	nutrition-sensitive agriculture intervention	accessibility	experience	Ethiopia	2017	Busse et al. 2017
42	Edible insects	alternative protein farming	consumption	object	Finland	2016	Kauppi et al. 2019
42	Edible insects	alternative protein farming	consumption	object	Austria	2018	Kauppi et al. 2019
42	Edible insects	alternative protein farming	consumption	object	Hong Kong	2018	Feleke et al. 2021

(Continued)

WS#	Design Outcome	Food Category	Design Category	Country	Year of Creation	Source
42	Edible insects	consumption	object	Benin	2021	Feleke et al. 2021
42	Edible insects	consumption	object	Democratic Republic of Congo	2021	Feleke et al. 2021
43	Edible mushroom	consumption	object	Benin	n.d.	Feleke et al. 2021
43	Edible mushroom	consumption	object	Democratic Republic of Congo	n.d.	Feleke et al. 2021
44	CEASE-DT	waste	experience	Italy	2021	Massari et al. 2021
44	Fleet Farming	waste	experience	United States	2014	Massari et al. 2021
44	Food Flow	waste	experience	United States	2016	Massari et al. 2021
45	High-quality cassava peels (HQCP)	waste	object	Benin	n.d.	Feleke et al. 2021
45	High-quality cassava peels (HQCP)	waste	object	Rwanda	n.d.	Feleke et al. 2021
46	SecondBite	waste	context	Australia	2014	Lindberg et al. 2014

Design outcome descriptions:
- Edible insects: alternative protein farming
- Edible insects: alternative protein farming
- Edible mushroom: circular bioeconomy intervention
- Edible mushroom: circular bioeconomy intervention
- CEASE-DT: design thinking approach to food waste prevention
- Fleet Farming: urban agriculture program
- Food Flow: food waste management app
- High-quality cassava peels (HQCP): Animal feed
- High-quality cassava peels (HQCP): Animal feed
- SecondBite: food rescue service organization

Quadrant C

Widespread, sustainable food design created by citizens

WS#	Design Outcome	Food Category	Design Category	Country	Year of Creation	Source
47	Aquaponics	Fish and vegetable farming	environment	agriculture	Bangladesh	2014	Sunny et al. 2019
47	Aquaponics	Fish and vegetable farming	environment	agriculture	United States	2008	Laidlaw and Magee 2016
47	Aquaponics	Fish and vegetable farming	environment	agriculture	Australia	2010	Laidlaw and Magee 2016
48	Community gardening	urban agriculture	environment	agriculture	Britain	2014	Kim 2017
48	Community gardening	urban agriculture	environment	agriculture	France	2012	Martin et al. 2017
48	Community gardening	urban agriculture	environment	agriculture	United States	2007	Corrigan 2011
48	Community gardening	urban agriculture	environment	agriculture	United States	2010	Gregory et al. 2016
48	Community gardening	urban agriculture	environment	agriculture	United States	2014	Furness and Gallaher 2018
49	Farm Hack	open-source farm tools information database for online/offline use across states	agriculture	systems	United States	2010	Smith 2016
50	Planetary Community Chicken	performance art installation to cross-breed chicken	agriculture	environment	Belgium	2016	Flood and Sloan 2019, 56-57
51	The Sausage of the Future	sustainable protein	processing	object	Switzerland	2014	Flood and Sloan 2019, 126
52	Food Activist Handbook	a handbook on food activism	production	communications	United States	2015	Berlow 2015

(Continued)

WS#	Design Outcome	Food Category	Design Category	Country	Year of Creation	Source
53	Banana Passport	communications	object	Iceland	2017	Flood and Sloan 2019
54	Food Futures Imagined	food futures participatory workshop	communications	experience	Finland	2020	Wilde et al. 2022
54	Food Futures Imagined	food futures participatory workshop	communications	experience	Sweden	2020	Wilde et al. 2023
54	Food Futures Imagined	food futures participatory workshop	communications	experience	United States	2020	Wilde et al. 2023
54	Food Futures Imagined	food futures participatory workshop	communications	experience	Australia	2020	Wilde et al. 2024
54	Food Futures Imagined	food futures participatory workshop	communications	experience	Denmark	2020	Wilde et al. 2021
55	Sun Mad	artwork	communications	object	United States	1982	Flood and Sloan 2019, 73
56	Supernatural	artwork	communications	object	Germany	2010	Flood and Sloan 2019
57	Fallen Fruit	residency art project	accessibility	experience	United States	2004	Flood and Sloan 2019, 19
58	Freeganism	dumpster diving	accessibility	context	United States	n.d.	Barnard 2011
59	Growing Food Justice for All Initiative	a food justice and anti-racism movement	accessibility	systems	United States	2006	Morales 2011
60	SONO filter	water filtration system	consumption	object	Bangladesh	1999	Ahmed et al. 2017

Quadrant D

Local, sustainable food design created by citizens

WS#	Design Outcome	Food Category	Design Category	Country	Year of Creation	Source
61	Food planning	urban agriculture	system	United States	n.d.	Pothukuchi 2015
62	Home gardening	urban agriculture	environment	United States	2010	Gray et al. 2014
63	Hoop house gardening	Indigenous agriculture	environment	Canada	2017	Thompson et al. 2018
64	Non-flower for the Hoverfly	pollen container	object	Iceland	2017	Flood and Sloan 2019, 53-54
65	Pā to Plate	food value chain loop	context	New Zealand	2016	Kawharu 2019
66	Sack gardening	urban agriculture	environment	Kenya	2008	Gallaher et al. 2015
67	Indigiearth	Indigenous entrepreneurship	context	Australia	2012	Ratten and Dana 2015
68	Mark Olive	Indigenous entrepreneurship	context	Australia	2008	Ratten and Dana 2015
69	Fresh Moves Mobile Market	mobile farmers' market	object	United States	2009–present	Smith 2016
70	Humane Borders Water Stations and Warning Posters	a system of emergency water stations and posters in the Sonoran Desert	system	United States	2000	Smith 2016
71	Community cooker (jiko ya jamii)	communal oven	object	Kenya	1993–2013	Smith 2011
72	Daily Dump	aesthetic pottery for home composting	object	India	2006	Flood and Sloan 2019, 37
73	Food rescue	citizen-driven, waste reduction initiative	experience	Sweden	2013	Zapata and Zapata Campos 2017

WS# = Wicked Solution Number

Appendix III

8E's of sustainability criteria: assessing
sustainability of design outcomes

WS#	Quadrant	Design Outcome	Is it equitable and just?	Is it environmentally-friendly?	Is it economical?	Is it ecological?	Is it enduring?	Is it effectuated?	Is it effective?	Is it ethical?
1	A	3-step solution	X	X	X			X	X	
2	A	Brazilian Mandala System		X				X	X	
3	A	Feeding Milan		X	X			X	X	
4	A	Food Access 3.0	X	X	X			X	X	
5	A	Rainforest preservation		X		X	X	X	X	
6	A	Seed to Kitchen Collaborative	X					X	X	X
7	A	Speculative and participatory design approach for facilitating bottom-up, smart urban food-growing futures	X	X				X	X	X
8	A	Pot-in-pot cooler		X				X	X	
9	A	Communicating food recall information to consumers	X	X				X	X	
10	A	EMERGE CT	X		X			X	X	X
11	A	Farm School NYC	X					X	X	
12	A	Food design cards				X		X	X	
13	A	Food packaging		X				X	X	
14	A	FoodPlanCNY		X	X	X		X	X	
15	A	Instock		X				X	X	
16	A	Neqa Elicarvigmun	X					X	X	
17	A	Project Daire	X					X	X	
18	A	Project SoL	X					X	X	
19	A	Reactivate Mobile App	X					X	X	
20	A	Yumbox		X				X	X	
21	A	Sustainable food tourism	X	X	X			X	X	X
22	A	Co-creating solutions in food deserts	X	X				X	X	

(Continued)

WS#	Quadrant	Design Outcome	Is it equitable and just?	Is it environmentally-friendly?	Is it economical?	Is it ecological?	Is it enduring?	Is it effectuated?	Is it effective?	Is it ethical?
23	A	Obesity Prevention Tailored for Health II	X					X	X	
24	A	Slow Food University of Wisconsin	X					X	X	
25	A	Urban farms GUI	X		X	X		X	X	
26	A	Free Food on Campus!	X	X	X			X	X	
27	A	Implementation of school gardens through the Healthy Hunger-Free Kids Act	X					X	X	
28	A	Umamification of vegetable dishes for sustainable eating	X	X				X	X	
29	A	Egg of Columbus		X				X	X	
30	A	Fresh boxes		X	X			X	X	
31	B	Carrot City		X				X	X	
32	B	Circular bioeconomy intervention		X	X	X		X	X	
33	B	Community-supported agriculture farm		X	X	X	X	X	X	
34	B	Grassroots rural producer movement	X	X	X	X		X	X	X
35	B	Urban rooftop farm		X	X	X	X	X		
36	B	Food safety info sheets		X				X	X	
37	B	Great food streets		X			X	X	X	
38	B	Why Cheap Art?						X	X	X
39	B	Memefest	X	X	X	X		X	X	
40	B	Food hub	X	X	X	X		X	X	
41	B	International Potato Center	X					X	X	
42	B	Edible insects		X	X	X		X	X	
43	B	Edible mushroom		X	X	X		X	X	
44	B	CEASE-DT		X				X	X	

#		Item	1	2	3	4	5	6	7	8
45	B	HQCP (Animal Feed)		X	X			X	X	
46	B	SecondBite		X				X	X	
47	C	Aquaponics		X	X			X	X	
48	C	Community gardening	X	X	X			X	X	
49	C	Farm Hack				X		X	X	
50	D	Planetary Community Chicken		X		X		X	X	
51	C	The Sausage of the Future		X	X			X	X	
52	C	Food Activist Handbook				X		X	X	
53	C	Banana Passport		X				X	X	
54	C	Food Futures Imagined	X	X				X	X	X
55	C	Sun Mad						X	X	X
56	C	Supernatural						X	X	
57	C	Fallen Fruit	X	X	X		X	X	X	
58	C	Freeganism		X	X			X	X	
59	C	Growing Food Justice for All Initiative	X	X	X			X	X	
60	C	SONO filter	X					X	X	
61	D	Food planning	X	X	X	X	X	X	X	
62	D	Home gardening	X	X	X	X		X	X	
63	D	Hoop house gardening	X	X	X	X		X	X	
64	D	Non-flower for the Hoverfly	X	X				X	X	
65	D	Pā to Plate	X		X	X		X	X	X
66	D	Sack gardening	X		X			X	X	
67	D	Indigiearth	X		X			X	X	
68	D	Mark Olive	X		X			X	X	
69	D	Fresh Moves Mobile Market	X	X				X	X	
70	D	Humane Borders Water Stations and Warning Posters	X					X	X	
71	D	Community cooker	X	X	X			X	X	
72	D	Daily Dump		X	X			X	X	X
73	D	Food rescue		X	X			X	X	X

Appendix IV

Food insecurity experience scale instruments

FOOD INSECURITY EXPERIENCE SCALE
Individually Referenced

Now I would like to ask you some questions about food.
During the last 30 days, was there a time when:

Q1. You were worried you would not have enough food to eat because of a lack of money or other resources? (if "Yes," go to question Q1a)	0 1	No Yes	98 99	Don't Know Refused
Q1a. Was this specifically due to the COVID-19 crisis?	0 1	No Yes	98 99	Don't Know Refused
Q2. Still thinking about the last 30 days, was there a time when you were unable to eat healthy and nutritious food because of a lack of money or other resources? (if "Yes," go to question Q2a)	0 1	No Yes	98 99	Don't Know Refused
Q2a. Was this specifically due to the COVID-19 crisis?	0 1	No Yes	98 99	Don't Know Refused
Q3. You ate only a few kinds of foods because of a lack of money or other resources? (if "Yes," go to question Q3a)	0 1	No Yes	98 99	Don't Know Refused
Q3a. Was this specifically due to the COVID-19 crisis?	0 1	No Yes	98 99	Don't Know Refused
Q4. You had to skip a meal because there was not enough money or other resources to get food? (if "Yes," go to question Q4a)	0 1	No Yes	98 99	Don't Know Refused
Q4a. Was this specifically due to the COVID-19 crisis?	0 1	No Yes	98 99	Don't Know Refused
Q5. Still thinking about the last 30 days, was there a time when you ate less than you thought you should because of a lack of money or other resources? (if "Yes," go to question Q5a)	0 1	No Yes	98 99	Don't Know Refused

Q5a. Was this specifically due to the COVID-19 crisis?	0	No	98	Don't Know
	1	Yes	99	Refused
Q6. Your household ran out of food because of a lack of money or other resources? (if "Yes," go to questions Q6a and Q6b)	0	No	98	Don't Know
	1	Yes	99	Refused
Q6a. How often did this happen?	2			Rarely (1 or 2 times)
	3			Sometimes (3-10 times)
	4			Often (more than 10 times)
	98			Don't Know
	99			Refused
Q6b. Was this specifically due to the COVID-19 crisis?	0	No	98	Don't Know
	1	Yes	99	Refused
Q7. You were hungry but did not eat because there was not enough money or other resources for food? (if "Yes," go to questions Q7a and Q7b)	0	No	98	Don't Know
	1	Yes	99	Refused
Q7a. How often did this happen?	2			Rarely (1 or 2 times)
	3			Sometimes (3-10 times)
	4			Often (more than 10 times)
	98			Don't Know
	99			Refused
Q7b. Was this specifically due to the COVID-19 crisis?	0	No	98	Don't Know
	1	Yes	99	Refused
Q8. You went without eating for a whole day because of a lack of money or other resources? (if "Yes," go to questions Q8a and Q8b)	0	No	98	Don't Know
	1	Yes	99	Refused
Q8a. How often did this happen?	2			Rarely (1 or 2 times)
	3			Sometimes (3-10 times)
	4			Often (more than 10 times)
	98			Don't Know
	99			Refused
Q8b. Was this specifically due to the COVID-19 crisis?	0	No	98	Don't Know
	1	Yes	99	Refused

FOOD INSECURITY EXPERIENCE SCALE
Household Referenced

Now I would like to ask you some questions about food.
During the last 30 days, was there a time when:

Q1. You or others in your household worried about not having enough food to eat because of a lack of money or other resources? (if "Yes," go to question Q1a)	0 1	No Yes	98 99	Don't Know Refused
Q1a. Was this specifically due to the COVID-19 crisis?	0 1	No Yes	98 99	Don't Know Refused
Q2. Still thinking about the last 30 days, was there a time when you or others in your household were unable to eat healthy and nutritious food because of a lack of money or other resources? (if "Yes," go to question Q2a)	0 1	No Yes	98 99	Don't Know Refused
Q2a. Was this specifically due to the COVID-19 crisis?	0 1	No Yes	98 99	Don't Know Refused
Q3. Was there a time when you or others in your household ate only a few kinds of foods because of a lack of money or other resources? (if "Yes," go to question Q3a)	0 1	No Yes	98 99	Don't Know Refused
Q3a. Was this specifically due to the COVID-19 crisis?	0 1	No Yes	98 99	Don't Know Refused
Q4. Was there a time when you or others in your household had to skip a meal because there was not enough money or other resources to get food? (if "Yes," go to question Q4a)	0 1	No Yes	98 99	Don't Know Refused
Q4a. Was this specifically due to the COVID-19 crisis?	0 1	No Yes	98 99	Don't Know Refused
Q5. Still thinking about the last 30 days, was there a time when you or others in your household ate less than you thought you should because of a lack of money or other resources? (if "Yes," go to question Q5a)	0 1	No Yes	98 99	Don't Know Refused

Q5a. Was this specifically due to the COVID-19 crisis?	0 1	No Yes	98 99	Don't Know Refused
Q6. Was there a time when your household ran out of food because of a lack of money or other resources? (if "Yes," go to questions Q6a and Q6b)	0 1	No Yes	98 99	Don't Know Refused
Q6a. How often did this happen?	2 3 4 98 99			Rarely (1 or 2 times) Sometimes (3–10 times) Often (more than 10 times) Don't Know Refused
Q6b. Was this specifically due to the COVID-19 crisis?	0 1	No Yes	98 99	Don't Know Refused
Q7. Was there a time when you or others in your household were hungry but did not eat because there was not enough money or other resources for food? (if "Yes," go to questions Q7a and Q7b)	0 1	No Yes	98 99	Don't Know Refused
Q7a. How often did this happen?	2 3 4 98 99			Rarely (1 or 2 times) Sometimes (3–10 times) Often (more than 10 times) Don't Know Refused
Q7b. Was this specifically due to the COVID-19 crisis?	0 1	No Yes	98 99	Don't Know Refused
Q8. Was there a time when you or others in your household went without eating for a whole day because of a lack of money or other resources? (if "Yes," go to questions Q8a and Q8b)	0 1	No Yes	98 99	Don't Know Refused
Q8a. How often did this happen?	2 3 4 98 99			Rarely (1 or 2 times) Sometimes (3–10 times) Often (more than 10 times) Don't Know Refused
Q8b. Was this specifically due to the COVID-19 crisis?		No Yes		Don't Know Refused

Appendix V
Public Fruit Jam by Fallen Fruit

Ingredients:

Fruit, picked, foraged, or otherwise supplied by participants, fresh or frozen
200 Jam jars
40 Packets of pectin
22 kg / 50 lb Sugar
Water (small amounts for jam making; large amounts for cleaning)
Bread and crackers for tasting the jam (try getting donations of day-old bread from bakeries)
4 or 5 electric burners
Pots (4–5 minimum), pot-holders, knives, cutting boards, and bowls
8 large tables as workstations
50–60 folding chairs
Labels for jam jars and pens to list ingredients

Method:

1. The basic combination for the jam is 5 cups (approx. 850 g) of fruit, one packet of pectin, and 5 cups (1 kg) of sugar. Keeping these proportions is important.
2. Cut the fruit into small pieces, removing seeds and stems. Put in pans with the correct quantity of pectin, bring to a boil, and add sugar. After a second, rolling boil, the jam is done. The best flavor results from the least cooking.
3. When the jam has boiled a second time, ladle it into jars, apply labels and write the ingredients on the lid. Take one of yours if you like, then leave the rest on the shared table for others. Consider swapping jams with other people. Put bread on one table for sampling jam. These jars will not be fully sterilized so the jam needs to be eaten soon when you get home; freeze long-term or keep refrigerated for up to three weeks.

Note:

Before you start, organize a team of deputies—volunteers to help you manage the participants and the cooking itself. Sociable people with some experience in making jams are the best. Plan how many people you'd like to include (these instructions are for 150–80 people over three or four hours). Find a suitable location (community center, art space, even outdoors can work). The kinds of jam will depend on the fruit that participants provide. We encourage you to try to look for radical and experimental flavors depending on your location. Participants are asked to join jam teams of three to five people and work with people they haven't met before.

Appendix VI
Fruit Salami recipe by food futurist and designer Carolien Niebling

Ingredients

500 g/18 oz Frozen or fresh fruit (forest fruits, apricots, mango, etc. or a mix)
500 g/18 oz Semi-dried fruit (prunes, apricots, figs, etc. or a mix)
Water or fruit juice
1 sachet Pectin or other gelling agent
200–300 g/7–10 oz Nut flour
200 g/7 oz Chopped nuts (without the skin)
Lemon juice to taste (depending on how sweet the fruit is)
Sugar to taste (depending on how sweet the fruit is)
Dried flowers (optional)
Sausage skin

Method

1. Put all the fruit in a pan and bring it to a boil. When your mixture is on the dry side add some water or fruit juice so that it is just covered. Simmer on low heat until the fruit is soft and mixed well.
2. Now you can add the pectin and use a hand blender to blitz the mixture according to your preference, which will determine the texture of the sausage.
3. Add the nut flour and stir well, making sure you have a thick mass that stays on our spoon. To achieve the right thickness you can add more nut flour. Add the chopped nuts, a squeeze of lemon juice, sugar (if necessary), and flowers. Try to keep the mixture quite tart because the sweetness intensifies during drying.
4. Choose which skin you want to use. I have chosen a vegetarian skin but there are also very good peel-off collagen skins available (my objective is to reduce meat consumption, rather than go strictly vegetarian). The diameter can vary from 20 to 50 mm, which alters drying time.
5. Fill the skins with the mixture to your desired length. The sausages can then be dried at 50 degrees Celsius in the oven. Leave the door of the oven open a little to let the moisture escape.

6. Drying the sausages depending on the thickness and desired softness, for 20–40 hours. When making the sausages for the first time, I would suggest taking one out of the oven every three hours after 20 hours of drying to test the texture.

Note:

When the sausage mixture is moist the texture is soft and almost spreadable. The flavor is slightly tart and fruity but the shelf-life is quite short. A drier fruit salami is sweet, chewy, and fruity but also lasts without refrigeration for about two years. The flavour of the sausage pairs well with wine, cheese, bread, or just as is.

Glossary

agri/aquaculture: planting and growing "raw food materials" and breeding and caring for animals that will be used for food. Other related activities include training and managing labor, land management, innovating or acquiring, maintaining and using farming technologies (Ericksen 2008, 238), and caring for "aquatic animals and plants" for food in "fresh, brackish and marine environments" (Pillay and Kutty 2005, 3). "A variety of factors determine these activities, from climate conditions to land tenure, input prices, agricultural technology and government subsidy provisions intended to protect or promote" (Ericksen 2008, 238).

agricultural agency: cognizance of one's power to grow and produce food and the resources to do so.

communication: the visual and verbal communication technologies like symbols, apps, and educational training programs that contribute to the food system's functionality.

communications: a design category defined by two-dimensional imagery accompanied by text (e.g., hashtags, package designs, a logo, an interface, or an app) that can evoke an array of emotions and actions and influence cognition and behavior (Heskett 2005, 82).

Community Supported Agriculture (CSA): a producer-consumer local production and marketing partnership that involves a subscription-based contract for the delivery of seasonal products from the farm.

consumption: choosing, purchasing, preparing, eating, and digesting food. Factors affecting these activities include price, income level, cultural traditions or preferences, social values, education, health, and household status among other things (Ericksen 2008, 238).

contexts: a design category of the professional organization and management of the knowledge set, scope, conduct, and playing field of a specialized activity, including but not limited to a program, professional organization, or governing policy (Heskett 2005, 166).

critical mapping: compiling existing design outcomes engaged in systemic interaction and organizing them visually towards identifying places to intervene in the system to design a more sustainable future.

designer: anyone, whether formally trained in design or not, who generates intangible and tangible outcomes through creative problem-solving.

distribution: moving processed food from one place to another, typically from place of origin to retail spaces for consumption. Activities in the distribution phase of the food system include various forms of shipping, governmental trade, and storage regulations (Ericksen 2008, 238).

ento-preneurs: new insect food companies.

environments: a design category of frameworks that facilitate activities, patterns of use, behavior, and expectations within living, learning, and working spaces (Heskett 2005, 102).

experience: a design form of the strategic orchestration of an engagement with something that is functional, engaging, purposeful, compelling, memorable, and enjoyable (McLellan 2000).

food accessibility: one's ability to acquire enough healthy food to sustain life. The factors and activities that influence one's ability to acquire enough healthy food include:

food affordability: one's "purchasing power" that depends on "pricing policies and mechanisms, seasonal and geographical variations in price, local prices relative to external prices, the form in which households are paid, income, and wealth levels" (Ericksen 2008, 240).

food allocation: governmental policies and social and political capital governing when, where, how [and how much] food [one] can access at a given time in a given private or public space (Ericksen 2008, 240).

food preference: social or cultural norms and values (e.g., religion, season, advertising, preparation requirements, human capital, tastes, customs) that influence consumer demand for certain types of food (Ericksen 2008, 240).

food agency: the human capacity to make decisions about what foods one eats and produces; how that food is produced, processed, and distributed within one's food system; and one's ability to engage in processes that shape broader food system policies and governance (FAO 2021, 190).

food democracy: 1) a strong ethical commitment to environmental sustainability, social justice, as well as individual and community health, 2) democratic governance through active participation of food citizens, and 3) a whole system perspective aiming to transform the entire food system (Prost 2019, 142).

food desert: a community that lacks convenient access to healthy and affordable food and is not able to economically sustain a supermarket (Fernhaber et al. 2018).

food design: design processes applied to products, services, or systems for food and eating.

food justice: ensuring that everyone has the right and access to healthy food.

food security: a state where all people, at all times, have physical, social, and economic access to sufficient, safe, and nutritious food to meet their dietary needs and food preferences for an active and healthy life.

food sovereignty: the human right to healthy food produced through ecologically sound, sustainable, and culturally appropriate methods, and the human right to define one's food and agricultural systems (Declaration of Nyéléni 2007).

freegans: a combination of the words "free" and "vegan," are often radical community activists who embrace community and, through minimal consumption, limit their participation in consumerism (Barnard 2011).

futures: a design form of a series of speculative or imaginary activities directed towards a desired outcome (e.g., a campaign or movement). See Taylor (2019) for other definitions.

generative justice: the universal right to generate unalienated value and directly participate in its benefits, the rights of value generators to create their own conditions of production, and the rights of communities of value generation to nurture self-sustaining paths for its circulation (https://generativejustice.org/ (Eglash 2016).

gleaning: collecting leftover crops from commercially harvested fields or on fields where harvesting was not economically profitable.

identities: a design category of any strategic combination of objects, communications, and environments that expresses meaning intended to shape, even preempt, what others perceive or understand (Heskett 2005, 125).

interaction: the design form of the shaping of use-oriented qualities of digital artifacts (Löwgren and Stolterman 2004) for a satisfactory or improved experience.

malnutrition: deficiencies, excesses, or imbalances in a person's intake of energy and/or nutrients. The term "malnutrition" addresses three broad groups of conditions: 1) undernutrition, which includes wasting (low weight-for-height), stunting (low height-for-age), and underweight (low weight-for-age); 2) micronutrient-related malnutrition, which includes micronutrient deficiencies (a lack of important vitamins and minerals) or micronutrient excess; and 3) overweight, obesity, and diet-related non-communicable diseases (such as heart disease, stroke, diabetes, and some cancers) (WHO 2021).

micronutrient deficiency: a lack of vitamins and minerals that are essential for body functions such as producing enzymes, hormones, and other substances needed for growth and development (WHO 2017).

objects: a design category of single- and multi-purposed, multi- and intersensory, three-dimensional objects (e.g., a saltshaker, refrigerator, or a farming tool) encountered in private and public spaces that function in some capacity that is intuitive or can be learned (Heskett 2005, 56).

processing: transforming raw food material (vegetable, fruit, animal) for trade by altering its appearance, storage life, nutritional make-up, and content (Ericksen 2008, 238).

production: harvesting crops and slaughtering animals (Ericksen 2008, 238).

service: a design form of a mindset, process, toolset, cross-disciplinary language, or management approach that improves a service or creates a new one (Stickdorn et al. 2018).

social innovation: a change process of recombining existing assets creatively to reach "socially recognized goals in a new way" (Manzini 2014, 57).

sustainability: "the long-term ability of food systems to provide food security and nutrition in a way that does not compromise the economic, social and environmental bases that generate food security and nutrition for future generations" (FAO 2021, 190).

sustainable: that which is ethical (i.e., does no harm to humans and communities), equitable and just (i.e., facilitates greater inclusivity in access to resources and benefits in an equitable and just manner.), environmental (i.e., improves and does no harm to nature), economical (i.e., permits value to return to all actors in the system thereby yielding "generative justice" (Eglash 2016)), ecological (i.e., contributes to the healthy balance of the social ecosystem), enduring (i.e., durable and lasts a long time), effectuated (i.e., implemented within a public context), and effective (i.e., evidence shows that the design outcome works).

sustainable food design: design outcomes and processes for any area in a food system that seeks to improve and optimize the environment, and the economy, and society, both individually and collectively, through a systemic lens that centers equity and justice.

systems: a design category referring to interacting, interrelated, or interdependent elements that form a collective and functioning entity (Heskett 2005, 145).

transdiscplinary research: includes focus on real-world problems, integration and transcendence of disciplines, participatory research, and the unifying of knowledge beyond disciplines (Hadorn et al. 2008), "trans-sector, problem-oriented research involving a wider range of stakeholders in society" (Klein et al. 2008, S117).

ujamaa: cooperative economics.

upcycle: creative repurposing and transformation of used materials or waste products to a higher value or quality material or product.

waste: composting, recycling, and disposal of expired and unconsumed but still-edible food and materials involved in its production and consumption.

wicked problem: a complex societal issue that exists within an evolving system of hyperlocal, context-specific, and cross-cultural and -disciplinary challenges (Buchanan 1992; Rowe 1986; Rittel and Webber 1973; Churchman 1967).

wicked solution: an interactive, multimodal visualization of design outcomes for identifying "leverage points" (Meadows 1999) that can shift the current state of the wicked problem's system towards a just future of sustainability and equity.

Bibliography

Barnard, Alex V. 2011. "'Waving the Banana' at Capitalism: Political Theater and Social Movement Strategy among New York's 'Freegan' Dumpster Divers." *Ethnography* 12, no. 4: 419–444. https://doi.org/10.1177/1466138110392453.

Buchanan, Richard. 1992. "Wicked Problems in Design Thinking." *Design Issues* 8, no. 2: 5–21.

Churchman, C. West. 1967. "Guest Editorial: Wicked Problems." *Management Science* 14, no. 4: B141–B142. https://www.jstor.org/stable/2628678.

Eglash, Ron. 2016. "An Introduction to Generative Justice." *Revista Teknokultura* 13, no. 2: 369–404. http://doi.org/10.5209/rev_TEKN.2016.v13.n2.52847.

Ericksen, Polly J. 2008. "Conceptualizing Food Systems for Global Environmental Change Research." *Global Environmental Change* 18, no. 1: 234–245. https://doi.org/10.1016/j.gloenvcha.2007.09.002.

Fernhaber, Stephanie A., Terri Wada, Pamela Napier, and Shellye Suttles. 2018. "Engaging Diverse Community Stakeholders to Co-create Solutions in Food Deserts: A Design-thinking Approach." *Journal of Public Affairs* 13, no. 3: e1874. https://doi.org/10.1002/pa.1874.

Food and Agricultural Organization of the United Nations (FAO). 2021. *The State of Food Security and Nutrition in the World 2021: Transforming Food Systems for Food Security, Improved Nutrition and Affordable Healthy Diets for All*. Rome: FAO. https://doi.org/10.4060/cb4474en.

Hadorn, Gertrude Hirsch, Holger Hoffmann-Riem, Susette Biber-Klemm, Walter Grossenbacher-Mansuy, Dominique Joye, Christian Pohl, Urs Wiesmann, and Elisabeth Zemp, eds. 2008. *Handbook of Transdisciplinary Research*. Vol. 10. Dordrecht: Springer.

Heskett, John. 2005. *Design: A Very Short Introduction*. Vol. 136. Oxford: Oxford University Press.

Klein, Julie T. 2008. "Evaluation of Interdisciplinary and Transdisciplinary Research: A Literature Review." *American Journal of Preventive Medicine* 35, no. 2: S116–S123.

Löwgren, Jonas, and Erik Stolterman. 2004. *Thoughtful Interaction Design: A Design Perspective on Information Technology*. Cambridge, MA: MIT Press.

Manzini, Ezio. 2014. "Making Things Happen: Social Innovation and Design." *Design Issues* 30, no. 1: 57–66. http://dx.doi.org/10.1162/DESI_a_00248.

McLellan, Hilary. 2000. "Experience Design." *Cyberpsychology and Behavior* 3, no. 1: 59–69. https://doi.org/10.1089/109493100316238.

Meadows, Donella H. 1999. *Leverage Points: Places to Intervene in a System*. Hartland, VT: The Sustainability Institute. https://donellameadows.org/wp-content/userfiles/Leverage_Points.pdf.

Nyéléni. 2007. "Declaration of Nyéléni." Accessed February 27, 2007. https://nyeleni.org /en/declaration-of-nyeleni/.

Pillay, Thundathil Velayudhan Ramakrishna, and Methil Narayanan Kutty. 2005. *Aquaculture: Principles and Practices, 2nd Edition*. Oxford: Blackwell Publishing.

Prost, Sebastian. 2019. "Food Democracy for All? Developing a Food Hub in the Context of Socio-Economic Deprivation." *Politics and Governance* 7, no. 4: 142–153. https://doi .org/10.17645/pag.v7i4.2057.

Rittel, Horst W. J., and Melvin M. Webber. 1973. "Dilemmas in a General Theory of Planning." *Policy Sciences* 4, no. 2: 155–169. https://www.jstor.org/stable/4531523.

Rowe, Peter G. 1986. *Design Thinking*. Cambridge, MA: MIT Press.

Stickdorn, Marc, Markus Edgar Hormess, Adam Lawrence, and Jakob Schneider. 2018. *This is Service Design Doing: Applying Service Design Thinking in the Real World*. Sebastopol, CA: O'Reilly Media, Inc.

Taylor, Damon. 2019. "Design Futures." In *A Companion to Contemporary Design Since 1945*, edited by Anne Massey, and Dana Arnold, 51–71. Oxford: Blackwell.

Index